Sleeping with Monsters

Conversations with
Scottish and Irish Women Poets

Research and Interviews by
Rebecca E. Wilson

Edited by
Gillean Somerville-Arjat
and Rebecca E. Wilson

WOLFHOUND PRESS

Published in Ireland 1990
by Wolfhound Press,
68 Mountjoy Square, Dublin 1.

First published in 1990 by
Polygon, 22 George Square, Edinburgh

Typeset in Sabon by Redwood Press
Printed in Great Britain by
Redwood Press Limited, Melksham, Wiltshire

British Library Cataloguing in Publication Data
Sleeping with monsters : conversations with
Scottish and Irish women poets.
1. Poetry in English. Scottish women writers – Anthologies
2. Poetry in English. Irish women writers – Anthologies
I. Wilson, Rebecca   II. Somerville-Arjat, Gillean
821'.008'09411

Wolfhound Press receives
financial assistance from The
Arts Council (An Chomhairle
Ealaíon), Dublin, Ireland.

ISBN 0 86327 281 9

COMHAIRLE CHONTAE ÁTHA CLIATH THEAS
SOUTH DUBLIN COUNTY LIBRARIES

SOUTH DUBLIN BOOKSTORE
TO RENEW ANY ITEM TEL: 459 7834

Items should be returned on or before the last date below. Fines,
as displayed in the Library, will be charged on overdue items.

Sleeping with Monsters

Scottish women of any historical interest are curiously rare...
our leading Scotswomen have been ... almost entirely
destitute of exceptional endowments of any sort.

– Hugh MacDiarmid
Cit. Margaret Bain
'Scottish Women in
Politics,'
in *Woven By Women*
CHAPMAN, 27/28,
Edinburgh
1980.

... the literature of the Irish literary Renaissance is a
peculiarly masculine affair ... it is in society that
women belong.

– Frank O'Connor
THE LONELY VOICE
Macmillan Press, London
1963.

A thinking woman sleeps with monsters.
The beak that grips her, she becomes.

– Adrienne Rich
from *Snapshots of a
Daughter-In-Law*
in SNAPSHOTS OF A
DAUGHTER-IN-LAW
W. W. Norton and
Company, New York
1963.

Dedication

To the memory of my parents, Dow and Barbara Wilson.

To my teachers, Ruth A. Borker, Donald Brenneis, Michael Harper, Wendy Owen, Adrienne Rich, Harry Kellet Roberts, Michael Roth, Marilee Stark and Herschel Tribbet, who all gave me more than they know.

For my friends and soul-mates, Consuella LuJoyce Brown, Lucinda Marie Toy, Nina Vincent, and my sister, Michelina Wilson – and so the dialogue continues.

Rebecca E. Wilson

Acknowledgements

Many people made this book possible. I wish to thank Nancy Y. Bekavac, Frances S. Orzechhowski and Martin A. Brody, of the Thomas J. Watson Foundation, for their continued support of me as a 'fellow' and a person during and after my research.

The following people assisted the research process: Tom Hubbard and Tessa Ransford of the Scottish Poetry Library; Rory Brennan of *Poetry Ireland Review*; Ruth Hooley, editor of *The Female Line*; and Jessie Lendennie, editor of *The Salmon*. I owe a special thanks to Pam Smith, formerly of Polygon Books, Edinburgh, for recognizing the potential of a book within a mass of raw, unedited material, and for starting the ball rolling.

I wish to thank my collective family, the Rand/Sterlings, the Wilson/Obertos, and the Page/Duncans, for their continued support and encouragement. Cheers.

I am indebted to my co-editor for her hard work, persistence and humour, which saw us both through many dark nights of editorial doubt and financial anxiety.

Though the following women do not appear in the collection, I wish to thank Elizabeth Burns, Chris Cherry, Moya Cannon, Glenda Cimino, Anne W. Gleave, Christine Hammond, Thelma Ingram, Jessie Lendennie, Patricia Mallon, Angela McSeveney, Sheila Mulveena, Joy Pitman, Rosemary Rowley, Maureen Sangster and Brenda Shaw, for they contributed to my greater understanding of women's poetic and personal experiences in Scotland and Ireland. I am grateful for their time and insight.

Rebecca E. Wilson

Contents

Introduction

A thinking woman sleeps with monsters.
The beak that grips her, she becomes. And Nature,
that sprung-lidded, still commodious
steamer trunk of *tempora* and *mores*
gets stuffed with it all: the mildewed orange-flowers,
the female pills, the terrible breasts
of Boadicea beneath flat foxes' heads and orchids.

from Adrienne Rich, *Snapshots Of A Daughter-In-Law* (1963)

MONSTERS SYMBOLIZE A FUSION of contradictions. Human and animal bodies, imbued with ideas and feelings, are joined in a single shape. In many cultures such creatures, appearing in dreams or visions, are associated with a *rite de passage*, the centre point of a transition from one state of being to another. The power of monsters is that they jar us out of our own realities. They can scare us, and they can encourage new emotional and conceptual possibilities; they can create, and are created from, both fear and freedom. The woman poet who seeks to name herself and the world around her necessarily sleeps with monsters. This book seeks to explore why.

I first encountered the idea of female and literary monsters while writing my undergraduate dissertation on the North American poet and essayist Adrienne Rich. In *Snapshots of A Daughter-In-Law* (1963), Rich wrestles with a separation of selves, woman and writer. The poet begins to unite the two identities and in doing so confronts the need for a new language and new images with which to express herself. When I began this book, I was surprised to find the same themes and images emerging, quite spontaneously, from the interviews in a myriad of subtle as well as overt ways.

I began the research for this project while completing my

degree in Cultural Anthropology. Until that time, my studies had focused on the language and symbolism within North American women's literature. I became curious as to the work of women outside my own literary tradition. At first, I found references to only three women and two poems and all of them were Irish. While poetry and analysis of American and English women were in abundance, that of Scottish and Irish women was virtually non-existent. I began to wonder whether there were women writing within the Celtic fringe, and if so, why were there no books or references to them? The less information I turned up, the more determined I became to find out why. Gradually, as a result of writing to various Arts Councils and libraries in Scotland and Ireland, I gathered a comprehensive list of contemporary names. I then turned my attention to the larger issue of the role of women poets within their literary and national heritage.

My studies in Cultural Anthropology had indicated to me that the role of the female poet in these three nations presented complexities which distinguished them from women poets working within other traditions. The complexity is twofold, encompassing both their female and national identities.

Feminist scholarship throughout the world has made us aware that the relationship of the female artist to her culture is potentially problematic; literature, its styles, subjects and symbols have been predominantly defined by men. Thus, many women writers are confronted with a creative tradition and a language that does not necessarily include room for their experience or modes of poetic expression. To quote Adrienne Rich again, '*this is the oppressor's language/ yet I need to talk to you*'. Although not each woman in this collection finds this to be true, nevertheless, each is working to hear the sound of her own poetic voice. This struggle for creative expression is also relevant in relation to the concepts of nationality and cultural identity.

There are writers and scholars better equipped than I to discuss the historical relations between England, Scotland, Northern Ireland and the Republic of Ireland. Nevertheless it is important to acknowledge, in most general terms, that both Scotland and Ireland share a history of domination by England. This history has had, and continues to have, political, physical, social and cultural ramifications.

In terms of language and literature, the British literary tradition has been represented, for the most part, by English writers (although it is often said that the finest English writers are Irish). Furthermore, Irish, Scots and Gaelic languages have been, and continue to be, marginalized in a variety of ways – from written to spoken expression. Writers who choose to work in Scots, Gaelic and Irish are faced with a literary structure that lends them little entry. The combination of these two elements results in a struggle for space in which a diversity of writing might develop and flourish. Again, each woman is searching for that space on her own terms, whatever her native language. This is the terrain I set out to explore.

As an interviewer, I designed my questions to cover a breadth of issues: When did these women start writing? What inspires them to write: images, sounds, concepts or feelings? For whom are they writing? In what forms are they writing: free verse, strict forms, or somewhere in between? What other kinds of writing are women involved in? Prose? Playwriting? Novels? And how does the process of writing poetry differ from other types of writing? Or for that matter, from other art forms women are engaged in, such as painting or music? How do women see themselves, as poets, female poets, feminist poets? In other words, do women see their writing as something upon which gender has no bearing, or is their writing influenced by their experience as women? Likewise, do women see themselves as being Scottish or Irish poets? If so, how is this expressed and explored in the poetry itself? For the women writing in Scots, Gaelic and Irish, what are their reasons for doing so? In addition, I drew questions from each woman's poetry with reference to individual styles and thematic threads.

The responses are diverse. There are women writing about monsters and women working through muses; some are confronting national sectarianisms while for others nationalism and nations are of no concern. Some write about the human spirit and others use themes of womanhood. There are women who are feminist and women who identify with a male poetic tradition; there are those who write directly from their personal experience and those who write in dramatic personas. The list goes on.

This book is not an analysis of these varied responses. What the interview format allows is for each poet to express in her own terms what her writing is about and what it means to her. For the reader, it offers an opportunity to listen in on how writers think, talk and feel about themselves and their work. In addition, by including poems with the interview text, we may begin to explore how ideas and feelings are translated from thought and speech into writing and art. This collection allows women poets to speak – whatever their perspective and experience – into the silence that has hitherto surrounded them.

Again, this collection is not an analysis of this process. Rather, it is an articulation of it. The women in this collection represent a range of approaches to creative poetic expression. Neither is this collection an exposé of women's personal lives; it is an acknowledgement that life and art are inextricably bound.

This book is about women. I say nothing new when I state that women's writing and its importance has been neglected in cultures throughout the world, from publication to criticism, acknowledgement to analysis. Scotland and Ireland are no exception. But whereas the feminist movement of the 1960s necessarily addressed the commonalities of women's experiences – economic, domestic, artistic, emotional, sexual, personal and political – feminism of the 1980s has moved on to examine the differences between women. As humans, our experience is informed not only by the particular events of our individual lives, it is affected by our race, class and nationality as well as our gender. The feminist dialogue has begun to expand and address such differences of experience, and the consequently varied needs, amongst women as well as between women and men. This book is part of that dialogue.

No writer operates in a vacuum; all artists are socio-cultural beings – the context in which one lives informs, in the broadest sense, the material and tools for creative expression. For the poet, this means working within a particular framework of symbols. These symbols include language, both sounds and words, as well as image, both colour and shape. Each poet combines language, image and subject matter in a unique and individual way, drawing from a wealth of personal and cultural symbols and experience. There is a movement, for the writer, between oneself and one's context, in order to understand as well as be understood.

This collection is by no means exhaustive. The interviews in this book, conducted between the summer of 1986 to the spring of 1988, represent a cross-section of established as well as emerging poets. I have also included those women of different nationalities, who live and work in Scotland and Ireland, for they shed additional light. As editors, Gillean and I have selected the texts to emphasize the range of views concerning the relationship between self and society, womanhood and writing.

There are twenty-five very different Scottish and Irish women represented in this collection. Their voices are like light through a crystal, reflecting a spectrum of experience. Their diversity can only add richness and colour to national and international literature.

Rebecca E. Wilson

A Note on the Choice of Poems

Monsters, once we started looking, cropped up everywhere – in how women perceive themselves and how they feel they are perceived, in their actual experience as much as in images from myth or legend or crude stereotype. Inevitably, being restricted in the number of poems we could use to represent each poet, we cannot have done anybody full justice. Some fine poems could not be included because of their length. Others ran into copyright problems or authorial veto. Throughout, our aim has been to try and give an indication of each poet's range – both serious *and* funny sides (as in Liz Lochhead's work for example), public *and* private themes, Irish (or Gaelic, or Scots) *and* English.

In doing so, perhaps we're beginning to make a map of what women today, in Scotland and Ireland, find significant. The women in this book confront personal relationships, as children, parents, lovers, spouses, students, artists. They reflect on the influences of education, religion, families, politics and the shadow of war. They engage with suffering and loss, with the experiences of childbirth, anorexia, infertility, rape, violence, emotional breakdown, with conflicts between domestic ties and responsibilities and creative and professional needs, with issues of race, language, national and personal identity. Eithne Strong, for example, finds a woman's lifelong experience of wiping bottoms as dignified a subject for poetry as the creaking of her ageing bones.

We hope these interviews and poetry selections will be of interest to readers not normally interested in poetry, or poetry as it is all too often defined by those who are in a position to influence taste and approve content. We also hope the confluence of thematic monsters which emerge, for the most part, from these pages, will remind readers, if they need reminding, of the diversity, strength and urgency of women's writing now.

Gillean Somerville-Arjat

Medbh McGuckian

MEDBH MCGUCKIAN WAS BORN in Belfast in 1950 and studied at Queen's University, Belfast, where she has been Writer in Residence. She is married and divides her time among teaching, writing and raising her three sons.

In 1979 she won the British National Poetry Award. Her publications include poetry in *Trio* (Blackstaff Press, Belfast, 1981) and four collections of poetry, *Single Ladies* (Interim Press, 1980), *Portrait of Joanna* (Ulsterman Publications), *The Flower Master* (1982) and *Venus and the Rain* (1984), both published by Oxford University Press, Oxford.

Medbh and I arranged to meet at Queen's. I went to the Engish Department and waited. And waited. No Medbh. Finally, I decided to go. I was just leaving the building when she came rushing up, a dark-haired woman with rounded features, breathless and apologetic. She couldn't talk then, but would I be willing to come and read to her creative writing class the next day? It was after the class that we actually had a chance to sit down. She was nervous but willing to talk; her hands fluttered up around her face whenever she spoke. I got a strong sense of the pressures she felt from the combination of teaching, writing and raising a family. We finally did the interview at her home late one night after her children had gone to bed. After two hours of talking, she took a deep breath and asked, 'Is that enough?

I WAS BROUGHT UP in Belfast. I wouldn't have been a poet, I don't think, if I had lived anywhere else. I don't write about 'The Troubles' but in 1968 the conflict did filter into me – did give me a sense of dislocation, a sense of being two people or a divided personality. I don't even read the news, I refuse to, but I can't get away from it. It's been going on for twenty years, and historically for five hundred years, but in my life, violence and tragedy have been inescapable. Also, I believe very strongly that you can't write without suffering, if it's not your personal suffering, then the suffering of your people, or the suffering of your nation.

What inspires you to write? Probably the desire to write inspires me all of the time. Did you hear about that murder (*The shooting of a young mother in Belfast*)? That doesn't inspire me, obviously, but I feel it is something I have to make a statement about. What inspires me are the things that happen and how you cope with them, or how you make sense of them. What I tend to do is gloss over them, or use poetry to control horror and evil, to make them, not less important, but to put them into their overall context. That's what I'm trying to do, not trying to cover it up, but trying to understand it, especially violent death, death imposed upon one human being by another. It's very difficult to do. It's a game of not facing reality, but if I didn't have it, I would be insane.

Inspiration works with me. It takes over, if it's a good one. I'm just a medium for it. I don't really have to work. If I have to do a lot of thinking and rationalizing, it's not going to be a great poem. I just take an assortment of words, though not exactly at random, and I fuse them. It's like embroidery. It's very feminine, I guess. They are very intricate, my poems, a weaving of patterns of ins and outs and contradictions, one thing playing off another. I guess there's a narrator somewhere, holding it all together, but I don't feel it's necessarily me. I feel there is someone else writing the poem sometimes.

Is it another part of you? I think it is some outside force, because sometimes I predict things in the poem and they come true, and how could I possibly know them? To me, this is fascinating. It's like witchcraft. Sometimes the poet is using very powerful influences when he's operating at his full potential. I think it is a 'he' very much when I'm writing – which is strange. I think of myself as not being male, but as much male as female, or as being sexless – not essentially female, anyway.

Who are you writing for? Principally for my own peace of mind, for my own sanity. I write for the approval of other poets and I don't write for the approval of other female poets. *Why is that?* Because most of them I don't approve of. Most of them don't exert themselves enough. Most of them have a different idea of what they're doing than what I am doing, whereas, when I talk to men, I feel that we have the same goals. *Can you give me an example?* When I was at a Women's Week I just did not feel that we were stretching ourselves in a way that men do. Their standards were limited – their perspectives were confined to each other. I just think that women should not sell themselves short, and sometimes they do.

In an artistic sense? In what kind of sense? They're content to be rated with second-rate male writers and I'm not. I have very strong ambition. I think that some women exploit their feminism to the detriment of their work.

How does this tie in with your own poetry, where many of the symbols that come up are traditionally images of femaleness – moons, flowers, houses, water? I think, again, it's a kind of tension. They are my world – I mean, I have a womb, I can't pretend that I haven't, I don't want to pretend that I haven't. I live in a house, I am a housewife, I like feminine things, I like beautiful flowers. But they're set in the context of their opposites. I wouldn't think of the moon without thinking of its opposite – I am always thinking of its opposite. I wouldn't think of a flower without thinking of the tuber, the root of the flower, and that seems to be a much more masculine thing. Those are the poems in which those tensions in me were unresolved. I was still a victim of my life, and was trying to work out certain kinds of freedoms, I'm not saying that I'm done with them, but they've lived out their meaningfulness for me at this point in my life. A house represents security, but it is a false security, because we know that a man can come into your house and shoot you. So there's not much real safety in a house. But insofar as the house represents the soul, the real inner you, that survives after death in some way, it can't be violated.

You talk about your pregnancies and births of your children as being very much related to your writing. Yes, in some senses. I think that, for me, to develop as a poet, I had to develop physically as a woman. My maturing physically goes hand in hand with my maturing in every other way, psychologically, emotionally. I think that women who don't have children always feel a kind of lack, lack of knowledge, or lack of awareness. A woman who's had a baby instinctively feels that she is part of some kind of secret, the sisterhood of motherhood, and it's something very special.

You said in your last interview that you felt that your poems are about male and female sides of yourself? How does that tie in? Not just in myself, but male and female sides of experience. There is an argument going on all of the time. In some poems it's more obvious, between the complementary roles; does the sun reflect the moon, or does the moon reflect the sun? Sometimes I turn things upside down and make the moon male because I get so tired of the moon being female. Why should it be, when it's just a piece of matter? Why shouldn't the sun be female if she wants to be?

I also said in that interview that I was afraid of women. I'm not frightened of them, but my experience of them was so bad. All of my early life was female. I went to an all-female school, I had a lot of sisters, and I had very little intercourse, of any description, with any man. I saw men at a distance, I had to revere them, they were priests, they did things, they had jobs. Women didn't. Women were just subservient slaves who went around the streets, gossiping about their children, and I didn't want that. When I went to secondary school, I was completely surrounded by women, nuns, and that was enough to put me off women for the rest of my life. I got sick of being part of this community that excludes men on what seemed to me very strange reasoning, that men were so different. I didn't feel that they were so malevolent, and at the same time, so flipping superior, that they were either going to rape you or own you, as a husband, or that they were going to look down on you, as a cleric, or a priest, or a pope, or a cardinal. I just got it into my head that all I wanted was to be free of this.

I basically see the role of the poet as a male role which I have adopted. I chose it for that reason. I didn't choose it because there were any female examples, because I didn't know about them then. I wanted to do something that would make me into a man, or give me the status of a man. And I'm proud of it for that reason, which is probably completely wrong, but I feel that I'm shifting. I think a lot of the motivation behind it was to gain status; I couldn't otherwise see how I was going to gain in any other field.

To survive in 'a man's world,' you had to be like a man? Not to survive, to be myself, to be authentic.

How do you then reconcile that perspective of being perhaps more comfortable in 'a man's world', or seeing poetry as a male thing, with what you said earlier, of having children and de-

veloping yourself emotionally as well as psychologically? It's absolutely opposite tensions. This is why I do tend to crack up, because one is the physical, sensual, instinctive, knowing thing – to be the passive recipient, to be the nurturer, to be the home, and the womb, and the woman, to give into the urges of your womb. And the other is the mind, the brain, not totally the brain, but the spirit as well. It's two different kinds of creativity, pulling against each other, and almost destroying each other. Polar opposites. But at times they gel, and when they gel, I'm happy.

What, for you is the relationship between form and content? For example, I recently wrote a poem that had the word, 'kilometre', to suggest infinite experience, a journey, a relationship that would be very long and fruitful. I had all the other lines fairly long, and then just 'kilometres', just one word, to suggest it filled up the rest. Sometimes the word, the content, will dictate the form, as in that case. But sometimes it's not so clear. Somebody pointed out to me the other day that he counted twelve prepositions in one sentence. I was starting off the poem, 'shape under shape, perfume under perfume,' that's the first line, but the content is almost dictated by the form.

And how does that relate to what you're trying to express? I'm usually trying to talk about myself, and the different poems and the different selves, and the mutiny of one self against another, the clash of one life against another. So, the prepositional form probably does suit it, 'shape under shape', perfume under perfume', that there's obviously something underneath. There's the superficial level, and then there are other levels under it all. I think it is related to those themes – a woman's hiddenness, her secrecies, her facets.

Would you consider yourself an Irish poet, and if so, in what sense? I'm not English but I write in English. I don't hark back to any Irish poets who were writing in Irish, I have no conception, no history of reading them, and when I've read them, it's been belatedly. So, there's no such thing as an Irish poet, really, divorced from the language that he works in. But I think my temperament is coloured by living on this island, my identity, my home, is very much fixed to the North. I certainly don't have any great feelings for the island as a whole in any romantic way. I'd like to see the whole thing sorted out amicably. But it's something that I don't understand. The fact that I spell my name in Irish is significant, because it's a re-Gaelicized version of what was previously anglicized. In a way I'm an English poet, trying to reverse into an Irishness that is an impossible dream. I was christened 'Maeve,' but my sisters were Dorothy,

Rosemary and Maria, and my mother, Margaret. They don't have
Irish names but I have this pseudo-Irish name, a pseudo-Irish iden-
tity. We're all just adopted. Ireland doesn't care about us, nor
England. We feel we don't have any roots.

My name, Medbh, is quite important, because I am repudi-
ating the anglicization of myself. And some part of me is desper-
ately seeking a spiritual reunion with my native, Irish-speaking,
peasant, repressed and destroyed, ancestors and ancestresses. If
to be Irish is to be Catholic, at the same time as you're trying to
get away from the anglicization of yourself, you are also trying to
get away from the colonization of your soul by Roman Catholicism. I can't accept that kind of restriction. I'm trying to re-
christianize myself, to get back to whatever true Christianity is.

You see, it's all very complicated. For example, the image of
Christ on the cross is such a disturbingly phallic image to present a
child with. If someone opened a book in front of my son with an
image of a man being hanged or bleeding, and said, 'Now, this is
what you must believe in,' I would find it shocking. I would think,
'What are you trying to do to this child?' but that's what was done to
me. I remember looking at bleeding hands and bleeding feet, the
sight of the wound – it's such a gory picture of manhood. Maybe it is
what life is about, but why that? There was no way we were allowed
to look at nude statues, or nude paintings by Reuben, but we were
allowed to look at that! Why am I allowed to look at that, but when
it comes to a representation of human love, of normal human delight
in the beauty of the body, it's not allowed?

THE FLITTING

'You wouldn't believe all this house has cost me –
In body-language terms, it has turned me upside down.'
I've been carried from one structure to the other
On a chair of human arms, and liked the feel
Of being weightless, that fraternity of clothes ...
Now my own life hits me in the throat, the bumps
And cuts of the walls as telling
As the poreholes in strawberries, tomato seeds.
I cover them for safety with these Dutch girls
Making lace, or leaning their almond faces
On their fingers with a mandolin, a dreamy
Chapelled ease abreast this other turquoise-turbanned,
Glancing over her shoulder with parted mouth.

She seems a garden escape in her unconscious
Solidarity with darkness, clove-scented
As an orchid taking fifteen years to bloom,
And turning clockwise as the honeysuckle.
Who knows what importance
She attaches to the hours?
Her narrative secretes its own values, as mine might
If I painted the half of me that welcomes death
In a faggotted dress, in a peacock chair,
No falser biography than our casual talk
Of losing a virginity, or taking a life, and
No less poignant if dying
Should consist in more than waiting.

I postpone my immortality for my children,
Little rock-roses, cushioned
In long-flowering sea-thrift and metrics,
Lacking elemental memories:
I am well-earthed here as the digital clock,
Its numbers flicking into place like overgrown farthings
On a bank where once a train
Ploughed like an emperor living out a myth
Through the cambered flesh of clover and wild carrot.

THE FLOWER MASTER

Like foxgloves in the school of the grass moon
We come to terms with shade, with the principle
Of enfolding space. Our scissors in brocade,
We learn the coolness of straight edges, how
To gently stroke the necks of daffodils
And make them throw back their heads to the sun.

We slip the thready stems of violets, delay
The loveliness of the hibiscus dawn with quiet ovals,
Spirals of feverfew like water splashing,
The papery legacies of bluebells. We do
Sea-fans with sea-lavender, moon-arrangements
Roughly for the festival of moon viewing.

This black container calls for sloes, sweet
Sultan, dainty nipplewort, in honour
Of a special guest, who summoned to the
Tea ceremony, must stoop to our low doorway,
Our fontanelle, the trout's dimpled feet.

Liz Lochhead

LIZ LOCHHEAD WAS BORN in Motherwell in 1947. She trained as a painter at Glasgow Art College then worked as an art teacher for eight years. Her selection to be the first holder of the Scottish/ Canadian Writers' Exchange fellowship in 1978 marked her transition to full-time writing. She was Writer in Residence at Edinburgh University from 1985 to 1987. She lives in Glasgow but spends much of her time travelling in Britain and abroad giving readings and performances of her work.

Her publications include five collections of poems, *Memo for Spring* (Reprographia, 1977), *Islands* (Print Studio Press, 1978), *Dreaming Frankenstein and Collected Poems* (1984), *True Confessions and New Clichés (1985) and Tartuffe* (1986), a translation into Scots from the original by Molière, all published by Polygon Books, Edinburgh. She has also written several plays including *Blood and Ice, Same Difference* and *Dracula*. At the time of the interview she was completing *Mary Queen of Scots Got Her Head Chopped Off*, which was premièred at the Edinburgh Festival in 1987.

I knocked on the door of Liz's office at Edinburgh University. She yelled, 'Come in'. I entered to find her clutching a pencil at her desk where she was working on her play, *Mary*

Queen of Scots Got Her Head Chopped Off. Various empty coffee mugs and smudged wine glasses stood on the desk and the window ledge. Before her lay sheaves of paper covered in large scrawling writing. She smiled, 'Oh, hello, come in. I was just working on my play and I'm stuck.' She ran a hand through her short blonde hair, making her bracelets jangle and clink. 'Should I come back later?' I asked. 'No, no, come in.' Despite the fact that I had arrived in the midst of her writing, she shifted into the interview with remarkable ease, often seeming surprised at her own answers. At the end, she said, 'I think you've got me going again. Sometimes it helps to talk about your work. It lets you look at what you're doing. I might be able to write now.' I thanked her and left her to it.

WHAT INSPIRES YOU? *What motivates you to write?* I don't know. I know what happens. I know what it feels like. A little bit of language goes funny. An ordinary phrase'll suddenly strike you in a new way. It'll turn itself inside out in some way.

Reading your work, I was very conscious of rhythm in it, of sound. I think that's what gets you going. It's always a phrase that sings out in your brain. You hear it with its own rhythm and that gives you the clue how to build the rest. But you've got to find all the rest. It's hard work.

Do you find playwriting is different from doing the poetry? At its best, no. Whenever I'm doing the ones I really love, it feels very like writing a great big poem. Like an adaptation of *Dracula* I did. But not plays like *Tartuffe*, which are just translations. I don't know why this one I'm working on's been such a slog. It keeps taking off and then grounding again. *What's it about?* Mary, Queen of Scots, which is quite a difficult thing to write about without being corny or romantic. It's really about Scotland, more about the present than the past, how those myths of the past have carried on into the present malaise of Scotland today. She was around when a lot of the things that rule Scotland today were forming and hardening, you know, misogyny, Calvinism, all sorts of stuff like that.

You draw a lot on mythology and history. Yes. I didn't in my first book. It was all about grey streets and rain and here and now and I didn't want to be allusive in any way. The next one was called *The Grimm Sisters.* I began to retell familiar stories from another angle. I didn't want the women to be the object in the stories, but the subject. And so there's irony there. And since then

I've been fascinated by familiar stories and myths and legends.

Does the content of your plays dictate the form? Yes, I think it always does in both plays and poems. I don't think there's ever that split. You might as well ask: Is the idea of giving birth different from actually giving birth to the real baby? It's all the one thing. I think that what's wrong when one isn't writing properly is that one can't find the form to put it in. Poetry is much more about waiting for it than other kinds of writing. With plays, if you waited for it, you'd probably wait a long time. You can't afford to wait. You've got to push.

Do you have an audience in mind? Not for poems, no. I feel a poem is like a message to yourself, telling you what you think and feel about certain things. One hopes coincidentally that it will also make a lot of sense to other people, but that's not what they're for while you're doing them. With plays I think about the audience all the time, because then I think, How will this work?

Do you have a clear intention when you're writing? No, I don't have a clear intention. If I had, I wouldn't bother to write. I think I write to clarify my intention. It's a process. I don't just write it once. I think my principal love is language itself. When I can't write it's because I can't find the right language. It's not the ideas. Any ideas I've got come already clothed in language.

You use humour a lot. Yes, I find language very funny anyway. Sometimes you laugh a lot when you're writing really sad things and sometimes you sweat blood when you're writing humour. They're not connected in terms of being fun to write. But the whole act of framing untidy old experience in language is inherently funny. *Is it a way of making things accessible to people?* It's not that kind of decision. It's just making it accessible to myself, I think. If something doesn't have irony in it for me it wouldn't be alive. The kind of amazement I have is often in simple language, how much of a giveaway it is.

Do you think of yourself as a Scottish writer? Increasingly. Ten years ago I liked being called a feminist writer because feminism was a new and helpful thing to be writing about and I was surprised to find how feminist my writing was. Now I'm happy to be called a Scottish writer because I'm surprised to find how Scottish it is. I don't write in standard English. I write in Scots English and sometimes actually in Scots. But it's a simple thing. It's defining what you really are so that you can more honestly relate with the world. Being a feminist writer was stopping writing as if I might be a man, so being a Scottish writer is stopping writing as if I might be English. It's a matter of taking on board certain things and letting them feed right through to the bedrock. It was probably the same for American writers when Mark Twain began to write in American English. For some reason 'a Scottish poet' sounds as if it's just something they're saying about you, whereas 'a feminist poet' tells a lot of people not to bother listening. It means to a lot of men that it's for women only and men shouldn't be reading it. I'm not interested in that. I wouldn't mind being called a female poet, because I think my poetry is a pursuit of the feminine. Robert Graves says all poetry is anyway, but mine is a female pursuit of the feminine, whereas his is about a male pursuit of the feminine. I think that's part of the problem. Adrienne Rich is very articulate about it.

Does Scottish for you as a writer mean the use of language, or language and experience, or geography or what? I think it's about what colour your English is. It's the same with being female. My language is female-coloured as well as Scottish-coloured.

It's almost as if your language is more reflective of your experience. You are Scottish. You are female. Oh, yes. But I can't think how your language could not be. It's a matter of realising that what you've got can be a tool. That's what Mark Twain discovered. You didn't have to learn this other language and then use it, so you weren't disadvantaged. You could use your own language that you talk in. That's the difference. To me prose is still not speech. It's a thing in black and white. And the fact that a lot of prose nowadays manages to capture speech and rhythm is one thing, but there's also that prose voice one feels one's got to master, that English-male-posh-grown-up-dead speech.

Often academic. Uhuh. Which is regarded as being the norm, voiceless and neutral, but these things are not neutral. My friend Tom Leonard has a poem about media language called 'This is the Six O'Clock News'. He thinks the text of that other language is KEEP OUT. GO AWAY. Which I think it is in a lot of ways. You feel that if you can't handle this clearly and elegantly then you haven't got the right to be a writer, which may be true. I love that people can write like that without worrying about it, because some people can. It's great. My interest in Scots was partly writing *Tartuffe* and exploring that kind of voice. There was a very clear voice I wanted to write down. It just invented itself. It wasn't like Scots I had read. It was like Scots I could hear. I felt there was a job to be done doing that. It was exciting.

How would you define yourself as a writer or a poet, a woman writer, a feminist writer or what? I don't identify myself as a feminist-writer. I'm I. I'm a feminist. When somebody asks me what I do, I usually say writer. The most precious thing to me is to be a poet. If I were a playwright, I'd like to be a poet in the theatre. I suspect some people might think of me as a writer/performer or a feminist performer or all kinds of things I wouldn't think of myself as. My work would never be anti-feminist, but I don't think of myself as a feminist-writer because I don't think you can write and sign up for anything. It's OK to call me a feminist-writer if men call themselves masculist-writers or macho-drunken-romantic-writers or whatever! I think I'm a sort of romantic writer. I'm definitely romantic rather than classical in my tendencies. Not a romance writer, however!

Do you feel the feminist-writer label means that you can only write about certain things? Yes, well, it insinuates you write about feminist issues. I do sometimes, but it puts a political framework round the writing that I don't find helpful. I think feminism's basically very, very simple. It's about equal pay, equal opportunities, abortion on demand, free childcare. So what could you write about these things? The other things, the things of the soul, which have to do with the way we screw up these simple things, and the reasons we screw them up. I'm interested in exploring, but not condoning. That's why the feminist bit doesn't fit with me the writer. I don't think anybody could have seen *Dracula* and called it feminist. I'm interested in exploring issues without apportioning blame. I'm interested in female masochism, for instance. I suppose it's a feminist issue, but it's also a human issue. It's more ambivalent than I would feel it to be in proper feminist terms. Maybe quite wrongly, I tend to feel that feminism's about things I'm sure about, so there's nothing much to be said about them. Sure I'm interested in exploring people suffering from the lack of these things, but it's not a potent thing for me to write about constantly. Whereas romanticism, masochism, horror, not necessarily correct or worked out things, seem to be potent whenever I'm writing about them. I'm happy to be called a socialist writer when I'm writing a bit of agitprop, but I wouldn't say I was a socialist writer. I don't mean that I don't want to take the isms', like socialism, feminism, and a slightly-gathering-steam nationalism that I feel, into my poetry, but I don't want to make my poetry have to sign up with them. Poetry is a bit greater than these 'isms'.

What about your interest in Frankenstein and Dracula?
That snuck up on me really. When I was in America I had a lot of time and wanted to write something more substantial and I decided I would like to write about Mary Wollstonecraft. All I really knew about her when I started was that she'd been Mary Shelley's mother and that Mary Shelley had written *Franken-stein*. It kept fascinating me, how this intellectual, rational woman, with all these incredibly powerful, almost too rational, views of female education, had been so haunted by bogeymen in her own life, and had tried to drown herself. And then it interested me that her daughter should have grown up to write *Frankenstein*, a horror book as far as I was concerned.

Once I started, that fact kept haunting me, so that I became gradually more interested in Mary Shelley, the heir to reason. It was quite like myself at that point. The feminism of the late sixties and all through the seventies had given me this sense that reason ought to be attainable and I still hadn't got very far with it in my own personal life.

Why would Mary Shelley write about monsters? I was haunted by that phrase from Goya: 'The sleep of reason produces monsters'. If you try to force things to be too rational the dark and untidy bits will well up and manifest themselves in quite concrete ways. So I stopped reading about Mary Wollstonecraft and began to read about Mary Shelley and became more and more interested in the companions she had who were pulling her in two different ways and what they meant to her, and the whole thing began to be written, a bit like a great big fat poem. All the different things it threw up were different aspects of self. When you read the book you're both creator and monster and a lot of the other characters as well.

The Dracula bit came up because the Lyceum Theatre Company in Edinburgh asked me to adapt it and I thought, Oh, no, I don't think so. That sounds awful. And I began to read the book and thought it was absolute crap. Then I read one thing in it which I liked, which was that with vampires, first you have to invite them in, and ever afterwards they can come and go as they please. But you have to invite them to cross the threshold first. So I was interested in people's darker natures, what makes some-body who has all the ingredients of a rational life turn to dark-ness. It's suppression. The more you try to suppress the dark bits of yourself, the more they well up. I'm very interested in repression of various sorts, linguistic, sexual, whatever. I keep thinking of a line from a poem by Adrienne Rich: '*A thinking woman sleeps with monsters* . . .' Yes, that's right.

THE BRIDE

I AM THE ABSOLUTE spit of Elsa Lanchester. A ringer for her, honestly, down to the zigzag of lightning in my frightwig and it's funny no one (me included) ever noticed the resemblance before, because this fine morning – jolted awake by a crash in the kitchen, the smell of burning and the corncrake domesticity of dawnchorus toast getting scraped – suddenly there's the me in the mirror staring back at me and me less than amazed at me all marcelled like Elsa Lanchester. Well, it's apt enough, this is my last morning as a single girl.

Despite your ex-wife's incendiary good wishes, there's the new frock I've been dieting into for more than a fortnight quite intact over the back of the chair. And because last night was my last night, last night I left you, left you to your own devices under our double duvet, left home and went home, home to Home home, to sleep my last night in my old single bed. I'd love to say I've my old toys around me, etcetera, and the same old old-gold counterpane, but is it likely? Is it likely, what with the old dear's passion for continuous redecoration? So not a Sunday-School prize that's not long gone to Oxfam, there's just one school photo, a wall-eyed teddy bear some rugby player gave me for my twenty-first, and an acrylic still life with aubergine I did in Sixth Year which, for a moment, I consider asking for (except where could we hang it) to take home to our home, our old home which today's nuptials must make our new home, take home to remind myself of what I can't remember which is what the hell the girl who did the picture and was (as far as I remember) painting-daft has to do with me, the me the bride with the Lanchester look.

Breakfast. Breakfast on a tray and like a condemned man I can have anything I want for breakfast but before I can lop the top off my boiled egg, before I can say 'soldiers' far less dunk them the place is bristling with sisters stripping me and unzipping me and down the hall the bathroom taps are pounding Niagra and bubbles. 'Buck's fizz, three fingers, Cheers Kiddo, cheerio' – this is Ellen the older one, the 'matron of honour', clashing glasses, knocking it back, in her slip and stocking soles, plugging in her Carmens, drenching herself in the Dutyfree Diorissima Dave brought back from that refresher course in Brussels with his secretary, unpacking Mothercare plastic carriers of maximum security sanitary protection from her Antler overnight case because she never knows the minute with that new coil she had fitted after Timothy. And Susan, sixteen, sly-eyes and skinny as a wand, she's always fancied you, ecru and peach, applegreen satin, she'll take all the eyes even though it's meant to be My Day, the bizzum's in kinks over the undercrotch buttons of my cami-knickers and I'm to touch nothing till the third coat of my nail varnish is dry and hands off my hair till Hazel comes to comb me out. Mother is being very mother-of-the-bride rushing around squeezing euthymol-pink shrimp-flavoured cream cheese on platters of crackers bigger than millwheels and though her daughters all agree a donkey brown two-piece is less than festive we're all thankful she's not drawing squinty seams up the back of her legs with eyebrow pencil in memory of her wedding in nineteen forty-three.

And here's the taxi and I stretch up my arms like one beseeching heaven, I stretch my arms like one embracing fate and four sets of arms help me into my dress, my dress I don't want to wear, my dress that after the whole caffuffle is really nothing special, my dress that should you jilt me, leave me in the lurch at the altar of the registry office, tilting my fragile psyche for ever permanently agley, the dress I'll have to wear as a penance till I'm dafter than Miss Havisham, in mourning for my life until it rots under the oxters. I should've chosen really carefully.

And then with Dad in the taxi and I know it's going to crash because there's got to be something going to stop me from ruining my life like this, but no, Dad winks and a quick swig from his hipflask and I'm on his arm and we're bowling gaily down the aisle towards you and the best man I've been knocking off for yonks with his grin and the ring (and his pockets bulging obscenely with apocryphal telegrams). Because we've opted for a quiet wedding and a civil sort of civil service the front four pews are chocablock with all our old lovers who – since we've taken so long to tie the knot – have all been married to each other, separated, been divorced so long they're on really friendly terms again and surely some one, some one will declare some just impediment to stop this whole ridiculous charade? I make my vows but all the time I'm thinking 'No, no, no' while I hear a voice I'm sure I recognise to be my own voice, loud as you like, 'I do'.

Despite the unfortunate business at the Reception with the manageress's Jack Russell depositing that dead rat right at my satin slippers underneath the top table which (the guests were animal lovers to a man) the company applauded, laughed and cheered; despite you and the bridesmaid being absent from the proceedings for a rather suspiciously long time, despite the fact that when we came to cut the cake the entire edifice collapsed like a prizewinning office block in a spectacular shambles of silver cardboard ionic columns and white plasterboard icing sugar we got into the going away car while the going was good and here we are, alone at last, in the plumbed-in twin-bedded room of the hotel where we told them we had booked a double – but the manager merely shrugged, said he had no record of that, and this was all they had, so take it or leave it, so we did.

We unpack our paperbacks. We scorn such sentimental institutionalising as making love on this our wedding night, and it's only after (sudden lust having picked us up by the scruff of the neck and chucked us into that familiar whirlpool) practised and perfect we judder totally together into amazed and wide-eyed calm and I lie beside you utterly content. I know for sure that this is never ever going to work.

DREAMING FRANKENSTEIN

She said she
woke up with him in
her head, in her bed.
Her mother-tongue clung to her mouth's roof
in terror, dumbing her, and he came with a name
that was none of her making.

No maidservant ever
in her narrow attic, combing
out her hair in the midnight mirror
on Hallowe'en (having eaten
that egg with its yolk hollowed out
then filled with salt)
– oh never one had such success as this
she had not courted.

The amazed flesh of her
neck and shoulders nettled
at his apparition.

Later, stark staring awake to everything
(the room, the dark parquet, the white high Alps beyond)
all normal in the moonlight
and him gone, save a ton-weight sensation,
and marks fading visibly where
his buttons had bit into her and
the rough serge of his suiting had chafed her sex,
she knew – oh that was not how –
but he'd entered her utterly.

This was the penetration
of seven swallowed apple pips.
Or else he'd slipped like a silver dagger
between her ribs and healed her up secretly
again. Anyway
he was inside her
and getting him out again
would be agony fit to quarter her,
unstitching everything.

Eyes on those high peaks
in the reasonable sun of the morning,
she dressed in damped muslin
and sat down to quill and ink
and icy paper.

Mary O'Donnell

MARY O'DONNELL WAS RAISED in County Monaghan. She studied German and Philosophy at Maynooth College and worked as a German teacher for several years; she is now Theatre Critic on the Dublin-based newspaper *The Sunday Tribune* and lives with her husband in Maynooth.

She has won a number of awards for poetry and has broadcast her work on radio and television. Her work has appeared in numerous Irish and American journals, including *Poetry Ireland Review* (Nos. 11,14,15,16; Poetry Ireland Press, 1984), *The Honest Ulsterman* and *The Midland Review* (Special Edition of Contemporary Irish Women Poets, edited by Nuala Archer, Oklahoma University Press, 1986). Her short story collection *Strong Pagans* will be published in 1991 by Poolbeg Press.

Mary's husband Martin met my bus at Maynooth. When we got to their house, Mary met us at the door, a tall woman, blonde, with an almost regal air. She led me into the kitchen where lunch was laid out on the table. As we ate Mary and Martin asked me about my family, my fellowship, and my education. I was the one being interviewed for a change which I rather enjoyed. Mary's work had proved difficult to get hold of and so after lunch, Mary gave me a stack of poems to read. I sat in her living room and read and made notes while Mary and Martin cleared up in the other room. About forty minutes later Mary returned and we began.

WRITING HAS ALWAYS GIVEN ME a sense of peace and coherence that nothing else has ever done. Only a love relationship obliterates all that. You forget about writing altogether then. But it's a language in which my way of seeing things is validated. I think it's just wonderful that there are other people out there, writing, using those codes, trying to name things that are difficult to name.

What about the poem 'Antarctica'? The experience of infertility really gutted me. I never would have thought it could have affected me so much. I have doubts about this maternal instinct business. I've no great experience of small children, although I quite like them. It was always a fairly intellectual thing. But when you find out that your equipment doesn't work as it's supposed to it's an entirely different matter. I felt my whole womanhood was under attack, that I'd failed my husband, and my husband's family and my own family. But I've long since shed that notion! That poem just burst out one night when another period had begun. I was desperate.

It doesn't matter so much now, funnily enough. I'm so committed to a writing career that I would definitely not welcome anything which would leave me with less time to write. And I've seen too many 'child-women', who spend their prime years chauffeuring children to and from school, to admire anything like that. Now I feel, 'Well, I'm at the end of a genetic line, and maybe that's sad and maybe it doesn't matter at all.' I used to cry a lot. At least I had that release. So did my husband. I still think of that poem as being pure, very distilled. It's OK.

I find other women poets' attitudes to maternity and fertility rather strange at times. There was some talk at the launch of *The Midland Review* about how we're all probably mothers and one of the women said, 'Oh, yes, women are already marginalized in poetry, but perhaps those who can't have children are doubly so.' I didn't have the guts to stand up and contradict her, but I was angry. I found it absurd. I know it wasn't meant like that, but I was annoyed at the assumption and its silliness. I don't feel marginalized. But there are all kinds of ambivalent attitudes towards the idea of motherhood within poets themselves.

*And bound up with ideas of creativity. I remember someone
saying to me she felt her creativity was very much bound up with
her children, and I was sitting there, never having had children,
thinking 'Does that then make my poetry less valid?'* Yes. This is
what I find difficult to understand. I suppose what you don't have
you don't miss. I don't feel amputated, but strangely enriched.
I'm very much aware of a creative process, the way a poem insists
on getting out no matter what. Whether it's our inner energies or
a psychic thing, I very much feel we're being worked through.

How would you name or interpret this muse, or this power?
I don't know. I think of it as a voice. I hear lines sometimes. It's an
asexual form, a white-robed figure. But in general a poem just
introduces itself. A line comes into your head. The thing is to
recognise that the mind wants to convey something ordinary
language cannot do. *Perhaps it's a process of learning how to
hear.* Yes, I think so, acutely.

Do you do other kinds of writing? Yes. I write short stories
as well. I need to write them every so often, although I think of
myself primarily as a poet. Sometimes I used to write them to
unblock myself if I was blocked for poetry, but now I don't.

Is that a different process from writing poems? Maybe I'll
have a more convoluted view of something and can't contain it
within a poem. My first published story was set in the future at a
stage when it did seem possible one could survive in a nuclear
shelter and there might even be something left when you came up
again. It's set in Ireland, in County Meath. A missile has gone off,
England and Bantry Bay have been hit and we're suffering the
effects up here. It's about a typical nuclear family and how they
experience things from the confines of a shelter 25 feet beneath
the ground for five weeks. They've everything worked out: their
sanitation needs and saplings for the brave new world they're
going to create. He has his blood pressure tablets, she has stocks
of Tampax! They have to forget about privacy. It's also about the
terrible tension that builds up and ends unresolved with the man
in his protective suit opening the hatch. He's going out with his
geiger counter to see what's left.

*How would you respond to the idea of poets walking a line
between reality and madness?* Sometimes I would say, yes, possibly some do. However, I tend to think that many poets walk a
romanticized line between what's real and what's imagined. It
isn't a bit romantic to be manic-depressive, but poets do romanti-
cize these things and imagine themselves dying of cancer or some

incurable wasting disease. It's all very nice for these 'victims' trapped in a 19th century mind-set! I don't know. I'm sceptical. I must say, though, I often think of Sylvia Plath. I'm 33 now. Was she 33 or 36 when she died? I get scared, I really do, and wonder if the thirties aren't dangerous years. There are so many hungers. *Hungers?* I think when one is chronologically in the prime of life there are all sorts of emotional hungers. Maybe status hungers. The adult can still have an infantile ego. My metaphor for life is The Great Search. It's a journey. Perhaps its purpose is to satisfy some of these hungers in self-discovery. I think the world with all its miseries can be a wonderfully celebratory place. It's the only place we know. That's why the nuclear problem concerns me so much. It's all very well for those who are convinced there's an afterlife. But here and now counts. It's every bit as valid.

I was looking at the forms you write in. You do different things with indentations. Is that conscious? That started in February this year. It sprang from a need to experiment a bit more. I was looking at some writings by American poets who were using these forms. I was told by a poet of some standing in this country who was looking over my work with an eye to publishing it that I made no concession to tradition in my forms. I had never thought of that. I always felt we were all part of some ongoing dialogue. He felt I needed to put a bit of 'discipline' into it. But I am actually a very disciplined worker and those lines aren't haphazard. I've thought them out for a reason. But of course it raises the question that maybe the women's tradition of poetry writing isn't the same as the male tradition, and some men do seem to doubly scrutinize what women write, without ever questioning the formal basis of their own work. Another man said to me, 'If you really want to broaden your range, you should be able to write a good love poem, a good political poem and a good sonnet.' I think those are very narrow prerequisites. The world is made up of an awful lot more. I've written a few sonnets, just to see, but I'm not that interested. I prefer my other stuff. I trust what I write.

Do you get lonely in this culture? Sometimes. And yet I don't feel alienated from it. I'm very much part of it. I feel it's the nature of poetry that most poets are lonely no matter where they are. They're full of contradictions. On the one hand you have the 'nobody understands what I want to say' school, and then when they *do* understand, you're absorbed by the establishment. But I don't think of poetry as a hobby. A lot of people can't conceive of an adult man or woman doing something like that other than as a hobby and that really bugs me. In general people will tend to patronise you or dismiss you. At work I prefer to keep the two separate. Either there's a complete overreaction or else a need to put you in your place. *Because you're a woman?* No. Just for being seen to be a little different. Poetry is always seen as something beyond the pale, even still.

Do you think of yourself as an Irish poet? Yes I do. I think of myself as an Irish person, though I've always tended to be a bit internationalistic. *What does that mean to you?* I write in English. I don't know that it means that much to me. It's only a label at the end of the day.

Do you think of yourself as a female poet, woman poet, feminist poet? Until now I've just defined myself as a poet, an Irish poet. I couldn't conceive of any feminist label. However, I am being forced, to some extent, to revise that. No matter where you turn in our society, you will be defined as a woman poet. And you are a woman. You're a woman first, as a man is a man first and then a poet. But you see, as soon as you call yourself a woman poet, it's a totally different vein you're prospecting. For example, Thomas Kinsella read a sequence of poems, *Brothers in the Spirit*, at a reading in Dublin recently and it struck me how wonderful, God, how *blithely* a man can use terms like that. Whereas, if I wrote a sequence called *Sisters in Spirit*, I'm instantly categorised, pigeonholed, trapped, no matter what I'm saying, no matter how broad or cosmic the poem is. 'Sisters' has a feminist connotation. And whereas I know 'feminism' is not a dirty word, more a clarion call, really, it is terribly misunderstood. My poetry comes first. I don't want to write propaganda. It's a problem. To deny feminism is to deny human rights.

Perhaps the word 'feminist' needs to be redefined. Yes, maybe it does. I'm not sure how, though. Any label is limiting.

I think people here categorize, if you say you're a feminist, you write about certain things, like your body, rape, abortion. But there are also other things. That's right, but people will see just what they want to see. There's a line in one of my poems, 'When winter scours this plain like a giant wire brush.' Well, I was in a workshop last year and the tutor remarked, 'Oh, yes, you can see the domestic thing there right away.' I don't have a wire brush and I'd never thought of it as a wire brush in a kitchen, but you see men can't prevent themselves from pigeonholing women's poetry, grounding it in a domestic vein. It's a reductionist view really. There are so many ridiculous assumptions.

You have written in your paper about the danger of all-women writing groups. Yes. There has been and probably will continue to be a need for those workshops. I certainly benefited from a couple. But you see some truly awful stuff coming out and there's no active form of criticism. People are a little coy, unwilling to offend. But one thing women can learn is from men's mistakes – for example, by adhering to an all-male, homo-admiring tradition. I really believe that women have been written out of literary history. I didn't believe it a few years ago, but I know it now to be actually true. I think men have suffered from this rather hostile tradition they have set up for themselves of all boys together. They're emotionally armoured. I just feel, let's not do the same by setting up women-only presses all over the world. I don't think it works. Men and women ideally have a symbiotic need of one another. It's a bit Platonic, this idea of the sphere, which Yeats talks about. We must avoid separatism at all costs. It's an anti-life gesture.

How do you feel about your erotic poems? I have always avoided writing love or erotic poetry because it's sloppy, self-indulgent rubbish sometimes. But those three or four just had to be written. The moment was right. The feeling was right. It's difficult to talk about them, because they're about the zones between what is acceptable socially and what is not. It's not a favourite subject in this country.

Are you worried about how they'll be accepted or understood? Not really. But I do find them hard to introduce. People wonder whom you are writing about. It's a bit of a problem. Anything in the margins, or the Checkpoint Charlie world, is bound to be.

I have difficulty writing love or erotic poems and I think it's because it's been done so much, and so much by men, that I'm not sure how the hell I'm supposed to write about it. That's true. They're so used to looking at our bodies through their poetry and concealing their own. I think a man's body is beautiful but you hardly ever see a male full-front or in an erotic scene. You might see a buttock or a thigh but to see a penis in a way that is intended to arouse is rather rare. That form of chauvinism still goes on, in films, in literature, in art. It's an unconsciously accepted way of keeping the male on a podium. It's a conspiracy of exclusivity.

Is your sense of being Irish in any part a sense of being

Catholic? I'm not a practising Catholic at all now. I sometimes fool myself into thinking I'm probably agnostic, but tendencies and attitudes stick with you even when you dispense with the structures. If you think of the concept of sin and guilt, all these steamy things Catholics go in for in a big way, I think it's good if you can achieve self-forgiveness. Catholics are still worried about sin. I don't know why. I just go my own way on that. We must stop being too self-critical. Lots of people wouldn't consider me Catholic and I don't care whether I have the label or not, but you don't shake off 16 or 17 years of basic grounding in Catholicism. Some of it's good, but it doesn't matter a damn whether there's a God-person at the end of the day.

Does your idea of the muse feel religious in any way? Perhaps a little. I don't know. Often I think there are two types of poets and one sort go in for transcendence, for moments of blinding insight. I often think of the creative process as something akin to a spiritual experience. But again I don't think it matters what you call it. I just write, and will continue to.

ANTARCTICA

I do not know what other women know.
I covet their children; wardrobes
stocked with blue or pink, froth-lace
bootees for the animal-child
that bleeds them.

Their calmness settles like the
ebb-tide on island shores –
nursing pearl-conch, secret fronds
of wisdom, certitude.
Their bellies taunt.

I do not know what other women know.
Breasts await the animal-child.
I want – maddened by
lunar crumblings, the false prophecy
of tingling breasts, turgid abdomen.

Antarctica: The storm petrel hovers;
waters petrified by spittled winds:
Little fish will not swim here.
Folds of bed-sheet take my face.
Blood seeps, again.

'But you are free', they cry,
'You have no child!' – bitterness
from women grafted like young willows,
forced before time. In Antarctica,
who will share this freedom?

REHEARSALS

Hen-toed puberty making me stumble,
I looked to transformation: Convent
basement. A solitary hour of piano,

goading myself, at fifteen,
to play Anitra's Tanz: Sprite-like
staccato of white feet, the halo

of wild silk, glint of silver,
discord – the breaking of passion.
Pale, an incandescence hexing

the hunter's fire; leaped, spun
the keyboard restlessly, fingers cold
in the blight of a convent winter;

arched, danced an unknown score,
the life-stab, thresh of music
on my flushing. Desire unleashed

the silences. Hours mounted.
'You play well,' the examiner said.
How well he'd never know.

The loneliness of reaching,
half-reined, stretching high,
readied for the stage:

Mistress of piquant nuance,
new desires, I learnt
the part of woman.

Maud Sulter

Photo: Martha McCulloch

MAUD SULTER WAS BORN IN 1960 in Glasgow and is a poet, journalist and artist. She holds a Masters Degree in Photographic Studies and facilitates creative writing workshops. She divides her time between London, Glasgow and West Yorkshire.

Her first collection *As a Blackwoman* was published in 1985 (Akira Press, London). Her work has appeared in *Let it be Told: Black Women Writers in Britain* (Virago Press, 1988); *Dancing the Tightrope, Watchers and Seekers* both by The Women's Press, 1987; *Through the Break* (prose), *Charting the Journey* (in conversation with Alice Walker), both by Sheba Feminist Publishers, London, 1987, *Original Prints3* (Polygon) and *The Pied Piper* (Only Women Press). She is also an editor and collective member of *Feminist Art News* 1988/90. Her second collection of poetry, *Zabat: Poetics of a Family Tree* was published by Urban Fox Press in 1989. A first novel, *Necropolis,* will appear in late 1990.

I sat waiting for Maud in the café of the Institute of Contemporary Arts in London. Maud was late and while I waited I rewrote my notes for my interview with Jackie Kay scheduled for later that day. A young woman walked in and looked me in the eye. 'Are you Jackie?' I asked. She smiled, 'No, I'm Maud.' From her manner on the phone, assured and to the point, I had expected her to be tall, thirtyish and the kind of woman who sweeps rather than walks into a room. To my surprise she was not much older nor taller than myself. I was nervous after my *faux pas*, but Maud carried on, with humour and clarity, to answer my questions. She had given a lot of thought to the relationship between the personal and the political in her writing. Thus the interview was short and intense.

DID WRITING FOR PUBLICATION CHANGE your writing at all? No, I wouldn't say so. If anything, it made me write more rather than less and it made me conscious of an audience. I think every writer should be conscious of their audience. *And who is your audience?* Anybody who reads my poetry! I'm not particularly precious about it. But at the same time, I very much hope it will be read by other Black women, both here and abroad, and that those contacts can be kept.

Being part of a network? Yes, very much so. Being within a very creative international network of Black women writers helps me to continue to produce – especially when there are difficulties with publication, or problems with royalties, or problems with the vociferous appetite for what I would term 'victim work'. I don't feel that my work falls into that category, and so sometimes there are attempts to marginalize it because of that.

Can you define 'victim work'? What is the difference between that and where you see your own work? I see my own work as primarily upwards and outwards. Its primary motivation is for constructive, radical change – and with an aspect of pleasure within that. But there's quite a resistance to that, for obvious reasons! You can't expect to effect change without encountering some obstacles, but I don't want to write to an audience who wants negative, depressing, long-winded commentaries on how hard it is to be Black. I think it's quite positive and constructive to be Black.

So what inspires you to write? How does that happen? Usually there's an emotional base point. Something will happen, either to me or someone around me, which tends to percolate, to work through a process. When the time is ready, I'll sit down and write something straight through, then put it away, and work on it later, when there's some distance between the writing and the editing.

Can we talk a little about anger? There's clearly a lot of anger in your poems. There's an anthropological saying, 'anger is object hungry', and therefore, empowering. Do you experience anger as empowering, or as overwhelming or engulfing? Well thankfully I don't get angry very often! But there are ways in which anger can be constructive. If it helps you confront situations or experiences, then it's worthwhile. But it must be directed. Mindless anger or violence is ultimately very destructive. We should be analyzing situations constructively in order to effect change. It's quite possible to want something to change without actually working out how that can be done. And if you don't take time to work that out, you'll work twice as hard and not necessarily get as far forward as you might.

Do you see your writing as very much part of that? It's analytical, and one of its main aims is to give voice to things that have been silenced, and to offer that up for recognition, and also for debate. So, yeah, it does serve that function.

You are a feminist, and very clearly involved in challenging White feminist assumptions about Black women. So, you're involved in a dialogue. But I also see you as not accepting the terms, necessarily, of that dialogue, in your writing. For dialogue to happen, there has to be engagement on both sides, and ground rules have to be worked out. They aren't given to us; we must work them out. And I would say it isn't just White feminist notions of Black women, it's actually White feminist notions of Black people that have to be challenged. If we are to work together it must be on mutually agreed terms. There are times when we must be prepared to listen as well as to talk. When women silence other women, on issues such as Palestine, or anti-Semitism, or racism, or sexuality, they do a great disservice to feminism as a whole. It's quite disheartening. But we continue to publish and to work inside and outside what could be seen as mainstream feminism. And, slowly but surely, it's being recognized that we will not be silenced.

This makes me think about a comment you made in your article 'Notes of a Native Daughter' in Let it Be Told, *that British publishers were going for the Black American women writers. And it also makes me think of, particularly in Scotland, the unwillingness to recognize the presence of Black and Asian people writing. Somehow it's safer when it's* ... Somewhere else. Yeah, that's a very important point. This whole dynamic of 'it's okay as long as it's from somewhere else' is endemic in British

society. Black people are okay as long as they come from somewhere else. It doesn't operate on a day-to-day level, but as many
people see themselves as leftist, or at least liberal, they try not to
hear anything that would make them change or challenge the
power they have.

And the fact that Black people have been in Scotland for
over four hundred years has also to be taken on board. What
could be politely called standing on the sidelines of an issue
people think has nothing to do with them has to come centre
stage, because the issue of race is very important in British
politics. It's another disheartening thing that in a country that
claims to have such a radical, rebellious nature as Scotland, there
is such a hesitation to take on board other people's voices. The
issue is there. It's not somewhere else.

There are spaces that should be opened up to Black artists
and Black people. And should the argument of standards arise,
which, unsurprisingly, it seldom does, because it wouldn't be
easily won, I would challenge anybody to say that they couldn't
be matched by Black people in Scotland.

When I read your poem 'Thirteen Stanzas', it seemed to me
that there would be a logical connection for someone who is
writing in Scots, which is very often associated with the working
class, and the kind of English you use, which is not 'standard
English' but real language, spoken language, and yet I don't see
that connection being made very often by other Scottish writers.
Reading those two interviews you sent me, I was quite shocked
by the idea that poetry was a male preoccupation. I don't think
culturally that is actually the case. The power of oratory, the
power of memory, the power of keeping lines of communication
open, is very much a role that women fulfil, and have every right
to do so. So I wasn't sure if my reaction to that was to dismiss it as
a White Western Bourgeois idea, that a poet must inherently be
male and that to be a poet one must adopt a male voice and stance
and perspective on life. I would challenge that very vehemently. I
would say that the importance of the conversation in the street, in
the kitchen, in the meeting, in the public or the private sphere,
was something that women hold very dear, and recognized the
value of.

That poem 'Thirteen Stanzas' enters a public, urban arena,
but has implications for all women – the importance of being
able to come together and have some sort of mutual exchange.
To cut yourself off from areas of communication like the shop-

ping centre and so on would be very sad. And it would be very sad
if you couldn't express it. I don't think there's any need for
women to be silenced in that way. It's self-censorship, the worst
act you can commit against yourself – because you're doing
somebody else's job for them. There are poetics in everyday life,
and in some ways, you can use a sense of poetics to survive.

So you can take a very painful situation, such as the way
women are abused gynaecologically, express it, and then ask
what we can do about it. You can also challenge some of the fear.
I like to think I can write about some things that we fear. In this
society you are trained to fear death, power and creativity itself.
And if we challenge that, we can move forward and enjoy the life
we find ourselves in.

*How do you see yourself, then, as a woman writer, feminist
poet, or what?* Labels are only constructive within set situations,
so I couldn't find an easy label with which to label any single part
of my life. I wouldn't label my work, because in different situations, in different places and times, the definition would be
different. I would call myself neither primarily a woman writer,
nor a writer who's a woman, because we'd spend too much time
discussing that, and I'd rather spend the time working!

*I was struck by your poem in 'Notes of a Native Daughter'
about Africa: 'Africa. Pale mother. Roots. / I am I / See me / Perceive me / But I / Shall name / My self.'* I don't think I would
actually define that as a poem. It was just a few words at the end
of the piece which the poems were appended to. It was a final
statement! In terms of the need to name oneself, for oneself,
rather than accept easy categorization by other people, I'd say it
was vital, for everybody. I don't hesitate to call myself a woman,
as I live as a woman! I'm more than happy to live as a woman, but
it's a very difficult word. It's a word that in this society has many
other connotations. A lot of stuff comes with the ticket. I don't
think there's any point reifying women. What a woman does is
important, and you must recognize the good and the bad in that,
and the power, too, the potential in that. And you must also be
able to recognize the women who will work against us much
more successfully, in many ways, than men do.

So what you're talking about is a complexity of self? You
have to take on board the contradictions of your life and your
experience, and live it! I don't see the appeal of an insular,
singular analysis. There are lots of communities you can operate

in. Which is why sometimes I worry about this 'growth' of one-to-one analysis, the idea that the answer to your problems lies in seeing your analyst three times a week. This has been creeping into some feminist circles, which is understandable given the pressures you're faced with. But living and interacting with other people is much more important than over analysing the past. You mustn't become fixated. You can't change things that have happened. You can't go back. You must simply find the best way to express yourself and to heal those wounds.

I was interested in the phrase you mentioned in relation to your grandfather, 'White Working Class Creativity'. Can you talk a little bit about that? It's very important not to be misled by concepts of class. Britain's the country I've grown up in and I have an understanding of issues of class here. I always find it very dangerous that people who have what is called 'an education' think themselves necessarily taken from their base if they are working class. It needn't necessarily challenge your class base. I mean, it does challenge your class base, but it doesn't necessarily change it. It's very noticeable that it's often those middle class people you have gone through that system with who are the first to tell you you are no longer working class because you have a degree, for instance. I've heard people say that to other people quite casually, and also quite calculatedly in a political sense. But you have the power to name yourself, recognizing the privilege you now have – if privilege is what it can be called! – and the advantages that you now have. *Options.* Options. But those can be played against. We have privilege, but it isn't necessarily permanent privilege. And the whole question of education as being something that separates you from other people is a myth that's perpetuated.

Can you talk a little bit about the recent development in your work, the mixture of images and text? I sometimes produce images with text which are complete poems in and of themselves, and then incorporate them into a piece, usually, but not always using photography. As an artist I find the need to choose the medium that I want to work in. I find that poetry is very useful for making short, sharp, literary statements within a frame, such as challenging media images. I would hope that that work will continue to develop.

How do you see your work developing in relation to the larger context of Black women writing? Having taken two or three years to complete another collection I've found that the work gets harder, not easier. One becomes more critical. One reads more. I have more contact with other writers on a one-to-one basis. Women whose creativity has spiritually influenced me include the African-Americans Ysaye Barnwell, Audre Lorde and Pat Parker, emotionally supporting sistahs such as my Surinamese friend from Holland Gloria Wekker, and of course, Lubaina Himid, the most committed and radical Blackwoman artist of our generation. And with the work of Black women writers being more freely available here, I'd like to see those networks continue to exist, whether it's poetry or simply a letter from a friend. I'd also like to see the hard work that's been done, say, in the last ten years, in terms of getting Black women's work published, continue. And for us to have a more international perspective on that, which means engaging in lots of politics, like what language we write in, which tongues we have access to and which tongues we don't. I'm very optimistic that we can continue to do that, and that in five years time, when this book's been superceded by another one, there'll be five more Black women poets to be included in it – and that each time the work of the foremothers will be recognized as well. Because that's a problem, too. It's very easy to imagine, if you sit here in Britain, that Alice Walker started writing five years ago, when the woman's been writing for twenty years! And there are women who were writing twenty years before that. So we must recognize that and search through the fragments to find the whole.

DELETE AND ENTER

Hey Brother. Nice seeing ya.
Travelling the contours of that
cragged not quite ebony face
through its valleys
now of death but still fine fine.
Journeying with you Griot
of our urban experience
voice rasps fingers gesture
from mere english futures are carved.

Our eyes met across a sea of black
and I foolish-like casually say
to myself Hey Brother. Nice seeing ya.
Promise to write you but the pen never
meets paper. I talk to you in my head.

Long distance. Sempiternal communication.
Walk with you. Hear the fury of Fire Next Time
sufferation plague pestilence starvation terrors
not of our making multinationals raping and
the cold war does not thaw though they
would like us to believe it. Hell
one Man believes in Armageddon
and does the other guy know God?

We ain't angry man we're mad
some mad bad niggers that's us
            'delete and enter if you must
            a more contemporary definition...
And yeah, There Be Dragons when and where
black faggotry and dykedom meet
            'delete and enter if you must
            a more contemporary definition...
coz time passes and skipping bullets diseases
poverty hate is real-life here. No one can be sure
to be here to see to the finer points of language
linguistics or typesetting errors – though I know we
call ourselves Black and I undoubtedly name myself Zami.

Our call and response wakes the world
voice no longer silent from fear but hungry
with passion. You make me Jimmy. You make me.

Ko na bra. Exile
is not a voluntary leaving.
We do not choose our birthing
nor perhaps our death but to die
knowing you loved me like you loved
the world hot hot as chilli-pepper
is a better way of living to the end.

You make me James Baldwin, you make me
and I will still cry bitter tears
feel my body disobey the command
to be brave. For true strength is all,
weakness a cold endless death.
And us? We will live forever at the tip
of each others vocabularies
at the edge of the Africa we know.
Fly back Jimmy. Fly back and wait

at the mountain top where family will
meet again someday; the Brethren and
the Sistren, to decide the naming
of the Sun. In our own tongue.

THIRTEEN STANZAS

trips tae the local – shoapin centre – dogshit – boarded up
    business –
capital before people – profit before
    need – hustle – bustle – cheery *hullos* –
how's it gawin? – how ra wains? – n the damp? – auld school
    pals

unrecognisable – under the weight – o lost dreams and
    illusions – other places –
other spaces – other possabilities – beyond the
    predictable – bloke – screw – n
how do ye do – quick jaunt up the aisle – offer a
    smile – bridesmaids in candy

pink – smirk – behind yer back – as the more experienced – in
    life n death –
sniff out the change – in the girlwoman body – in defence
    some consume –
colourful pages of gloss – throwaway gestures – at a
    liberated life – anyway.

up tae the shoaps – in the past – a'd look forward – tae
    seein – that tall gaunt
figure – appear – running fae hir hoose – tae hir mithers – the
    fishvan – tae the
butchers – never too busy – to stoap fur a chat – a natter – a
    rap – steamin hoat

tea – in the bakers – sit doon – roll n sausage – a confectioners
    nightmare –
bilious – mysteriously hued – sugar fuels hollow bellys – we
    remember hunger – or –
the hunger of others – talk o the family – the new kids – the
    strikes – lay offs –

shut downs – heroin runnin – inglorious put downs – of life
    on the dole – Gien

examples tae many – other sisters – in a struggle – wi the
    council – the welfare –
the dhss – in ten short years – a never heard – a cross word
    or rebuke – at your

fellow travellers – on a road so shell shocked – it makes yi
    sick – oh carrie –
you never knew me – or you knew me too well – still – this
    visit's been dif'rent –
auld habits n aw that – glance up – scan queues – gaze in
    windaes – in the hope

o seein yr neat coiffured head – above the crowd – last
    christmas – was like nae
other – wi lost ye carrie – let the game get the better ae
    us – one o the best –
ae us – couldny believe it – hysterectomy – naw couldny
    believe it – hysterectomy –

not you the fighter – survivor – o open heart surgery – that
    hit n run accident –
on the way hame fae the bingo – wi used tae go the
    gither – regular – a huvny
been since – it wouldny be the same again – here we ur
    wimmin in the 80s –

bodies still abused – an no ony bi others – the loss o yr
    womb – sae late in the day – too late in the
day – a violent act by violent men – in the name of medical
practice – medikill theory – anyway sister – you bore two fine
    sons – n a daughter –

stole awae – bi the reaper – too swiftly – too soon – our power
    to bear children –
oppresses us wimmin – only as things staun – at the
    minute – in a control valve –
of a society – that wants no understaunin – o ir
    wimminhood – hey carrie – will ye

remember me? – did the self-same cancerous
    quellings – silence me back then? –
it may be too late tae sae it – bit a love an respect ye – bear
    forth – these
flowers – gold n white tokens – bright – like the lights in your
    hair – here in

remembrance – of yir fair self – of a friendship between
    women – white working
class woman – black working class girl – a cross – the divide
    of race – we were
women in struggle – women in struggle – women in
    struggle – united –

Catriona NicGumaraid

Photo: Scottish Television

CATRIONA NICGUMARAID WAS BORN on the Island of Skye. After studying at Glasgow University she taught Modern Studies and Gaelic for a couple of years before becoming Writer in Residence at the Gaelic College in Skye. She is married with two children and has lived in Dundee, but is currently in Glasgow.

She is both writer and poet in Gaelic and has published one book, *A Choille Chiar*. Her poems have appeared widely in literary magazines in Scotland. In addition to her poetry she has written and acted for the BBC.

I went to Catriona's home late one afternoon. She was still living in Dundee at the time. She apologized for the mess, which was actually non-existent, and explained that she had been working hard and things were kind of frantic for her just then. We had a cup of tea and started the interview in her living room overlooking the street outside. She was nervous but friendly and I was tired, having done four interviews in the past three days. It seemed to both of us that we talked in circles. After forty minutes, we finished. 'My goodness,' Catriona said, 'I hope you can make some sense out of that jumble! I afraid I'm not very clear today.' 'That's okay, neither am I. I'll let you know if there's a problem.' In my opinion, the interview, despite us both, turned out fine.

GAELIC IS MY FIRST LANGUAGE. I had some English when I went to school but certainly English is my second language. It's strange. I know of no one who is able to write equally in both languages, apart from maybe Iain Crichton Smith. But I think there is one language to which you are more emotionally attached, and Gaelic is certainly mine. Yet I don't think I'm any more fluent in Gaelic than in English. There are certain things I would find easier to talk about in English, like political ideas or something scientific, because I've been educated in the language of English to do so. When I was at school they always taught native speakers of Gaelic through the medium of English which is ridiculous. Now they don't do that.

How much Gaelic is still spoken in Skye? The last census found 80,000 Gaelic speakers and that Skye is fifty per cent Gaelic-speaking. It's declining lately among the young people, but a lot of people are learning the language. In Dundee there are three Gaelic university courses. So there are quite a lot of learners of the language, but the number of native speakers is going down.

So you're trying to do something about that? Yes, well, I've tried to bring up my children bilingual, but with so few native speakers in Dundee it's quite difficult. You're talking to them in a vacuum. My daughter, who is eight, is Gaelic-speaking, but when she went to school she became less fluent in Gaelic. My little boy, who's three, has got some Gaelic, but I wouldn't say that he's all that fluent.

You said there are things you would find more comfortable talking about in Gaelic. What kinds of things are they? If I were to talk about something where emotions are involved I would prefer to talk in Gaelic. As far as poetry is concerned, I've never written in English. But I find it easier to write a letter in English.

Tell me about the poem, 'Roag – 2000 AD'. Roag is English for Rodhag, which is three miles from Dunvegan, and like a lot of Gaelic-speaking areas, there are mostly old folk. There are very few young people in the village, and, of course, there's a great influx of what they call 'White Settlers', not a very nice term, but people coming in who are mostly English. I'm not anti-English at all, but I do worry. If they come in at a trickle, that's not bad, but I do find when I go home, that there's almost a clash of people, as incomers are coming in too quickly. It's not happening in my village yet; it's just that native people will die off very soon and I can see that there will be none of the native population left. For someone who is a language loyalist as I am, it sets off feelings of guilt, being away from a Gaelic-speaking area. But maybe things will change.

What does it mean to you to be a 'language loyalist'? Well, I feel myself in complete isolation in Dundee where there are so few Gaelic-speaking people. I think in my imagination I'm living in a Gaelic world all the time. I know that most of my thoughts are concerned with Gaelic, and certainly as I go about the house, I always sing Gaelic songs. Though I read English literature as well, I do try to keep in touch with Gaelic speakers and writing.

When did you start writing? When I was in my early twenties. I'd always been very, very interested in old songs, and I had a traumatic love affair. I wasn't that interested in modern Gaelic poetry, to be quite honest. I didn't understand it very well. But when I was in the Celtic class at the university I came across Sorley Maclean's work and it had a tremendous impact on me. Had I not come into contact with it I might have written songs. Who knows? If you're a poet, it might come out any way. So I just started writing down poems. They just had to come out. I'm certainly not a disciplined writer, though I think I'm getting more disciplined now that I'm not writing so much personal poetry. I used to write in a complete frenzy. If a poem wasn't right in about ten minutes I'd tear it up. People used to think I was very odd because I would only write at night, in the very small hours of the night, when I felt no one was watching. But now that I'm writing more political stuff, I'll say, 'Well, I'll try and write that.'

I don't write a lot. It's maybe the particular age my children are at. You're so shattered from things like nappies all the time. Nowadays I manage to write in a very short space of time. I can't stay up all night working because I've got small kids to see to in the morning.

You said 'political poems'? Yes, like what's happening in Skye under the influence of people from outside. And I'm very, very concerned with the decline of Gaelic. Indeed, it may be extinct in the next few years.

We talked also about your love poems. The book I'm publishing some time next year hasn't got any love poems in it. I haven't written any love poems since I got married! But I've got a book I published with my sister, *A Choille Chiar*, that's completely love poems. That's how I started writing poetry. It is very private. I think a lot of people who start writing do go in for confessional writing. I look at these poems now and I cringe because they are so indulgent. I don't think I could write a love

poem now, unless there was something wrong with my relationship with my husband.

What is your intention when you're writing? To get rid of
this feeling inside me, whether it be anger or whatever. To get rid
of the emotion. If the poem is successful I feel I have exorcised the
emotion. I'm more of an intuitive poet, and in some ways I would
hate to become more self-conscious, because, if I have a strength,
it is that I tend to be spontaneous. I think it's very good to sit
down and translate a poem using a set form, but for me, I prefer
to do my own thing, if that doesn't sound too arrogant.

Gaelic poetry is traditionally very formal. Yes, with the clan
society, which came to an end in 1745, each clan had a clan poet.
They wrote to a set form and each poem would have a certain
name and scansion. I wrote one once, for a laugh. It's quite good
fun as an exercise, but I find them boring.

Nowadays there are 'village poets' who write about events
in the village, and songwriters still writing in the old set forms,
and then you have the modern poets writing in free verse. I think
that maybe I fall between the two stools in that sometimes I write
in a complete tizzy and sometimes I write something that will
take three years and be more formal. We talked about content
and form. They're closely linked. The content would dictate the
form. I wouldn't feel happy unless the form fitted the content. I
know it instinctively. I know the movement. If I were writing a
satire, I would want it to be quite quick. If I were writing a love
poem, it would depend on the kind of love poem. I'm not good at
describing this sort of thing. I just sit down and do it. I often use
internal rhyme, which, I think, is because I'm very influenced by
old songs.

In Gaelic society a lot of the songwriters were women. Yes,
in Gaelic society the better poets were the women. They wrote
the wonderful work songs when they waulked the tweed, when
there would be only women present. The waulking songs, and
the keenings, which are used as waulking songs now, were
usually women's songs. They are much more emotionally heightened. There wasn't much difference then between a song and a
poem. It would be very difficult to put music to a modern Gaelic
poem.

You write in Gaelic for the BBC? Well, I've acted in a few
radio plays and a Gaelic teaching show. I've only written two
plays. One was a drama documentary for the BBC on Mairi
Mhor, a songwriter from Skye who was very much concerned

with the agitation leading up to the Crofters' Holding Act – this is its centenary year (1986?). But more than that, she was wrongly imprisoned for allegedly having stolen some money. She didn't start writing poetry until she was fifty. Her songs are still sung.

How different do you find writing plays from writing poetry? It's a completely different activity. It's not so intense. I mean, you can put the pen down. With poetry I tend to write in a very intensive way. With playwriting I found that I could leave the sketch I was working on and come back to it. With a poem I have to finish it.

Sometimes I don't write for such a long time that I think, 'My goodness, maybe I've lost it. It's gone away.' That makes me go into a panic because I don't want it to go away.

You've published one book of poetry? Aye, but I tend not to send stuff to publishers. *Why is that?* I'm disorganized. I'm in such bits and pieces. The married woman with children that you're taken to be: you're rushing off to school; you're being a housewife; I'm teaching a Gaelic class on Wednesday nights; and working for the BBC. So there's a lot happening, and my time tends to be short. It's easy to say. 'Och, I'll think about it tomorrow.' Also, there's not all that much demand for Gaelic poetry. There are only two Gaelic publishers. There's just not enough money. *So there aren't very many options?* There aren't. A lot of people are interested in Gaelic poetry with English translations and I do a lot of readings using translations, but few Gaelic readings on their own.

How do you feel about reading with translations? I'm quite happy about it. A lot of people don't read Gaelic but they can read the poems in English. My own English translations are poor. They only give you the gist of what I'm saying. But with a lot of learners of the language, translations open up new possibilities. They may not be able to grasp the whole poem in Gaelic, but with the help of the English translations they can.

How would you define yourself as a poet? Do you see yourself as a poet, a female poet, a feminist poet, or what? I don't know if I think of myself as 'a poet' because I do quite a lot of other things. I think of myself as a person who writes poetry. And certainly I wouldn't think of myself as a feminist poet. Not that I'm not concerned with feminism. It's just that I haven't written anything on it as yet. I may very well do, but I feel I'm most concerned with Gaelic. I don't know. I may be wrong about this, but it seems that in cutting yourself away from men in writing, you're almost saying that women are inferior. But certainly I haven't explored the feminist side of things. Maybe I should, because I get quite angry about it, the unequal status of women, which is certainly virulent in marriage.

Who are you writing for when you are writing? First of all, I'm writing for myself, and, I hope, for people who understand what I'm trying to say, and that in a hundred years' time there will be people to read what I've written.

RÒDHAG — 2000 AD

Nuair a bheir an fheannag
an t-sùil as a' chaora mu dheireadh,
bidh mi ri didearachd air d'uinneagan:
bidh iad an sin
a' cluich chairtean
's ag ol Beaujolais,
poodle a' dannsa mun casan;
fhaileadh blàth a' bhainne air falbh as na bàthchannan,
's iad làn thruinnsearan fuar cruaidh pottery
airson an luchd-turais;
fuaim nam brògan tacaideach 'nan samhla
a' coiseadh air monadh;
na croitean uaine fasail
gun bhristeadh spaide.

Nuair a bheir an fheannag
an t-sùil as a' chaora mu dheireadh,
bi mi ri farchluais
air d'uinneagan,
ag eisdeachd
ri di'osagan ag ochanaich,
's na guthan cruaidh' Sasannach
a' dol an aghaidh na gaoith.

ROAG — 2000 AD

When the hoodie-crow takes
the eye out of the last sheep
I will be peeping in at your windows
they will be there
drinking Beaujolais
a poodle prancing around their feet
the warm smell of milk

will have left the byres and they'll be full of hard cold pottery
for the tourists

the sound of tackety-boots
ghosts walking on moors
the crofts green and unproductive
without spade-breakings

When the hoodie-crow takes
the eye out of the last sheep
I will be peeping in at your windows
listening to your breezes sighing
and the harsh English voices
clashing with the wind

EILIDH

Bha duil a'm gum biodh tu agam
measg chreag is tiurr' is ghlinn,
's gun ionnsaicheadh tu cainnt Dhiarmaid
gu siubhlach bhuamsa fhin –
chan ann an seo san ear-bhaile,
far nach tuig mi cleas na cloinn';
ach a-nochd gur dluth an daimh, a chagair,
's tu torghan air a' chich.

EILIDH

I thought that I would have you
midst rock, sea-wrack and glen
and that you would learn Diarmid's language
fluently from myself
not here: in this east city
where I don't understand child's play
but tonight the understanding is close
as you gurgle at the breast.

Rita Ann Higgins

Photo: Joe Geoghegan

RITA ANN HIGGINS was born in Galway where she has lived all her life. Her literary career began when, ill in hospital at the age of 22, she read Orwell's *Animal Farm* 'because it was a small book.' She conducts guided tours of historic Galway and lives in Ballybane with her husband and two daughters.

Her poems have appeared widely in literary magazines in Ireland and the United States and been broadcast on the radio as well as dramatized by the Galway Theatre Workshop. In 1986 she was awarded a writing bursary by the Irish Arts Council/An Chomhairle Ealaion. Her first collection, *Goddess on the Mervue Bus*, was published by Salmon Press, Galway, in 1986.

Rita invited me for dinner. She picked me up in Galway and drove me to her home in Ballybane, a housing estate outside the town. When we got there, the dinner was almost completely burned; Jennifer and Heather, Rita's daughters, had forgotten to turn off the oven. We salvaged what we could and ate in the warm, crowded kitchen, observed by several young cats, who sat outside the window. Later, Rita and I adjourned to the sitting room for the interview. In contrast to the kitchen, this room was quite bare except for the furniture. I set up the tape-recorder and we started. We got through the interview with much laughter,

Rita stealing an illicit cigarette from me now and again when her daughters weren't looking.

I REALLY WANT TO WRITE but I go through long periods without writing. Then all of a sudden, like last night, I had a hectic day, my husband went away and I was emotionally withdrawn. I wrote a very long poem which had absolutely nothing to do with my husband or my kids or anything like that. I couldn't have imagined yesterday morning that I would write a poem. I had no intention. I wasn't interested. We really don't have an awful lot of control over this end of it.

How do you feel in the periods when you don't write? Disappointed, because I know I have an awful lot to say. It's easier to write than to communicate on a one-to-one basis. But I try to read a lot. I feel compensated if I'm learning something in the meantime. I didn't start to read until I was 22. I had tuberculosis and went into a sanatorium. I read *Animal Farm*, because it was a small book and I could read it from cover to cover! Then I went on to *Wuthering Heights*. These two books got me started. It was such a revelation. But it was late. Everything has been slow. It's still very slow. It takes me forever. Even now I couldn't say five novels I've read. Most of the books I read are books I pick up and read some and close them, like poetry anthologies and *Marx for Beginners*. I'm trying to study history. There's so many periods I know nothing about. It's getting easier and it's certainly fascinating, and the fact I can write in between is marvellous altogether.

Are you doing it on your own? On my own. I'm just lucky I woke up. My imagination was always with me, but I didn't have the words to back up feelings, so it was necessary to start reading. Then in 1982, I went to the Galway Writers' Workshop and was encouraged. Someone said, 'You've got something there'.

What inspires or motivates you to write? Most are character sketches. People and everyday events. Nothing too technical. I don't deliberately try to keep it simple but I think it communicates directly. That suits me. *Who are you writing for?* I don't think that comes into it. It's just an angry voice inside yourself that has to say something. It needn't always be angry but a lot of the time I'm annoyed about something. The last poem is about the traveller situation, the way they're treated.

Do you think of your poetry as being read aloud or on the

page or both? I'm sure it sounds better when I read it myself because you can emphasize certain words. I have a problem with punctuation and the same with spelling, so I think it sounds better when I read. But I think it communicates on the page as well, so I'm not too worried about it.

Do you find the content dictates the form? Definitely. I don't know anything about form. It just happens. I rewrite everything about eight or nine times. I know when it's finished. I've lost interest in it. It's out of my system. *You feel better when the poem is done?* Absolutely. I was high as a kite last night. *Is it different when you write about other people rather than yourself?* It's easier to write about other people. It's more interesting, too.

Do you think of yourself as an Irish poet? I'm just an ordinary woman. But an Irish poet. I don't know what that means. I just love it here. I love being Irish. I'm glad I'm Irish.

Tell me about 'Seventeen Times'. It was inspired by my daughter, Heather, and I dedicated it to her. It's about story-telling, but more than that, it's about this draining process that goes on between mother and child. You can love your children to pieces, but they can drain the living bejesus out of you. She has this favourite story about the stolen canes of Brierhill School. She keeps saying, 'Tell me about the stolen canes.' So I tell her and she'd say, 'Again.' And I'd just decide she was happy and contented with it and be creeping away and there she'd be, tapping away at my brain. That's what it's about, this taking from that children have the power to do.

Does being religious come into your sense of being a writer? I was brought up in the Irish Catholic situation. My mother was extremely religious and my father was extremely drunk. My mother was very good-living. We never cursed. We never heard a curse in our house. And we seemed to spend all our time praying for other people, saying novenas and rosaries. Then all of a sudden this guy was coming home drunk all of the time. It didn't tally. We were so good and this guy is having a ball! So I'm not religious in myself at all, but at the same time in the back of my mind and heart there's a finger being pointed. I don't know what that means, or if it's conscience. You'd have to have some residue from the past with a background like that. All the religion on the one hand and the rakes of alcoholism on the other.

Tell me about 'Middle-aged Irish Mothers'. I associate my

childhood very much with middle-aged Irish mothers, my own and all these others that would come in and out of the house and in and out of the church, especially the church. I would see them hanging around the church after Mass and I always wondered what they did. So I figured they must be praying for the Tommics and the no-hopers, the guys with the shingles and the women with the veins. I haven't seen them for a while because I haven't been there, but all through when I was a kid it was an image that stuck in my mind. They're great singers, too, You couldn't see them, but you could hear them from behind. Germinating sopranos – 'Glo-o-r-r-i-i-a-a!' Our churches are riddled with these women.

What about 'Old Friend'? That's another one about a middle-aged woman who would be friends with my mother who is dead now. I associate her with nice things from the past. A friendly old woman. I would meet her in the supermarket and we'd start reminiscing. I didn't mind these middle-aged mothers and the prayer. It wasn't offensive. They all had this incredible faith and prayed all the time and it worked for them. So I associate something good with them. There were no nasty characters. I like old women and I like middle-aged women. Just something about them. They have their own power. One of them used to give me brown bread with butter and sugar on the top when I was young and I absolutely loved this treat. I would hang around her house until she saw me and then she'd call me in. So I like old women forever more. Though I suppose the association with my mother would be the strongest connection with them.

Have you ever written about your mother? Not directly. But she's in all those poems about the old women and the middle-aged Irish mothers. I've no desire. There's nothing there I want to eradicate. On the other hand, my father. I don't know how that would go. One poem, 'Almost Communication', is about him. Maybe I'll write more, but I'm happy enough with that one. It communicates as much as I want to say. This humour in our home, it isn't enough. It's good and it's great, but at the end of the day, when all the laughing is over, you must be able to look at a person – as I say in the poem, 'I haven't seen his eyes for years.' There was always lots of laughs, but no real communication.

When you write humorously, is that different from when you write more seriously? I haven't really got power over that.

It's not a decision I make. When I start to think about a poem, the humour isn't necessarily there. It just sneaks in.

Do you hear poems in your head as you're writing them? Yes. Wordfall is important. It's delightful even. *Do you see the poem in your head, the person or the thing?* I'm not so familiar with that, but surely it must happen. When I wrote about Mrs McEttigan I could definitely see her outside the Post Office.

It seems that your poems are very much giving a voice to working people. You can't write what you don't know. At one stage I started to write what I thought were intelligent poems and they were so disgusting. I never use any big words because I don't know any. But I tried to use them early on and it was a great lesson to me. I'll never do it again. It works much better the natural way. Lack of sincerity seeps out of poems. You can feel it when someone's bullshitting. It's unnecessary. We all have such a wealth we can draw on.

This is a great poem, 'Poetry Doesn't Pay'. Do you like that one? So do I. If I'm here penniless and can't pay the rent or can't pay the light, what good is poetry to me then? You have to be practical if your soul is to survive. You can't get carried away! But I don't always feel that way.

How do you feel when people come up to you and respond to your poems, when something in your poems speaks to them? That's good. That's confirming that I'm not a freak. They thought that. They had that experience. It's all just repetition, what we're writing. It's happened before and it will happen again.

So you're not aware of a critical audience when you're writing? Not at all. Sure, who's interested in poetry anyway? About five people in Galway out of a few thousand! *And certainly not the rentman.* Certainly not the rentman!

MIDDLE-AGED IRISH MOTHERS

Germinating sopranos in conservative head squares
are the middle-aged Irish mothers in heavy plaid
coats, who loiter after Mass in churches

Lord make me an instrument of your peace;
Where there is hatred, let me sow love;

to light candles for the Joes and Tommies of the drinking
world, the no-hopers, that they might pack it in,
if it's the will of God,

> Where there is injury, pardon;
> Where there is discord, union;

to pray for Susan's safe delivery, Bartley's gambling,
Mrs. Murray's veins, that they would not bother her
so much, not forgetting Uncle Matt's shingles.

> Where there is doubt, faith;
> Where there is despair, hope;

Soon, not out of boredom, they will move diagonally through
their cruciform sanctuary to do the Stations
in echoing semi-song whispers,

> We adore thee O Christ we bless thee, because by
> thy cross thou hast redeemed the world

sincere pleas to dear Jesus, that the eldest might get
off with a light sentence, pledges of no more smoking,
and guarantees of attendance at the nine Fridays,

> Where there is darkness, light;
> Where there is sadness, joy;

finally, for the Pope's intentions, Mr Glynn's brother-in-law,
the sweeps ticket that it might come up,
but only if it's the will of God,

> O Sacred Heart of Jesus, I place
> all my trust and confidence in thee.

I like these middle-aged Irish mothers, in heavy plaid coats,
one of them birthed me on the eve of a saint's feast day,
with a little help from Jesus and his Sacred Heart.

> I tell you most solemnly, anything you ask for
> from the father he will grant in my name.

POETRY DOESN'T PAY

> People keep telling me
> Your poems, you know,

you've really got something there,
I mean really.

When the rent man calls, I go
down on my knees, and through
the conscience box I tell him.

This is somebody speaking,
short distance, did you know
I have something here with my poems?
People keep telling me.

'All I want is fourteen pounds
and ten pence, hold the poesy.'

But don't you realise
I've got something here.

'If you don't come across
with fourteen pounds and ten pence soon
you'll have something at the side of the road,
made colourful by a little snow.'

But.

'But nothing,
you can't pay me in poems or prayers
or with your husband's jokes,
or with photographs of your children
in lucky lemon sweaters
hand-made by your dead Grand Aunt
who had amnesia and the croup.

'I'm from the Corporation,
what do we know or care about poesy,
much less grand amnostic dead aunts.'

But people keep telling me.

'They lie.

'If you don't have fourteen pounds
and ten pence, you have nothing
but the light of the penurious moon.'

Valerie Gillies

Photo: Bruce Cockburn

VALERIE GILLIES WAS BORN in Canada in 1948 and brought up in Scotland. She studied at the Universities of Edinburgh and Mysore, South India. She lives in Edinburgh with her husband and three children and is currently Writer in Residence at Dundee College of Art.

In 1976 she won the Eric Gregory Poetry Award and in 1976 and 1987 was awarded Scottish Arts Council Bursaries. Her publications include *Trio: New Poets from Edinburgh* (New Rivers Press, New York 1971), *Poetry Introduction 3* (Faber, London, 1975), *Each Bright Eye* (Canongate, Edinburgh, 1977), *Bed of Stone* (Canongate, Edinburgh, 1984), *Twelve More Scottish Poets* (Hodder and Stoughton, 1986), *Tweed Journey* (Canongate, 1989) and *The Chanter's Tune* (Canongate, 1990).

I went to Valerie's home to interview her. It was an early summer evening and the night, for Scotland, was warm. It was one of my first interviews and I was nervous. Valerie put me at my ease immediately, making me a cup of tea and chatting effortlessly about this and that. She told me that she was currently working on combining both harp and violin music with her poetry and asked if I would like to hear some. She then introduced me to her son Lachlan, who played the violin, and her daughter Maeve, who played the harp. They were polite and shy with me, stealing glances at me and at one another. But when they got out their instruments and began to play both children became quite professional and played remarkably well. Each played in turn with their mother as she read poems, some of which had been designed to go with music, and others to which the music became more of a backdrop for the words.

YOU STARTED WRITING WHEN *you were fourteen?* Yes. After that I couldn't stop! I just wrote when I found the inspiration until I went to Edinburgh University. That was the first year that Norman MacCaig was Writer in Residence and he encouraged me to write every day. He explained that was how he worked and how other artists and musicians worked, that you had to keep in practice, do something every day and look over it afterwards.

How does the creative process work for you? I think it's happened differently at different stages of my life. When I was younger I would write very much in the fire of the moment. Now I can see something or be in a particular place and I can feel the presence of the poem there. Then I leave it alone. It's present in me. Even if it took me a year I wouldn't want to write that poem until I focused the whole of my concentration on it. For a time I worked a lot on what I would call poetry of meditation and that meditation technique is still with me. Very often now it's about places, and when I come back to writing about them, the whole thing can take off and I know it's right. But it can be a long time between being in a place and deciding what it was I saw or understood and want to write about.

It's really interesting the way you do music and poetry together. It's very powerful, because your poetry has in itself such a musical quality. How did that idea come about? It really began with the harp. My daughter Maeve plays the clarsach and the girl who teaches her, Savourna Stevenson, who is certainly the finest virtuoso harper in Scotland, had been composing a lot of new tunes. She and I began to operate by a series of challenges. She would challenge me to write something to go with a piece of music she'd written, or I would challenge her to write a piece of music which fitted the mood of the poem. I love her music so much and she likes the poems, so we ended up weaving the two together. Sometimes the poem comes first and sometimes the music.

We use a lot of new material. Savourna says she finds it very refreshing and stimulating to work with poetry. I think it's probably to do with the historic link between poet and harper. You feel part of an ancient tradition. I feel that as far as lyric poetry is concerned, that's what it's all about. Savourna lives in the Borders and a lot of her music is atmospheric of this tremendously beautiful countryside where the passion and heroism of the Border ballads were acted out. We're trying to say it's like a landscape painting. We go out and paint it in music and words.

Then you can make your poetry to be read aloud rather than to be read on a page? Yes, it has become more so. The fact that the paper is there with the words written on it is not very important to me nowadays. If I lost them all I would be able to remember them. Savourna doesn't look at the music and so I have gradually moved away from looking at the words. It comes alive somehow if you're not hanging on to that piece of paper. You're trying to make it new in the sense of putting it across to an audience.

So how do you juggle having kids and doing your writing? I don't! I can't! Everything is for them at the moment. And in these years which no doubt will be shortlived, it's very difficult for them not to come first. I suddenly find poems lying around that I hardly remember writing because there's been no peace to write, though as often as I can I will get up a good while before breakfast and write when nobody else is up. I'll maybe go out and take a walk, but I don't let myself make the broth or sweep the floor or iron a shirt, because once you start on these things ... !

It's also difficult if the man is the main breadwinner and has his own creative work to do and you're not also nurturing his talents some of the time. In a way poetry is easier because it's not a long canter like writing a novel. And I've found in recent years that I don't need to have peace. I had a lot of peace in the first part of my life. I was an only child with busy parents and stayed a lot of time with my grandparents in a very lonely place. Occasionally I played with other children, but I had a kind of adult life in miniature. I had a contemplative nature. I read books and did drawings and roamed around the moors. So in a way I've moved back. I'm suddenly going through the playfulness of childhood and enjoying my own children.

I was very impressed by this poem 'Infertility Patient'. How did this come about? It's one of my persona poems. I had a couple of friends who waited a long time to have babies and I wondered what that would be like. Then I got to thinking of Katherine Mansfield. I think she had an abortion when she was about 18 and she could never have a child. Now she's got so many stories in which she does wonderful cameos of childhood. She was obviously fascinated by children and felt her whole being immersed in what children were experiencing when she was amongst them. What they could experience she also felt. And obviously she would have loved to have her own children. And yet, how could she have written so much so well if she had? It's one of these unanswered things.

Then there's the suffering of so many people you meet in life, people who've tried and who've lost children and who want to hold your child, and you wonder what it must be like for them to hold someone else's child. Women today are, I suppose, as tortured by their own fertility as at any stage in the past, although it's getting more excruciating as the 20th century rolls on!

Women's lot nowadays, with work outside the home as well as raising a family, is something I really only saw first in India among the poorest of people, where a woman would step aside into the ditch and have a baby and then climb back into the field and keep working. That is more or less the state into which the middle class Western woman has brought herself. So, whether it's an advance from the days when your husband did the earning and you had the peace and quiet in which to have 16 children! (laughs). It's a peasant way of life. It's lots of hard work. The only advance is that we don't lose as many children as an Indian village woman would in the course of her childbearing years, through epidemics and so on. And of course she has to have a number of children in order to be sure that some of them survive.

When you write about other women do you put yourself in their shoes, so to speak? This infertility poem, for example. You've had children, so you're speaking about a very different experience. Well, I'm not pregnant at the moment. So there are barren times in your life. Sometimes they have to be. And they can be times of suffering that nobody else sees. It's the call of the womb ... It's something, I suppose, you don't appreciate until you've had one or two children and then you begin to understand about these people who never have any and are never going to get any and they're in their forties and they realize their fertile time is past.

It's strange what people do to themselves. Maybe they're avoiding fertility for years and suddenly they want to be fertile after a long time of not being. And then they think, Why is this not happening? And maybe it's too late. I was reading that in the

States two-thirds of all couples are sterilized, one partner or the other. That is a very strange society if you think of it as an anthropologist. Think of the Masai fertility cults. Or in India, you'll take this garland and your *prasad*, your coconut and your banana, and you bring it to this *lingam*. In south India there's a great cult of Nandi Bull, a symbol of fertility. Infertile women will go and crawl beneath the forelegs of the statue. They'll come from miles and miles away. They'll walk or they'll come by bullock cart or village bus. They'll go sunwise round the statue and then crawl underneath the foreleg. It's a tiny space. It's like being born. Even a tiny slender Indian woman has to push hard to get through. And there's a wonderful brahmin who looks after you and casts eyes on all the women that come! And I feel that probably women today in the west are wondering why they're all twisted up and why there's so much of themselves that they're obviously feeling guilty about and yet there are these women who are just the same as these Indian village women going to a place where there's a famous *lingam*, begging for a child. Because very often in the subcontinent temples, if you're a woman, that's what you're there to ask for. You may have plenty of other children, but you look the god in the eyes and say, That is my request, not immortality, not wealth, but a child. There are a lot of places in prehistoric monuments in Britain which have much the same atmosphere, henge monuments and chambered cairns and places. I think we've lost touch with that nowadays in the west.

When you think of yourself as a poet, do you think of yourself as a female poet, a Scottish poet, or what? I suppose my feelings would be that in any art there's neither man nor woman, there's only the maker. I think it's hard. I like to think there are things I've written where you wouldn't know whether it was a woman or a man writing, and then there are other things, to do with children, or love poems. Yet men write poems about children as well. Probably they couldn't write the birth poems, but you never know! I suppose I've a lot of male heroes in my poems – my grandfather, for instance. He was a big strong man, a symbol of protective power! When I was a child he was the person who played with me a great deal, and because he spoke 'braid Scots' I've a strong feeling about Scots, but I've never written in Scots.

Why is that? At the time I ceased to speak Scots I ceased to think in Scots. Then, at secondary school, Scots was definitely not acceptable, not even a Scots accent. The Scots I had been exposed to was very strong in vocabulary. It wasn't just an accent. It was a whole language, dealing with the countryside and work and daily tasks. That had to be excluded from life in Edinburgh, so it never really occurred to me to write in Scots. I'm not saying it could never happen. I'm still enough in touch with the language.

This summer, when we were on holiday in Galloway, my children went out to play with the children of the estate workers and farm people who lived nearby, and it was the first time they had heard Scots used in play by other children of their own age. As I say, this is the expansion of the English language, that has taken place over many centuries. They don't hear it, unless I read to them in Scots, and I'm concerned they do hear it, for it's their linguistic heritage.

YOUNG HARPER

Above Tweed Green levels
Maeve first raises the harp.

Prosper her hand that plucks
then clenches fist like a jockey.

Grip inside thighs
the colt with a cropped mane.

Turn blades on the curved neck
bristling with spigots.

Out from the rosewood forest
came this foal of strong nerve.

Stand in your grainy coat,
let her lift elbows over you.

Keep her thumbs bent
and fingers hard to do the playing:

Eight summers made them, clarsach,
I freely give you my elder daughter.

THE NEGATIVE

He's come for the pipe-band,
being just big enough
to put on his sporran.

My son is a scrap
of his own tartan:
he is all kilt, save for his brown knees
and the bloodied old scars on them.

It's his everyday kilt, but here, today,
it makes a tourist trample through the crowd:

'Move *there*, little boy.'
She fires the camera, conspires
to steal his virtue into a picture.
He flashes a dour and warring glance
that must be perfect for her.

Now that it's taken, he ought
to spring to life,
flash out a knife,
ask for her money or the negative.
Yet he must know
that will develop into something
different from the youthful Lachlan.

No,
the negative will show
a stony moor,
a twisted tree,
and all around them
the ragged map
of Scotland.

INFERTILITY PATIENT

'I could never have enough children.' Katherine
Mansfield

To lift another woman's child
is like carrying a bundle of barbed wire.
And one who will let himself be held
stirs every bereaved desire.

Between collarbone and breast
his hard head makes an impression:
a dent in a white quilt
someone's secretly been sleeping on.

My hands fall empty in my lap
when she lifts him away.

I can share, as I give him up,
only his backwards look with no wave.

She's the fertile one while I am not.
Inject a dye and see my tubes are drawn
blocked and scarred, death's first print I've got
in me: you month, rat's jaw, I see you yawn.

Mary McCann

Photo: Margaret Christie

MARY McCANN WAS BORN in Kilmarnock in Ayrshire in 1942. She studied Physics at Glasgow University and worked in Physics research and teaching until 1976. Since then she has spent her time studying art, writing and illustrating. She is a member of two women's writing groups and lives in Edinburgh.

Her work has appeared in *Changing Rooms*, an anthology by Pomegranate Women's Writing Group (1981), *Women's Writes*, a broadsheet published in connection with Feminist Book Fortnight (June 1985), and *Edinburgh Women's Liberation Newsletter*. She exhibited with *Fireweed*, a women's anti-war exhibition, which toured Scotland and Northern England from 1982–84. Recently she had poems in *Fresh Oceans* (Stramullion, 1989) and had a play *Thunderbirds and Snakebites* performed by Catch Theatre Company.

I met Mary in the Edinburgh women's writing group, Pomegranate. Thus, our initial contact with each other was to do with our own poetry, which gave me an opportunity to become familiar with her writing. When I asked Mary if I could interview her she wanted to look at my list of questions, as she was nervous as to what I might ask. I gave her the list and she seemed quite comfortable with them. I invited Mary for lunch and she came, bearing a carrier bag filled with oranges and yoghurt. Mary had brought written responses to my questions, but as the interview progressed began to talk freely with me.

I GAVE UP DOING SCIENCE when I was about 36. I really couldn't cope with it any longer. So I became unemployed and started writing a while after that. *How did that come about?* There were two strands to it. I wasn't terribly well. I had a lot of anxiety and depression and I needed to make sense of my life, especially having been on a very narrow track since the age of 18. So I read about things like keeping intensive journals and I decided to keep one myself because I needed to record my moods and find out why I was so moody. Also I met people who were going to writing groups and they sounded really interesting. So I went to a Theatre Workshop writing class run by Brian McCabe and other young male Scottish poets. I started writing reminiscences and then I started writing poems. I really needed a means of expression. I also started doing art again which I hadn't done since I was 15. At school I really loved painting and drawing and was good at it, but I gave it up because I was supposed to be 'an academic'.

  Do you do other work in addition to your writing? Well, I've been holding off getting any straight work for a long time. I really didn't feel able to. I'm still unemployed. I've done different kinds of unpaid work, illustrations, exhibitions, producing the *Women's Newsletter* and organising *Women Live*.

  What inspires or motivates you to write? A lot of different things. The themes I tend to come up with are: domesticity, which is to do with my mother's life; roots, where I come from, which are very tangled in my case; my own childhood; nature; feminism; anti-war; city life; and memories of Catholicism.

  I was very interested in the poem about Donegal. Yes. My grandmother came from Donegal and it's a current obsession of mine to find out how she lived. Both my parents' families had strong connections with Ireland and I don't know much about where they came from, so I want to learn a bit more about it. They must have had such strength and endurance to have made those journeys.

  Could you talk a bit about your background? I was very lucky in my childhood in many ways, growing up by the sea and in a small town, not a city. I've made a lot of changes in my life, but all the things I've changed from are still there inside me. I grew up a very devoted Catholic in a traditional, conservative, Irish Catholic community. Then I left that behind to go to the city to study Science, a completely different dimension from being a Catholic, except that they're both authoritarian! I also got involved with various men, which I think was a kind of search for personal freedom. And then I left all that and started writing, became a feminist and moved towards relationships with women. But I wonder where the roots of it are. Some of them are in my mother's life and what she got from her mother. My mother's very intelligent, very creative and imaginative. She's led a domestic life for 46 years. She's still cooking dinner for my dad and things like that. That's her priority. They were both very anxious about me giving up my job, but recently she's come round. She's supporting me. She has always told amazing stories and I recently found out that she writes poems. It means a lot to me that she's backing me at the minute. I've also been in mental hospital, which is another dimension I write about. That has shown me that the imagination I had has been rather squashed, to put it mildly, at school and everywhere else. There was no place for it, except in the art class.

How do you work with an idea? I still keep this diary and I write down dreams and what I see happening around me. And every so often, I get an idea for a poem or a story. If I'm writing a poem it usually happens very quickly. I just let it flow. I listen hard to what's forming in my mind.

Do you think of yourself as a Scottish poet in any sense? Yes, I must be, mustn't I? I have vague feelings about that. Scottish women haven't done enough writing. Most writing in English has been done by American and English women, and there's exciting writing in English from other nations, from India and Africa and so on, and Scottish women should be in there too.

What does the Scottish thing mean to you? Is it a sense of geography or what? It's hard to say. There's a chip on the shoulder, of course. In my case it's a complicated chip. I remember when I was a child wanting to know: Was I Irish or was I Scottish? And my dad said, 'You're Scottish with an Irish background.' Then we were Catholics as well. That was a minority, an oppressed minority for a while, but they're rapidly becoming more middle class now, compared to my dad's family which was working class. The community I grew up in was mainly working class and poor, although both my parents went to university, which was unusual for their generation and their immediate families. Since I've become a feminist I've gone into another minority. I seem to have lived in minorities all my life! And I'm interested in that. It's very inspiring in feminism to see different groups of women saying they must be represented too, disabled women and women from ethnic minorities. So we should have Scottish women writing, and there should be Scottish women from the islands who have a different tradition, and Scottish women from the Irish immigrant tradition like me, and the Italian, Asian and Black Scots, and Scottish women from the built-in, bricks-and-mortar, lowland Scottish middle class and so on. There are all these different dimensions.

And it's not only working class-middle class, or Scottish-Irish, but also rural-urban? That's right. I don't feel able to tackle all these huge themes, but they hang about there. Another one is men's work and women's work. My mother was totally immersed in women's work as dictated by society. She gave up her work when she got married and had me. I was the oldest. She had seven pregnancies, five of which survived. She just worked and worked and worked. I remember her being tired the whole time. I remember deciding, in the arrogant way you do in your teens, I do not want to be like my mother. And I ended up choosing a masculine field of work and really trying very hard in that field and deciding in the end it wasn't for me. There had to be something more balanced. Part of my changing was to appreciate just what my mother did for us as children. She is very loving and puts people first. My values have now shifted more towards hers.

That's so often a dilemma for women. How do I do something that's not like my mom and then choosing something that's defined by society as a masculine activity? Yes, I went to extremes when I did that. I'm very surprised to see that I've gone to extremes in quite a lot of directions, but I suppose I just felt very constrained, by the possibility of my mother's role and my background, and it's been the result of my various attempts to break out of that.

How do you define yourself as a poet? I think I'm a feminist and a poet. I find it hard to call myself a poet. That's a bit of a laugh! But I'm definitely a feminist and there was a big change in my feelings about writing when I got into Women Live in 1982. I was at Art College part-time, and everything was these correct little drawings and correct little photographs, and when a few women produced 'feminist art' it was like a bolt from the blue. They had the courage to tackle feminist issues and suddenly there was this great feeling of excitement about what creative women were doing, instead of going to mixed writing groups and trying very hard to get into the Edinburgh literary scene! It was like a conversion experience and very addictive. We were all getting a buzz off it. That made me feel it was worthwhile, that I wanted to take part in it, that I wanted to be a writer and a feminist and to write about women's concerns and feminist concerns.

I wrote these strong anti-war poems around that time and I've made efforts to write political poems since then, but now I find it harder. It's still there as a dimension, but I want to write about more complicated things now. My first political poems were too simple. I don't think you should have to go around tearing yourself to pieces asking yourself if you're being politicaly correct. I can't be bothered with that. I think there should be plenty of freedom and I like the idea of discussion between women who have different viewpoints. In general I'm against the idea of feminism holding women down or stopping them doing things out of some idea of political correctness. There's a lot of different strands. And having grown up in a very conservative social group, I understand the temptation to try to get everything cut and dried, but if you do this, you have to realize that it means the end of growth.

When you talk about doing art on feminist themes, could you give me an example? I could give you examples from other people's work, like Beverley A'Court, for instance. Her work at that time (1982) had references to things like rape or menstruation, these kind of realities. In *Fireweed*, she did beautiful collages out of feminine materials, like muslin or rose petals, and when you looked at it, it was actually about Agent Orange in Vietnam. *I loved your poem about Greenham Common.* Yes. I wasn't able to go. It was too cold! And I hate long bus journeys! But I thought I'd write a poem about it because I was very moved by it. I watched it on TV in tears. That's what it's like, when feminist things come to life. You actually see people doing something very brave and taking a risk for something that a lot of us feel but never have the nerve to do. That puts it in a nutshell for me. I like that spirit. The poem was influenced by having read people like Adrienne Rich. I tend to pick up what I'm reading. I've picked up from Liz Lochhead too. She uses Scottish words and her own background. I'd like to do that too, but probably more in stories than in poems. I don't seem able to do that in poems. My poems seem to be very 'English'. But there is a vague connection with Celtic things. I love Celtic legends and the Hebrides. The Celts really loved nature. If you look at the Book of Kells, you've got all these wonderful illuminations of birds and beasts, and that's pre-Christian. My father is a gardener and passed on his love of Nature to me. In my poem 'Dream' you have this idealised version of living on a small farm in Ireland or on the west coast of Scotland. It was the dream of all the Scottish and Irish exiles, this little self-sufficient farm.

It reminds me of people coming to America. Yes, well, they all sang sentimental songs about Scotland and Ireland. And the sad thing was, the land here wasn't able to support them, and that had a political dimension too. I love the transformation images you get in Celtic legends, like growing a garden in the sea, and so on. I find that sort of thing very beautiful and inspiring.

What about the dragons? That came out of a Women Live art group and a game of Consequences. We were looking for a theme for an art exhibition and dragons began to emerge. So we decided to draw dragons and all these teeth appeared. Really angry drawings! Some were very pathetic, with captive maidens and things. And I did this flying red dragon, like a big red greyhound, with a woman on its back. It was taking her for a ride through the sky and she was extremely happy. Then I went home and woke up in the middle of the night and wrote this poem 'Red Dragon'. The others followed later. 'Dragon Nonsense' was slightly different, in that the speaker can't accept the flights of imagination the dragons represent. But she's suspicious of the old style knight in shining armour as well. It just seemed to be a game, writing these poems. It was for fun. Dilys Rose, whom I met in Pomegranate Writing Group, had written a set of doll poems, so I thought I'd write a set of dragon poems. It came from that picture and a surge of energy, having discovered that image and somehow relating to it. I can't explain that process very well. I wasn't alone, though. I did it with other women.

In anthropological terms dragons can symbolize putting together old things in new ways. That's right. That's Frankenstein. Those dragons are made up of pieces of information, myths or images from other places. They became interesting because you could do anything with them. Nobody really knows what a dragon's like. Liz Lochhead goes in for monsters, very exciting, passionate monsters. Frankenstein's monster is such a tragic monster. *It was very interesting, in her interview she talked about Mary Shelley in relationship to her mother, the feminist and rational philosopher and the daughter who writes about monsters.* Well, it was also to do with childbirth, wasn't it? Not being sure about what she could bring forth as a writer. I got a lot out of Liz Lochhead's play about Mary Shelley. Anybody would be interested in Frankenstein, it's really powerful. And I like to think of it in terms of Science and what Science does.

Your poem about lying in bed and remembering Hiroshima is a very strong combination of the immediate relationship with a loved one and thinking about something so terrible. Yes. It was a very emotional poem and very important to me to write at the time. It came out of having been a nuclear physicist, I think.

At first I enjoyed Physics. I liked the idea of it being new knowledge. I was also a sort of intellectual snob. Physics was riding very high about 1960. That was what bright people did. There was a lot of social pressure to do it if you were going on to university. Some of the men who taught me had worked on the Bomb, but as they never referred to it except as a joke, you felt there was something odd about that. I read *Brighter than a Thousand Suns* when I was a graduate student, but there weren't an awful lot of people you could talk to about it. I first tried to get people interested when I became a teacher. For a long time it was one of my great interests, reading up the history of the Bomb. All the men who worked on the Bomb were regarded as heroes, and I thought, this is knowledge that's gone wrong. It was a horrible feeling. Those big teams of men were usually working away on accelerators, and I worked on accelerators, I worked on reactors. There was this wonderful sense of conquering the frontiers of knowledge all the time, but they did it with exactly the same spirit as the Bomb makers back in Los Alamos. So I always felt there was something I had to understand there and protest about. I got very upset about Hiroshima every time I read about it. Then in the Women's Movement we did Hiroshima Day marches and things like that.

Now I've moved on from worrying about what scientists can do in the way of atomic weapons to what they can do in ecological terms, racing on to make new genetic species, and the use of fertilisers and pesticides, and the creation of deserts and so on. Also, about 50 per cent of the scientists in this country are working on defence-related projects. The whole thing's gone completely crazy. I didn't think that while I was still in it. I wasn't political at all while I was a scientist. I went through the sixties without noticing! I was working. It's one of the things they do to scientists: they make them work hard. You never have ay free time. And it's still true. You basically end up with very right wing people. It's very hard for a scientist not to be, although I think more of them are questioning scientific ethics now than they used to do.

You've got through some amazing changes. Yes, well, I think I've stopped changing now. I think I've got a bit where I ought to be now. I worry about not having a job. I'll need to get that straightened out. I'll see. I've stopped feeling guilty about wanting to do creative work. For years and years I felt I ought to be doing something socially useful, but I think I'm growing out of that now.

What's your intention in writing? I find it hard to say. It's something that excites me and it's a satisfying process to discover things. It may simply be a form of therapy, but it has helped me. I'm much happier with my own self and my own feelings than I was. I was told constantly in mental hospital that I wasn't coping with feelings. I think that was because I grew up in a traditional Scottish setting, where you didn't talk about feelings, and then went on to Science, probably still in flight from feelings. So I had all that catching up to do. I'd like to see more women, and more Scottish women, using their imagination and feelings, because we have been very held down in Scotland. We've been very repressed. But things are changing.

DRAGON NONSENSE

listen I can't think of dragons just now
I've got the dinner to cook
dragons what do you mean dragons
load of nonsense
I've got to get the potatoes on
stir yesterday's mince
run to the shops for extra marge
set the table AND
do the washing so's
I'll have half an hour to myself after ...
DRAGONS
away you go what are dragons anyway
scaly monsters
fire shooting out their mouths

rescuing the girl no sorry
that was the hero wasn't it
kills the dragon
marries the girl
happy ever after
washing his socks eh
and cooking day in day out
bit like myself
makes you wonder
not much choice either way
dragon or drudge
bit of a con
huh

ON NOT GOING TO GREENHAM COMMON,
DECEMBER 1982

December.
one crimson rose survives
by the mellow brick wall
of my landlord's garden

alone in my room
I am talking to suffragettes

the house roofs are white with frost

I am talking
with prisoners of conscience

home. peace. tiny brown sparrows
peck bread on my windowsill

I am painting a picture
made from Hildegarde the nun's visions
in 1165

pale women come to me.
they are emaciated. they are martyrs
they are smiling

the sky is full
of grey pigeons with green and violet necks

this woman is from Chile. electrodes
still tangle in her hair
she puts out her hands to me

the seagulls
make world lines of freedom in the air

my grandmother is here, with eleven children
and her hands worn down to the bone

the lilac tree is scant black wire
with green buds

oh seagulls   oh white   oh red rose
oh sky   oh lilac   oh winter

my friends are getting ready
for Greenham Common
they wish to kiss
the death weapons goodbye

they wear green and violet scarves around their necks
I am not with them

in my room, staying at home, coward,
I talk to sparrows and seagulls

and to all these women who enter me
without knocking

who will not leave me
alone

Eva Bourke

Eva Bourke was born and educated in Germany. She now lives with her husband and children in Galway.

She writes in both German and English and has published poems in Ireland, Germany and the United States. Her first book of poems, *Gonella*, with drawings by Jay Murphy, was published by Salmon Press, Galway in 1985. Her second collection *Litany for the Pig* appeared in 1989, also by Salmon.

Eva met my train at Galway station. She was late and I waited, nervously, not having met her before. Finally, she came rushing up, a slight, dark woman, breathless, grinning and waving to me. She took one of my bags and we went on a tour of Galway, the canals, the Spanish Arch and the market place. We talked about Irish, German and American politics and women's rights. Two days later we did the interview in her living room. I liked her so much it was difficult to settle into my interviewing role. Nevertheless, we managed to get started.

I started writing seriously only about six years ago. I can't remember how it happened. It was just a general dissatisfaction with things in Germany. But I had started long before that. I wrote a lot in the States in my teens and I found the confrontation with the new language very stimulating. But that all went underground afterwards. I felt there were far more relevant things to do than write poetry. I became interested in it again in Ireland when I suddenly had a lot of time to myself which I hadn't had before. I didn't take it seriously at first. It was just for my own amusement. But I enjoyed it so much that I continued. I'd say that's fairly typical when you're coping with life, with money problems and children, with jobs and changing countries. You don't have the tranquillity to sit down and write a poem.

Do you feel in limbo? As a writer, as a poet, I'm in limbo, because I'm not Irish and the Irish identity topic doesn't concern me personally. I'm also in limbo as regards language and I often wonder should I be writing in English at all? It feels almost arrogant to be writing in another language. I feel I ought to be writing in German. That for me is a personal struggle which the other poets in Galway don't have. I want to write in German very much, but I can't because I haven't got the living contact with the language. However, this summer I'm going back to Germany and I'm going to try to write in German again. My first publications were in German and if they hadn't happened I would never have continued.

When did you switch from writing in German to writing in English? It has gradually happened more and more. Until a few years ago I used to write in German. Then when we came back from a sabbatical in Munich I felt a bit isolated. I needed an audience. So I started translating a few things and from there I started using English more and more. Now most of the time I write in English.

Is it a different process, writing in English? Yes. It's less automatic, less spontaneous. I have to think and search more and the play with words is almost eliminated. My writing in English is almost reduced to imagery and I'm beginning to hate that. I like language as a material, almost like something tactile. I would love to use English like that, but I have the feeling I can only do it in German. I'll have to find some compromise in English if I'm going to continue here at all. Have you come across this bilingual split before? *Yes, the women who write in Scots and Gaelic have consistently said that those are experiential and emotional languages for them, whereas English is conceptual and abstract. One woman said that if she was going to write 'from the heart' she would use Gaelic, and if she was going to talk about politics she would do so in English.* Yes. Writing is such a spontaneous process. You can't direct yourself. Sometimes a poem comes out in German. It's there in my head, finished, before I actually sit down at the typewriter. Sometimes it's in German and sometimes in English.

What inspires or motivates you to write? That's a hard question. Often it's simply a word or a phrase. Sometimes it's an idea that you follow up and try to distill. Sometimes it just comes out of the blue. And it's totally different each time. Sometimes you work on something for ages and ages and sometimes it's suddenly there, quite complete. I have so much other work to do, I can't type it out at once, so I have to keep it in my head and work it out there first. Sometimes it's an experience you want to talk about that will set you off. Conflict, of course, brings out a lot.

In your book Gonella *there are a lot of strong statements about the way we live, for example, the poem 'The Fish'.* That's because of this rupture in the world no one seems able to handle. The fish used to be an acronym for Christ and so it became the symbol for Christianity, but it also has multiple layers of meaning and association. It can be symbolic of life as well as of fertility. I'm using it, not in the Christian sense, but in the life-affirming and fertile sense. I'm juxtaposing these two ideas of the Judaeo-Christian tradition, because it seems to me that those two religions are deeply involved in the mess we are in at the moment. The poem is a play on how it could have been otherwise. I am also playing with the patriarchal and matriarchal concepts of the world. A female fish might have made a difference.

There's also the old anthropological polarity between nature and culture, men being associated with culture and women with nature, culture being dominant over nature. Exactly. This poem is turning that all around and asking if we can't do better than this.

Do you have an audience in mind? No. I've written a few poems with my own children in mind and I've written one or two specifically for children. That's about the only audience I've ever thought of. *Are you writing for yourself then or for other people?* Initially you don't think of anyone ever reading or appreciating what you write, but after a while the audience intrudes whether you like it or not. Will they understand or misunderstand it? It's really terrible when somebody misunderstands something you've written, or uses it for their own purposes.

When you write, does the idea or the content dictate the form? There's a tension. There's not too much attention paid to the form. I'm delighted we live in an age when form is not a prerequisite. Sometimes it intrudes. I've written sonnets in German, just to see whether I could do it!

How would you define yourself as a poet? I'm a poet. I'm a woman. I'm a feminist. But I wouldn't say I'm a feminist poet. These definitions usually coincide. I'm also interested in other things, like biology. Does that make me a biological poet? As for 'woman poet', I thought it was redundant, merely another term for 'poetess'. But I am a woman poet in that I write also about women's experience.

You said something earlier about writing about people who are powerless. Yes: children, old people, people who are powerless or suppressed.

This poem 'Two Times Two in Domestic Interior' is very different from the other poems. You're allowing the pictures to speak. Were you conscious of that? Absolutely. It's about the Japanese print and woodcut-maker, Utamaro, who was persecuted by the Emperor for making woodcuts of ordinary everyday themes, such as women washing themselves, combing their hair, breast-feeding, cooking and so on, which at that time was against the law. Artists had to stick to representations of the high-class geishas and the Emperor's court. But Utamaro's prints were reproduced all over the place and were particularly influential in the 19th century. The French Impressionists were inspired by them. Utamaro was arrested and never recovered from this humiliation. He died as a result. In that poem I imagined him on the run and described what might have happened to him. What the poem is saying is that some artists are nourished by simple, everyday things, and because they celebrate such things, they can return to them as a kind of safety net in times of need or duress. The image of the women preparing his meal at the end of the poem is not about a physical meal, but about inspiration, what he draws on as an artist. I love his work. He portrays women cooking and peeling vegetables, like in the poem. I felt in the end that he just had to be there. That's where he belongs. So it's a social statement as well. It's also against censorship, or imposed forms of aesthetic criteria, such as the idea that a poem has to be well turned out, that it can't have any roughness, that it has to be beautiful and acceptable to a certain class, a drawing-room thing.

I was very struck by this poem, 'The Lamentations of Annie', and particularly those lines where she says: 'I am the

*Madonna of the cardboard box / Of the broken back at thirty-
five.'* Do you think it's completely resigned? *It's very sad. Very
enraging. If you had written it as 'She' it would have felt very
powerless, but the fact you put it in the voice of an 'I' gives it
some sense of power. She's very defiant, but I wanted her to do
something at the end.* That would be unrealistic. A lot of people
in Galway have actually been very offended by this poem. Certain people I know are extremely religious. It's the reference to
the Pope and her turning away from the Bleeding Heart in the
hospital.

That's what's going on right now with the itinerant people?
She is a travelling woman. I know her well. I've only really put
together what she told me over the years. It could have gone on
for another twenty pages but I had to cut it short. I'd love her to
do something too. But she can't. She won't. I read it at a festival in
Galway and some people got up and left. It hit a nerve because
the church really doesn't do anything about the situation of the
travellers.

*Do you find it different writing from your own experience
than as a persona?* There are very few poems involving myself.
It's not that I want to hide behind personas, but that I often find
other things more interesting.

Tell me about this poem, 'Advice on how to Hibernate'.
That's a very German poem. It came out first in German and then
I translated it. The imagery of ice, of winter, of hardening despair
and frost, cropped up in the 19th century, when a lot of progressive painters and poets used it after the failure of the French
Revolution. Whether consciously used or not, it has overtones of
the restrictive legislation of the subsequent Restoration, when
the old order re-established itself. There's a famous romantic
painting by Caspar David Friedrich of a tiny ship in the middle of
all these icebergs. It's called 'Stranded Hope'. Enzensberger, a
West German poet has a collection called *The Sinking of the
Titanic* and he uses the iceberg image in almost every poem to
represent this threat to all progressive ideas. Now the pack ice
seems to be everywhere.

THE FISH

And what, if it had been a fish
in the beginning,
not the word, or the power, or the deed.

A fish,
sky-blue,
or pre-cardinal red,
or sienna brown,
(before Troy was ever heard of).
A fish in the sky with diamonds
And sapphires.
A fish whose fins
brush the equator.
A fish full of milky tits
suckling the stars
(There would never have been a thing
like Ganymede,
half ice and half cosmic dust
circling around a barren planet.)
There would have been streams
and tropical seas
at a very habitable temperature.
The fish would have seen to this,
for even god-fish want to survive.

There would have been no need
for anyone's son's sacrifice,
no need for supplication and betrayal
in any particular olive grove,
none for the gathering of blood
in chalice or grail,
none for holy wars,
nor genocide.
Can you imagine
fish roe begetting a field
of steely warriors.
Never.
No baby fish would thrive
in the type of soil
that threw up armies.

We would have been lanterns
of finely beaten metal.
Drifting lights,
children of wave and alga,
children's children of the salts,

constellations in a glass world
of aquamarine and indigo,
with the spice of seaweed and ocean foliage
in our mouths,
yellow-ringed, with fragile gills,
moving opalescent fins
as showers of sparks
through sea-caves,
fireworks descending on cushions
of chrysoprase
in coral woods.

Why did we not choose the fish
when we were still able to?
Why did we love our own image so,
Armoured in steel,
at best full of misery,
too heavy to float,
always busy
sowing dragon teeth.
The chance was gone
at the flick of a tail fin.

TWO TIMES TWO IN DOMESTIC INTERIOR

I
One peels vegetables
letting the curling peels
drop into her lap.

The other,
drying a lacquered bowl,
cares for the child on her back,
whose forelock rises like a brush
on his shaven skull.

On the stove stand an iron kettle
and a covered dish.
The water-bucket beside it
is made of varnished wood
and tied with ropes of braided rush.

Tortoise-shell combs and pins
pull back the women's hair
and hold it in place.

There is little room to move
inside this 'floating world'.
No window opens on trees,
no screen gives shelter
from the sun.
There are neither depth,
nor shadows.
The scene is so clear, you can see
the grain in the wood,
the threads in the cotton jackets.

II
One crouches before the fire,
blows through a bamboo pipe
to kindle the flames.

The other, ladling tea
into her cup,
holds up her left arm to her face
and closes her eyes
against the smoke.

III
In the garden
two men use indigo
to print irises and kingfishers
on a piece of silk
stretched between two poles.

A troupe of travelling musicians
goes past.
Two acrobats wearing demon masks
casually walk beside them
on their hands.

It is rumoured that the man
who made these woodcuts
is on the run
from the emperor's secret police.

He broke the law
against portraying the life
of the lower class.

But the two women know
his whereabouts:
this moment he is sitting
cross-legged on the porch of their house,
waiting for his bowl of rice
and fried cormorant.

Eavan Boland

EAVAN BOLAND WAS BORN in Dublin in 1944, educated in New York, London and Trinity College Dublin. She is married with two daughters. She teaches creative writing and works as a freelance journalist and reviewer for the *Irish Times*.

Her publications include *The War Horse* (1975), *In Her Own Image* (1980), *Night Feed* (1982), published by Arlen House Press, Dublin, *The Journey* (1987) and *Selected Poems* (1989), published by Carcanet Press, Manchester, in conjunction with Arlen House Press, Dublin.

Eavan asked me to come to her home for the interview as one of her daughters had the flu and she wanted to keep an eye on her. We sat in the living room and had a long conversation about the American poet and feminist theorist, Adrienne Rich, and comparisons between American and Irish poetry. When I started the tape-recorder, she became very professional. She had obviously given a lot of thought to my lines of questioning. Her answers consistently related her own writing to the larger Irish tradition. I found myself having to work hard, not only to keep up with her, but to pick up on the thoughts and ideas she was handing to me.

I CAME FROM A VERY bookish household. My mother was a painter, and once said to me with great candour, that she had never passed an exam in her life. My father was a very educated, articulate man. Both of them loved literature, and so it was natural, when I was a child, that I should write stories and poems. But I didn't really connect with it in a way that I understood until I was eighteen or nineteen.

What inspires you to write, or do you believe in inspiration? No, not really. I think I'm influenced by my childhood, by the fact that my mother was a painter. And, of course, painters' lives are governed by light. The sense of a writing world, governed by practical disciplines, has always appealed to me. I have never been sympathetic to the idea of inspiration.

So what happens when you write? Do you see something, come up against something? I always think of myself as working at a rock face. Ninety days out of ninety five, it's just a rock face. The other five days, there's a bit of silver, a bit of base metal in it. I'm reasonably consistent, and the consistency is a help to me. It helps me to stay in contact with my failure rate, and unless you have a failure rate that vastly exceeds your success rate, you're not really in touch with what you are doing as a poet. The danger of inspiration is that it is a theory that redirects itself towards the idea of success rather than to the idea of consistent failure. And all poets need to have a sane and normalized relationship with their failure rate.

What do you mean by 'failure rate'? Things that don't work, material that you can't handle, obsessions that you don't have the ability to deal with. Adrienne Rich, in her article *When We Dead Awaken*, talks about her early formal training as giving her asbestos gloves to lift hot material. Sometimes you can't handle the heat of the material.

Has that been true for you, working with particular material? Yes, it has. It's never easy to clarify why something is difficult to handle. I suspect that as a lyric poet, you're always working with time and perceptions of loss and just common down-to-earth disappointments or irretrievable segments of human experience. You're trying in some way to formalize them, and not just technically, but also imaginatively so that you shelter them from further depredation and loss.

Can you say more about this? You write a lot about your experience as a woman, writing very much in the voice of an 'I'. Yes, the voice is me. It isn't just the voice of an 'I'. It's me in the

Yeatsian sense, in that it's the part of me that connects with something more durable and more permanent in my own experience. It isn't, to paraphrase Yeats, the 'I' that sits down to breakfast. I don't think of myself as writing in the voice of a woman. I am a woman and I write in terms of what defines me. Very often I think that I am a human being whose window onto humanity is womanhood. But I make a clear distinction between feminizing material, which I think is unethical and restrictive, and humanizing the feminine parts of an experience, which are very often potent, emblematic and powerful parts of it.

What do you mean by 'feminizing material'? If you take an experience and 'feminize' it, you give it its meaning within a sociological or a political context. If you examine anything that you do according to its purely feminine importance, then you lose a good deal of the myth and power of that experience. A lot of what we now call 'feminine experiences', or 'women's experiences', or 'women's issues', within poetry, are in fact, if people would only look at them closely, powerful metaphors for types of humiliation, types of silence, that are there throughout human experience. But you need to unlock the metaphor and you can't do it by feminizing the material. You can only do it by humanizing it.

Say, for example, your poem 'Anorexic'? Yes. I always worry about the ethical basis of poems like 'Anorexic'. Anorexia didn't happen to me. On the other hand, I hoped that I had some rapport with a state of suffering which has seemed to me to have roots in perfectionism, rather than just in a state of morbidity. I hoped that as an artist, I could understand it and see what was restrictive in it.

Are you very conscious of using formal strategies when you are writing? No. I'm very conscious of what I do technically, but I wish there were formal strategies. A lot of humbug and mysticism is talked about the technical aspect of poetry. I wouldn't be able to handle a strictly formalist approach. I could never sit down and approach my material with a sense of how I might shape it. In all honesty, I think that formalism is, and can be, manipulative to material. I'm a hand-to-mouth technician, and either I have enough for a poem, or I don't. I wish there were strategies and manoeuvres. But very often it's just the rations of the day, technically.

And what is your intention when you are writing? Purely to resolve the material as best as I can. It's all so intuitive, so instinctive. I remember having a sick child and someone saying, 'You won't know that the child is better until the fever comes down.' In something of the same way, I don't know that the poem is resolved until the fever comes down. I don't have any way of knowing what I have done until I have done it. For that reason, it is an entirely instinctive area.

Are you writing for a particular audience in any sense? I am writing for a particular constituency within myself, from which the poetry comes. You can call it a 'vision'. I think the area of private vision in any artist is impossible to find and almost impossible to define. It is the difficulty of finding it that gives the tension and energy to the poems that do find it.

And are you trusting of that inner vision? Does it stay with you consistently? More trusting than I used to be. It doesn't stay with me in any sense of a pillar of fire or a cloud or an accompanying force or anything like that. But for somebody like me, who thinks of herself as a lyric poet, writing is not an expression, it is an experience. I make a clear distinction between the writing I do, which is expressive of a subject, and the writing I do that is the experience of it. I experience certain things through my poems, which is why I write them. I write them as a method of experience, not as a method of expression. *And is there any sense of resolution with the experience when you've finished the poem?* No, I don't think so. They are all glimpses, perceptions, sometimes senses of healing, although I'm slow to say that. I don't think that healing is in any way a monopoly, or indeed, a chief property of poetry. You can find very good, very wounding, and very wounded poems. But certainly I am conscious of that area of experience within myself.

How about In Her Own Image *relating to the particular consciousness of dealing, say, with poems like 'Anorexic' and 'The Exhibitionist'?* I have to say that I think that *In Her Own Image* is a misunderstood book. Perhaps I shouldn't say that. Writers are constantly putting their hands over their hearts and saying they are misunderstood. I wrote it with a puritan perspective, but it was taken to be a confession of a number of diseases which I had had and neuroses which I was clearly giving evidence of! There are certain areas that are degraded because they are silent. They need to be re-experienced and re-examined. Their darker energies need to be looked at. That is exactly what *In Her Own Image* is about, seeing the image by looking at it. It is not some kind of free-fall through feminist ideology. Only in Ireland would it have been taken to be so. It is an examination, which I came back to in *The Journey* and in *Night Feed*, of the responsibility of the poet to the silences which surround human experience.

So giving voice ... Yes. They are not areas of feminist commitment. They are unresolved areas within myself. Their lack of resolution allows me to understand the silences around me, by the light of the silences within me. To me experience is power. The way that the Romantic movement understood poetry was to gain power. I don't want that. I want to use the poem to share the experience.

How do you feel, then, about the idea that there is power in the act of naming, in writing about a silent area? I think that the power is already in the experience and the naming doesn't add to the power. It shares the power, but it does not create it.

You are married and have two children. How do you juggle that with your writing? It has been nourishing and restoring for me to be with a family. When I was young I moved around a lot. We were split up because of my father's diplomatic career. I have relished and loved family life because of that early experience. It has seemed to me to be strangely and intimately connected to the work I do, not antithetical to it. I make no division between them. I don't have difficulty working when the children are in the house. When they are young you may deceive yourself as to how much energy you have, but there are things going on in you that are better − types of information, types of understanding, types of responses in yourself. Wonderful tribal echoes come in when you are raising a family.

Say more about the tribal echoes. This is an area where Adrienne Rich might disagree. She has an interesting passage where she speaks about the traditional roles of women being oppressive to the imaginative function. But I think there's another way of looking at that. I don't for one moment deny that what she calls the traditional roles have been agents of oppression and distraction to a lot of gifted women. But they do also have a strong, tribal relationship to the past. Nothing has changed in them. No industrial revolution has wiped them out. The advent of the washing machine doesn't change certain things that are constant and enduring and simple. By doing them you restore your continuity with those feelings, those emotions. You can't participate in them and not have a wider sense of connection with the whole human experience.

Would you consider yourself an Irish poet? Yes, I do. It is something of a convention here, if there are people to whom poets are introduced, to say, 'Here is so and so, he's an Irish poet, and here's Eavan, she's a woman poet.' It can be made clear that there is a distinction: an Irish poet is a male poet, and the Irish poet who is a woman has to be described as 'an Irish woman poet.' Again, it's part and parcel of the categories that exist.

And what does being Irish mean to you? Apart from the fact that it connects me with a past, I find it a perspective on my womanhood as well. Womanhood and Irishness are metaphors for one another. There are resonances of humiliation, oppression and silence in both of them and I think you can understand one better by experiencing the other. I am not a nationalist. It isn't always in linear time that nations flow along and define themselves. They crystallize in different individuals, at different times, in different voices and with different echoes. A 'nation' is a potent, important image. It is a concept that a woman writer must discourse with. I have that discourse and I like to think I have it partially on my terms. But no poet ever discourses with such a powerful image on his or her own terms. There has to be some contact between my perceptions and the national perceptions in Irish literature. When I was a young writer I wasn't willing to do without the idea of nationhood. And I knew that, as a woman, I couldn't accept the idea of nationhood as it was formulated for me in Irish literature. Therefore, I had to find some way of resolving those two things.

And what would you choose about being Irish? I would always choose a past that was real and actual and was composed of private, enduring human dignities. I don't want songs to be sung at midnight, but lives that were lived and lost and lived again. What is valuable in the past for me is a sense of all those things which you guard as precious and detailed in the present. And if you come along and smooth all that into some ballad or into a simplified image, you have wounded a truth that lives in the present as well as the past. That is what a nation means to me.

You are a feminist. Would you define yourself as a feminist poet? No. I am an absolute feminist. And when I say 'absolute' I'm aware it's not the right word to tag in front of feminist, but for many women of my generation, the feminist movement was the adventure of that generation. I have a real sense of the meaning of feminism as an enlightenment to men and women in this generation. I have come to a clearer understanding of human responsibilities through my feminism. But I am not a feminist poet, in the sense that feminism or socialism could be used to suggest that there is or could be, a programme for poetry. Poetry is not feminism by other means. As W. H. Auden said it hasn't saved anyone from death, and it doesn't change anyone in a direct way, whereas there is no doubt in my mind that feminism is a real agency of change.

You work with other women, with their writing ... That is a very conscious feminist commitment on my part, one which I not only wanted to undertake, but which I felt I owed to my own sense of survival. There are ways in which I have survived the stresses that other women have had to endure in Ireland, not through any virtue in myself, but simply because I happen to have been born in Dublin, and not eighty miles from it in a small town, without a library and with, perhaps, a bus that came twice a week. Those things can be very decisive in people's sense of isolation. I was born in a city, close enough to the energies and centres of information to be able to make up my mind about them. I had more options than many gifted women in Ireland who are very stressed by the circumstances that they live in. Workshops don't solve all that, by any means. But they do very often modify a sense of isolation and give people just a bit more confidence.

In your workshops, you work with men as well as women? I do, and I have the same feelings for the man who has been oppressed by diffidence and timidity. I have the same tenderness for that experience in a man as in a woman. For sociological reasons, there are patterns that have made me close some of my workshops to men. The simple fact is that, in Ireland, the emergence of the woman writer and the male writer are radically opposed. The male writer tends to emerge in his early twenties, economically independent, usually quite mobile, and for that reason, able to lay his hands on some of the things that nurture the young writer, from books to company. The woman writer tends to emerge in her thirties, perhaps having a job, but more likely having a young family. She very often has no money of her own, very little free time, and so is uniquely vulnerable to all the pressures that make people stop writing. My workshops are really for the woman who is single or married, and who is vulnerable to the pressures which suggest to her that she has nothing valuable to say, when, in fact, she doesn't have the circumstances in which to say it.

Someone once said to me that women's writing was very much judged as being 'poor' because women had neither support nor skill. Would you see this as a phase? Funnily enough, I think that when people say, 'Oh, God, that's women's writing,' they are not actually talking about the writing. They are very often talking about the womanhood. When you have societies in which the lives of women are devalued, as the *Harvard Studies* on psychology argue, those societies store in the very idea of womanhood many of the associations which they are least re-solved about. If those unresolved associations then come into a poem which makes that society confront them and say, 'Oh my God, another woman's issue!' – then that is a defective dialogue between a society and a poem by a woman. That has to be changed. A society has to become more self-knowing in its per-ception of that poem, which, in fact, can be a light on its own evasions. In turn, I think the woman poet has to become more understanding of the deprivations of the society which finds it difficult to judge her work.

Have you experienced this judgment with your own work? Yes I have. It comes and goes. The dialogue with me as a poet in Ireland is definitely influenced by the dialogue with me as a woman. What happened to me as a young poet was that I was a woman and a poet in a society which had the greatest difficulty connecting the two concepts. When I was praised as a young poet it often happened that the poem was praised and the woman-hood was edited out. When I was criticized as an older poet the womanhood would be decried and the poem would therefore be distorted. The society was struggling and I was struggling and there was inevitably a clash. Historically it was on the cards that I was going to pick up that tab as a woman poet.

But to be effective and useful as an Irish woman poet you have to be willing to pick up that tab. You have to understand that you enter a society and a history at a point where it is urgently talking to itself about the meaning of this experience in its own life. A woman poet is part of Irish history. She is, first, part of the ordeal, and second, part of the meaning. And that society has to argue out the ordeal and the meaning in terms of poetry by women, just as much as poetry by men. But it brings to the poetry of women a greater measure of its own tensions.

It can be difficult, for instance, to be a woman poet in a nation whose poetry on women consistently simplifies them. The Irish poetic tradition provides powerful, simplifying fusions of the feminine and the national. And you have to enter that field of force, as a woman poet, bringing a lot of complexities with you which are thoroughly unwelcome, into a tradition which has simplified women.

What are the ways in which they have been simplified in Ireland? Irish poets of the 19th Century, and indeed their heirs in this century, coped with their sense of historical injury by writing of Ireland as an abandoned queen or an old mother. My objections to this are ethical. If you consistently simplify women by making them national icons in poetry or drama you silence a great deal of the actual women in that past, whose sufferings and complexities are part of that past, who intimately depend on us, as writers, not to simplify them in this present. I am conscious of bringing my own perspective into the debate. 'Mise Eire' is certainly the poem in *The Journey* that states it.

We were discussing before the difficulty of working within a male tradition. Yes, but I don't take a passing view of it. I don't believe you can take a male tradition and say, 'That is my tradition.' I take Eliot's view that each voice that comes in, if it is its own voice, rearranges that force, and everybody has to look again at the assumptions on which they work.

We talked, on the phone, about the tendency for women writers to slide into sentimentality. Yes. I think that comes from the temptation to believe that, because it is by or about a woman, it must therefore share in the power of the female experience. It may not. No writing shares in any power unless it has been privately understood. You can't take a public understanding of feminism and apply it to a private vision of womanhood. It is the private truth which makes good writing. I think that sentimental writing tends to occur when people import public realities into what should be private work.

Public in the sense of 'writing for . . .' Yes, absolutely. Preordained audiences and meanings. *And are you conscious of working with people against this?* Well, I may point it out to them. Women's writing has been a revelation to the women of this generation. They can draw on it to help them, to confront themselves, but after that, they are just where they were. They have to draw on private fortitude and private knowledge and private hard work to reach some kind of self-knowledge in their own work.

For myself there were certainly times when it was a bit wearing and it could certainly be isolating. Now I see them as having been instructive. There was a point when I realized that, as a woman poet, within the tradition of Irish poetry, I was at best marginal, and at worst, threatened by it. It took me quite a while to interpret the exact meaning of that marginality within the tradition. But I did look at Black writing in America and dissident writing in Europe, and came to see how powerful those images were and how visible that invisibility could be. And I came to understand my own tradition and my own work better because of that.

ANOREXIC

Flesh is heretic.
My body is a witch.
I am burning it.

Yes I am torching
her curves and paps and wiles.
They scorch in my self denials.

How she meshed my head
in the half-truths
of her fevers

till I renounced
milk and honey
and the taste of lunch.

I vomited
her hungers.
Now the bitch is burning.

I am starved and curveless.
I am skin and bone.
She has learned her lesson.

Thin as a rib
I turn in sleep.
My dreams probe

a claustrophobia
a sensuous enclosure.
How warm it was and wide

once by a warm drum,
once by the song of his breath
and in his sleeping side.

Only a little more,
only a few more days
sinless, foodless.

I will slip
back into him again
as if I had never been away.

Caged so
I will grow
angular and holy

past pain,
keeping his heart
such company

as will make me forget
in a small space
the fall

into forked dark,
into python needs
heaving to hips and breasts
and lips and heat
and sweat and fat and greed.

MISE EIRE

I won't go back to it —

my nation displaced
into old dactyls,
oaths made
by the animal tallows
of the candle —

land of the Gulf Stream,
the small farm,
the scalded memory,
the songs
that bandage up the history,
the words
that make a rhythm of the crime

where time is time past.
A palsy of regrets.
No. I won't go back.
My roots are brutal:

I am the woman –
a sloven's mix
of silk at the wrists,
a sort of dove-strut
in the precincts of the garrison –

who practises
the quick frictions,
the rictus of delight
and gets cambric for it,
rice-coloured silks.

I am the woman
in the gansy-coat
on board the 'Mary Belle',
in the huddling cold,

holding her half-dead baby to her
as the wind shifts East
and North over the dirty
water of the wharf

mingling the immigrant
guttural with the vowels
of homesickness who neither
knows nor cares that

a new language
is a kind of a scar
and heals after a while
into a passable imitation
of what went before.

Kathleen Jamie

Photo: Irene Reddish

KATHLEEN JAMIE WAS BORN in Renfrewshire in 1962 and grew up in Midlothian. She studied Philosophy at Edinburgh University.

Her first publication, *Black Spiders*, published by Salamander Press (Edinburgh, 1982) won a Gregory Award and a Scottish Arts Council Book Award. Further publications include *A Flame in your Heart*, written with Andrew Greig (Bloodaxe, Newcastle upon Tyne, 1986) and *The Way We Live* (Bloodaxe, 1987). At the time of the interview she was completing her first novel and was Writer in Residence for Midlothian District libraries and Lasswade High School. She was then married to mountaineer Andrew Black and lived in Fife.

Kathleen and I corresponded before I arrived in Scotland. I wrote her that I would be researching in the Scottish Poetry Library and that she could find me there. While browsing one day in the Library, I bumped into a small young woman. 'Sorry,' I said. She stared at me. 'Are you Rebecca Wilson? I'm Kathleen Jamie.' It was my turn to stare. 'Well,' she said, 'fancy a cup of coffee?' Over coffee we stared at our feet and made chit chat. Finally she asked, 'How old are you?' 'I'm twenty-four. How old are *you*?' 'Twenty-four,' she answered. Silence. 'Well,' I said,

91

'you're much younger than I expected.' 'Well, so are *you!*' she retorted. Over the next few months we became friends. Finally, I dragged Kathleen out to lunch and an interview. Getting her to talk was like pulling teeth, but after several glasses of wine, she began.

WHEN DID YOU START WRITING? I used to get gold stars – two at a time! – for writing stories at school. I was taken to the head-mistress at the age of five to show this story I'd written. It was my only talent and I clung on to it. I started writing outside school when I was fourteen or so. *Was that poetry?* Yes. At school we were given poems to read and I kept thinking, I can do better than that! Sheer arrogance. So I went home and would write three poems and have a cup of tea and then do another three!

Have you ever had any formal training? Oh, God, no. I don't know if you can. I don't know where it came from. There's never been any books in the house. The only books in the house are the ones I've brought in.

You were the first – the only – child in your family to go to university? That's right. Mum and Dad certainly never went. Mum would have liked to have gone, but when she was young circumstances wouldn't allow it. *Did your parents encourage you in your writing?* They didn't discourage me. The family's attitude has always been that whatever you want to do, unless you're bombing children's hospitals, they just leave you alone to get on with it.

How old were you when you first got published? Nineteen – twenty. *How did that come about?* It was quite funny. People were encouraging me to take this manuscript to this chap because the word was he was looking for a new young poet. That was the Salamander Press, which was in Edinburgh in those days. It's defected to London now. So I just took it round and dumped it on his doorstep like an abandoned baby. I walked the streets round his house, then just left this envelope on his doorstep and ran away! He wrote to me a week later and said, 'Come and talk to me about this.' He seemed dead keen to do it.

So you didn't have any difficulty getting published? I've always found it as easy as falling off a log, but I suspect this is an aberration.

Valerie Gillies had the same experience, so it seems to me it might be easier here, or taken more seriously? It was a happy coincidence. They were looking for a female poet. It suddenly

became very fashionable, more so when you're young and
especially if you're not a feminist poet!

*When you think about your work how do you think of
yourself?* As an artist. As a writer, then an artist – as a sensibility.
I certainly don't think of myself as a woman poet. I don't even
think of myself as a poet. I've only recently started thinking about
what I do. It was pretty much intuition before then. *Black Spiders*
is now juvenilia to my mind. I'm only beginning to realize the
depths and the expanse of poetry, and my own strengths and
weaknesses, what poetry's for and what I can do with it. The new
work is opening up, I like to think. It's emotionally more accessible. I'm not playing tricks with the reader just for the sake of it.
The word 'true' keeps coming back to me, true or honest. All one
can aim for is truth.

What inspires you? I don't know. I don't think I am 'inspired'. I think of it as a sort of imbalance in the mind sometimes.
Do you know how a Van der Graaff generator works? I remember them at school. You had two poles. One of which would
build up a charge of electricity, and when it got too great it would
discharge, and you got a little blue flash – beautiful little things! I
think of 'inspiration' as more like that. That flash of lightning is
discharging this extra energy or restoring to harmony what's
going on in the mind. It doesn't mean it's unpleasant. I actually
love it when I know I'm building up to something. But 'inspired'
is not the right word. I don't see it as anything like 'Oh, I must
write a poem about that!' I'll get this notion, something I want to
say, but it's inarticulate. What I'll end up doing is fetching round
for material to do that with, and I might happen to look out the
window and see something I can use. I suddenly become open to
everything. For example, there's a poem in the folder which I
wrote after Andrew went off to the hills. I was thinking about a
poem for a departing mountaineer and I literally just looked out
the window and there was this beautiful skyline with these four
little figures on. I honest to God couldn't tell what they were and
I've just used all I could see in that poem. *So the idea began with
your trying to write about his leaving?* And then I draw in
whatever's kicking around.

How long do you work with a poem? It might be a week. It
might be three months. I've got one on my desk I've been at for a
year and a half. It's still not right and never will be.

Do you use any poetic forms at all? No. I don't know any.
That's what the lack of formal education does for you. I just

don't know what a sonnet is, or a villanelle. And they don't interest me. But sometime I'll have to read into it, because I've got to know the craft.

What does it mean to be a Scottish poet? I suppose you're inevitably Scottish, like you're inevitably female, but there are other things more essential. That's why I'm keen to think of myself as an artist. Being female, being Scottish, is more accidental. I'm sure if I was born a male in Paraguay I would still be an artist. I'm going against the grain in saying that, because the fashion now is to see being female particularly as being essential to your nature. That's the bottom line. But I don't know if it is for me.

Tell me about the play you're working on. It's a monologue. It's a story I read in the newspaper years ago about this French-woman who had been looking after her son who had been in an accident. He was almost a grown man and was in a vegetable state. She had fetched him home and looked after him in a two-room flat for something like twenty-seven years when he finally died. And I thought, Did she talk to him? I was trying to imagine what this would be like. The play is her speaking to her son. Then I realized that on radio the listener is in exactly the same position as this boy in being a passive listener. So what I've done is make the sound of her voice come and go as his gyrations of consciousness come and go. Sometimes it's deadpan, sometimes slightly woozy as he's perceiving it, sometimes it's crystal clear. He can't do anything about it, except understand that she's taking his hand.

What's the difference between using a persona to write about something and in writing directly from your own experience? You use such different voices. This woman's got a working class Scots voice, which is not mine. It's like when you tune in to a radio. If you hit the radio station a little light comes on. I just tune in to different people's voices. I do the fine tuning in my brain and I know when I've got the voice perfect or slightly off. There are innumerable personas in my mind that I use, like the character of Katy in *A Flame In Your Heart*. How accurate that is I'll never know, but one of the best compliments I've received is when the BBC did the new book as a radio feature. We gave the tape of it to Andrew's mother. Being blind, she relies all the time on radio. When she took the tape from Andrew she said, 'She's 23. What does she know about the War?' But when she played it she was absolutely knocked out. She came back to Andrew and said,

'She's got it right, you know. That's exactly how it felt in 1940!' So I was very pleased. But I can't hear dialogues. I can't hear two people talking together.

Would you ever write in a man's voice? Should I ever hear one. I certainly haven't heard one yet. *So you hear mostly female voices?* Mm. I didn't actually realize I was writing in female voices until recently. It's just so natural. Who knows what goes on inside men's heads? Not me!

Do you do a lot of different kinds of writing? No. Only poems. Even the play's like an extended poem. But I want to write a children's book. *About what?* I don't know. I've got a lot of strange ideas. Oh, I'll tell you one thing I've got. In England in the fourteenth century there was a mystic. Every village had its mystic, a hermit figure. They all seemed to like them very much and kept them fed and watered. And there was a particularly famous one in Norwich, called Dame Julian of Norwich. She lived for most of her life, forty years, walled up in a cell. She communicated with the world only through a little window which most of the time she kept curtained. Everybody loved her. She was like an agony aunt. Everybody used to come to her for religious advice and personal advice as well. She went into se-clusion after a very grave illness, which she prayed to have, in which she had an extraordinary series of visions, revelations – 'showings', she called them. She spent the rest of her life meditat-ing on these visions and wrote the first book in English by a woman, as it happens. T.S. Eliot discovered her. She came out with that wonderful quotation: 'All shall be well and all shall be well and all manner of things shall be well.' She was getting on at God. She kept harking back to the problem of evil. The plague was going on at the time, and she was saying, 'Here, if you're so good, why is this all happening?' And eventually God or what-ever, said to her, 'Look, it'll be all right. Everything shall be fine. Just let go and let me deal with it.' And she took great solace in that. I'd love to write a series of poems in her voice. She had this gorgeous vision when she was ill. I can remember her words: 'In the palm of my hand the size of a hazelnut and I said, What is this? And the answer came, It is all that is created.' Isn't that beautiful? I think it would work very well. It would be nice to do a voice which is a bit offbeat, being fourteenth century, a bit wayward, completely scatty – she was obviously away with the fairies half the time – but at the same time so warm and human. She keeps banging on. I think it takes a woman to keep banging on at God saying, Why evil? Why death? *Why is that? Why a woman?* I don't know. It just seems she'd be more involved in a way. I think male religious and male mystics, with honourable exceptions, seem to have avoided that. They've been more into knowing God than banging a lot of questions at him.

Are you religious yourself? Difficult. I was brought up a sort of liberal atheist, but when I was eighteen I went to Jerusalem and I saw these major world religions at each other's throats – Jews, Christians and Muslims, all very closely related religions. And I thought, What is this thing that drives people to such passions? Then when I came home I took a course in comparative religion and in philosophy of religion, and so I went into it in an academic way. But reading more and more about it made me accept things that I'd been taught to deny. I haven't got much of a faith, but I feel that if I lost it I'd be pretty desolate. I remember once up in the Himalayas, coming back down safely off this glacier, I turned round and saw K2, and at that point I was just giving my thanks that we were all right. That's from the heart, actually praying, you know. But it's certainly interesting, religion as phenomenon rather than faith. But philosophically, once you learn everything is a leap of faith, then why not go the whole hog? There's some quotation, maybe you know it, about a little philosophy turning you into an atheist and a whole lot turning you into a believer. But I couldn't be a Christian. I'm more of an idealist, an absolutist.

Does your attitude towards religion affect your work in any way? No. That sequence of poems about Dame Julian of Norwich: using her voice would be my vehicle for talking about any religious feeling I could have, and my feeling for how she understood God and her relationship with God, which is a voyage of exploration for me,

What about the stereotype of the crazy poet? That doesn't affect you at all? It alarms me. If so many poets are mad, have I got a good chance of cracking up? I think it's more solitude than being a poet. It would do for anybody. Certainly if I'm on my own for a long time I can feel myself going a bit wobbly.

What is your intention when you write? Are you thinking about publishing? Are you thinking about other people looking at your work? Not really. What I am is a writer. But what I do in terms of a job, the teaching and the publishing and the promoting, I could dispense with all that, and still have this process in me.

So you write primarily because you need to write? Yes. If anything threatens that I go loopy. I feel like a pioneer though. *Really. How so?* Trying to work out a way of living which allows me to write. I must sound absolutely hysterical to other people. If I'm short of cash and have to get a job, I say, 'It'll stop me writing!' That's my greatest fear, having to stop, or not having space, or whatever. I'm so bound up in material problems.

So when you say you're a pioneer, does that mean you're referring to other artists or to your peers, your family or whom? I think it's isolation in a way. I don't know many other women artists to ask, 'Look, how do you manage materially?' And although my family are really good about it and quite proud, they think it's a bit strange. They're quite shocked. But just for myself, I must be hell to live with, sorting out how to combine these elements of housekeeping and relationships and writing, always writing. For instance, I'll say to Andrew, 'Go AWAY for six weeks and let me write!' So he goes away for six weeks and I'm saying, 'What do you mean by abandoning me for six weeks?' CLASSIC! CLASSIC! That's isolation. Artistic isolation. There are a lot of 'poets' around, but gey few I can relate to. It's commitment. I don't know if I've met in anyone else the commitment I feel in myself. That's why I'm so attracted to people like these climbers. I can see somebody who's working his guts out so that he can go off and climb a mountain. That I can understand. Writers and climbers might just get on very well, because there's a mutual understanding.

This is an assumption, even built into my project, that poets have something in common with each other, which is not necessarily so. No. I feel more in common with my climbing friends or with one or two devoted doctors than I do with other artists. It's that commitment that relates.

POEM FOR A DEPARTING MOUNTAINEER

Regarding the skyline longingly
(curved as a body, my own, I desire you)
where ink-coloured cloud masses
and rolls on the ridge,
I pick out silhouettes. Deer
dolmen, trees, perhaps tombs
raised through the bracken and weird
midsummer nights by the ancients.
Or men. I can't discern, and mustn't wonder
whether the figures are vibrant, stone,
setting out hunched under loads
of turning home. I must be distant,
draw the curtains for bed,
and leave them, like you who left
with your grave-goods strapped to your back
alone to the lowering cloud.

THE WAY WE LIVE

Pass the tambourine, let me bash out praises
to the Lord God of movement, to Absolute
non-friction, flight, and the scary side:
death by avalanche, birth by failed contraception.
Of chicken tandoori and reggae, loud, from tenements,
commitment, driving fast and unswerving
friendship. Of tee-shirts on pulleys, giros and Bombay,
barmen, dreaming waitresses with many fake-gold
bangles. Of airports, impulse, and waking to uncertainty,
to strip-lights, motorways, or that pantheon –
the mountains. To overdrafts and grafting

and the fit slow pulse of wipers as you're
creeping over Rannoch, while the God of moorland
walks abroad with his entourage of freezing fog,
his bodyguard of snow.
Of endless gloaming in the North, of Asiatic swelter,
to launderettes, anecdotes, passions and exhaustion,
Final Demands and dead men, the skeletal grip

of government. To misery and elation; mixed,
the sod and caprice of landlords,
To the way it fits, the way it is, the way it seems
to be: let me bash out praises – pass the tambourine.

Joy Hendry

JOY HENDRY WAS BORN in Perth, Scotland. She came to Edinburgh in 1970 and studied Philosophy and Literature at Edinburgh University. She lives with her husband in Edinburgh.

She began co-editing the literary magazine *Chapman* in the early seventies and eventually became its sole editor. She is a freelance journalist and reviewer and divides her time between editing and writing.

I knew Joy for over a year before we ever got round to doing the interview. When I first met her she had, quite rightly, a healthy suspicion of American researchers. Gradually we got to know each other as we continued to rub elbows at poetry readings and all sorts of literary and social events. We finally did the interview one night in her dining room-cum-office. Her computer sat in the corner of the room, and all the surfaces and large sections of the floor were covered with books, articles and stacks of poems that had been submitted for *Chapman*. Over whisky and coffee, we talked. Halfway through, I exclaimed, 'I am so sick of these questions!' Joy responded, 'So ask me some different ones.' So I did.

IF PEOPLE CALLED ME a feminist poet I wouldn't object unduly, but I wouldn't go out of my way to call myself that. I would even hesitate to call myself a poet. People have to earn the right to use that word about themselves. But I wouldn't reject the term 'feminist'. I think the feminist movement is extremely valuable. I've learned a lot from it and I'm sure I still have a great deal to learn. When I began writing I saw myself almost as a genderless poet, although paradoxically I wanted to write about what it was like to be a woman, which just shows how unthought out my ideas were! But I felt that the idea of being a female poet was almost a stigma, because I had been indoctrinated by certain ideas about woman poets and felt that most of what they wrote was pretty inferior stuff and I didn't want my writing to be associated with that.

In your article 'The Double Knot on the Peeny', you talked about the need for feminism to be both international and for women to explore a sense of themselves within their own cultures. Yes, I think that's very important. I don't see any contradiction in this. In trying to liberate women from certain aspects of social conditioning, feminism has tended to snip them off from their native roots, from giving them another context within which to see themselves, a very valuable context, where a whole new set of insights come into play. Particularly where you've got a country like Scotland, where there's such a struggle for identity going on, it's tremendously important for Scottish women to see themselves as functioning within a Scottish tradition. Even although it is a male-dominated culture, there are feminine roots within this tradition which will be useful to women. Then there's the whole egalitarian tradition of the Protestant reformers. They thought women should be educated alongside men. It's very important that Scottish women learn to understand themselves both as women and as Scots and not as a deracinated international phenomenon. Scotland needs to redress the balance between the masculine input and the feminine input and if feminism merely distracts women's attention from the problems of Scotland and Scottishness, it will impede the development of the nation as a whole.

You write in English and Scots? Yes. I've just begun to write in Scots.

Is it different from writing in English? There's a different kind of energy behind it. It's much more physical, much more gritty. It's hard to rationalize what I feel is missing from English that I find in Scots. It's partly that it's a relatively unused

language and therefore it's fresher. English has become ab-
stracted from ordinary life whereas Scots retains a sometimes
rather quaint relationship with real things. Take a clock, for
instance. In Scots you have the 'wag at the wa''. There's a picture
there. Pictures leap out of the words, either pictures or sounds. In
English these have been flattened. You don't see the pictures any
more and the sounds are so extenuated you're hardly conscious
of them.

When I'm writing in Scots I have to sit with a dictionary. I
use the *Scots Word Book* and *The Concise Scots Dictionary*.
Some people think if you have to do that, it invalidates the whole
exercise. I think that's just nonsense. I've no qualms about doing
it.

It's an act of reclaiming. That's exactly it. It's an unnatural
situation we're in, having lost the language in the first place. It's
been a combination of deliberate policy and a series of historical
accidents. It's been a deliberate policy to discourage Scots and to
make people feel crude and clumsy using it. The Scots have done
it to themselves to quite a large extent. I'm not blaming outside
forces for this entirely. All I'm doing is turning the clock back and
saying I don't want the English equivalents for these words, I
want the Scots originals. Scots is the original and English is the
intruder, the incomer. That's an act I have the right to make. Just
as a woman has the right to say, I see myself as a woman first and
a social being second, or whatever. It's the same with nationalism. A lot of people will say, I'm proud to be a Scot, but I'm even
prouder to be British. It can be just as valid for me to say that I
regard myself as a Scot and I don't want to regard myself as
British in the slightest. It doesn't, however, mean that you cut
yourself off from the rest of humanity. It just means you're
concentrating on something specific first. You can take the
parallel quite far really. For example, when you suddenly realize,
perhaps in your early twenties, that an awful lot of your attitudes, intellectual and emotional, have been male-dominated
and you begin to wonder, What do women really think or feel? –
you won't know, because your head's been stuffed full of nonsense all your life. So you have to say, 'To hell with this, I've got
to discover something new.' So with Scots and Gaelic.

*All the women I've spoken to who write in Scots or Gaelic
talk about them as emotional languages and see English as a
conceptual language. You bridge both nationalism and feminism. Most of the nationalist women I've interviewed were very*

anti-feminist. I think that's because they haven't thought their way through the Scottish tradition. It has to be thought through. There are some very bad aspects to it. It's a fairly traditional Scottish attitude: I don't need feminism. It's also a sort of intellectual backwardness. Scotland is a backward country, let's face it. We're about ten years behind London and twenty behind New York! There's a lot of conservatism in the Scottish tradition. In contrast to the wild, passionate, adventurous Scot, there's also the canny, plodding, very crafty, careful kind of person who doesn't want to risk losing everything. And you get these two things operating very often within the same individual. But I would say that with most nationalist women, especially the older generation, their passion goes into nationalism and they've simply never been exposed to feminism at all. They have an inbuilt defence against it. On the one hand they don't need it, and on the other it's something they've outgrown without ever going through, which makes no sense at all.

Do you see yourself then as a Scottish writer? Oh, yes, absolutely.

Is writing criticism, articles or reviews a different process from writing poetry? Yes and no. I like to think I write prose as carefully as I would write poetry. Obviously, doing journalistic hackwork, you can't be as meticulous as you would like, and there isn't the same degree of emotional input, and you're not always writing for yourself. Poetry is a much purer form of expression. You can brush away these social limitations, peripheral attitudes and so on. Poetry is a way of setting yourself free to be much more individual, perhaps even irresponsible, except that there's an even bigger responsibility in writing poetry than writing prose criticism.

Are you writing for an audience? For me the audience is irrelevant. I can't get over the feeling, and I may be wrong about this, that the writer who is writing for an audience is writing for the wrong reasons. The moment you start to write for an audience it's bound to have an effect on what you say and how you say it. You're likely to be compromised before you even begin. You have to be true to yourself. You shouldn't be influenced by commercial or social considerations. That's terribly important. At the same time of course you have to be intelligible. Obscure writing is bad manners. The act of writing is necessarily an act of communication and you've got to perform that as perfectly as you can. Sloppy writing is never excusable, nor is disappearing up your own arse. That's where the audience comes in for me: the fact that you have to communicate successfully. Sometimes of course you'll be saying things that are very difficult to comprehend, that perhaps haven't been said before, or you're trying to use language in a new way, but still you should do your job of communicating as well as you can.

In these poems about death I was interested in the way you made death a persona. Did that give you some sense of having worked through the experience? This one was written about six months before my father died. I wrote it one night after he'd gone to bed early. Normally we'd be sitting up chatting over a dram and putting the world to rights, but he'd just come out of hospital after another session of radiotherapy and he wasn't up to sitting up late any more. I was conscious of how much he had deteriorated. I felt so angry, so full of despair and sorrow. It's a protest, a rather futile protest, I suppose. I wasn't conscious of thinking, Well, I'll turn Death into a persona. It was much more spontaneous than that. It came out more or less as it is. I thought it was very rough and rudely written. I was amazed to find it stands up.

This one is quite powerful as well, moving from talking about the moon to this particular instance, 'I sleep in your bed', and then back again. Yes. It wasn't conscious. It just flowed out like that. I work very intuitively, so I find it very hard to talk about my poems. I feel they either speak for themselves or they don't. I wonder about that image. It makes me cringe slightly. It might be a bit much for people to take. When my mother died I had to sleep in her bed. I had no choice because there were no other beds to have, and I actually enjoyed the experience. It wasn't until a long time after that I actually went back to my own bed in the house. Then after my father died I felt this impulse to sleep in his bed, as a way of, I suppose, at once recognizing the fact that he wasn't there any more and secondly, just to have this feeling of closeness. I didn't make a habit of it. I only did it the once.

It's a wonderful example of what we do to try to let go and also reclaim. Yes, that's why I feel I'm embarrassed about it for the wrong reasons, which is why I've left it in. That's what I mean about being honest. That was the experience as it was. If I thought it might make the audience uncomfortable then that would be the wrong reason for changing it. If, however, it interfered with the development of the poem, then I should change it.

How do you see the status of poetry in Scotland? High in

theory and low in practice. Poetry's supposed to be important to our culture because of Burns and the importance of song. There shouldn't really be a distinction between poetry and song. It's a formal difference, that's all. It just breathes out of the ground in Scotland, this impulse to poetry and song. And yet, because Scotland has become so anglicized, so divorced from its own self, it's now extremely suspicious of poetry, except when it's been sterilized, like Burns has to some extent. It's amazing how many people are genuinely interested in poetry, but they don't do anything about it. They don't read books, they don't read magazines, but if you go up and stick something under their noses, they'll buy it and they'll read it and enjoy it. Potentially Scotland could be a tremendous country for poetry. It's an art Scotland has always excelled at. Poetry is Scotland's great gift. But bookshops have a lot to do with it. And the whole establishment. People don't know about Scottish writers or Scots language and they don't look for Scottish poetry because they don't know it's there. And the bookshops don't stock it because they think nobody wants it. It's a vicious circle. We've been saying the same thing for years and years and it's still true. But progress is being made. And a lot of people are writing. I'm amazed at the comparative quality of stuff I'm getting from England. I accept almost none of it. That could, of course, just be my blinkered judgment, but I don't think so. It's actually not as good as the stuff that's homegrown. It lacks a dimension that even the more mediocre offerings from Scotland have. A kind of passion often differentiates the Scottish contributions from the English ones.

This is a vast generalization, an anthropological leap, but given that poetry is an act of power, could the confusion about supporting Scottish poetry be linked with the confusion about Scottish identity? Oh yes, I'm sure it is. Just as people don't really know much about what it is to be Scots, so they don't know to look for Scottish poetry, and if they find it, they don't know how to respond to it. It's a process of bewilderment. Often, too, you'll find the very people who're most Scots in their speech looking at a piece of Scots poetry and saying, 'Och, I dinna ken whit that says. I canna read that.' But if you can get them to sit and listen they will see that it's something they can relate to, and something quite intimate to their lives.

It's this business of being a stranger to yourself. It's tragic when you think about it. We have lost the ability to be natural with ourselves. Important aspects of our natures have been suppressed or diffused or expressed in quite alien strange ways. Take Scots cuisine, for example. Now you could set up a French or a Chinese or a Turkish restaurant in Edinburgh and people would be rolling in, but set up a Scots restaurant and most Scots wouldn't want to know, because they don't know what it is. Put a Scots dish in front of them and they probably wouldn't recognize it. And the same is true across the broad span of Scottish life: embroidery, painting, music, everything, except perhaps golf and football. Cloth, the making of cloth – it takes you a very long time to realize that tweed is not only warm but actually very beautiful, whereas you tend to think of something that's home-spun as being somehow crude and undesirable. So poetry and language is just like all the rest, a part of the identity problem which I see as essentially political.

And how would you see that resolved? There are two possi-bilities. Either Scottish traditions will continue to be more and more diffused and you'd be as well to participate fully in a fairly healthy British umbrella tradition. If there's very little left that's genuinely different, what would be the point in preserving a corrupt tradition? Or the current upsurge of interest in the Scottish cultural heritage will increase and lead to a de-mand for political autonomy. I think we're at the turning point now.

Do you see the reclamation of a Scottish tradition as com-patible with something new? Oh, absolutely. One of the greatest innovators in 20th century poetry, Hugh MacDiarmid, went through this process of rediscovery of his own Scottish identity and moved on from there to all sorts of things. There is a tradition of innovation in Scotland. Bring the two together and you'll get even more exciting things happening. There's no con-tradiction. You don't have to accept everything that's there just because it's Scottish, but at least whatever you decide to do will have a context.

You're not a member of the Scottish National Party? Well, actually I got signed up recently. My husband did it when I wasn't looking! I do, however, like to stay outside the SNP. I find it difficult to belong to any political party because I don't like what they do or say most of the time and I think it's better for my purposes to be a bit of a maverick and not allow people to stereotype me, because they do, they try to diminish what you say. It's like feminism again. They try to refuse to look at what you say because they want to dismiss it as feminist. The magazine also takes a non-partisan stance. It's basically nationalist and socialist, but you won't find me hammering any party policy in it. The magazine has to be bigger than any one ideology. I've even published poems whose politics I detest because I thought they were good poems. I think that's important. That's the sense in which literature transcends politics.

DEATH-EVE

Why is it only tonight I understand
the moon was in eclipse that night.
Driving southwards on the motorway,
I watched its bitten shape
through the car window,
afraid to look too close and long.

Why did I not recognise it?
I did not see the eclipse,
but thought instead it was
the old moon in the new moon's arms,
and puzzled that it seemed
the wrong way up.
Looking for a portent, perhaps,
I remembered Sir Patrick Spens
and that maiden's voyage to death.

Tonight, one moon month later, father,
I sleep in your bed,
to be near you again,
perhaps to hear you call.
The moon will be full
by your death-time tomorrow.

The eclipse passed:
death the unbitten has no quarter,
no phase, no reconstruction.
Its full moon blazes across centuries
across the myriad layers of the dead,
whose lives have passed
as quickly as a shadow across the moon,
leaving no trace.

Each full moon sets its face
over the deepening layers of the dead,
and the dead give never an answer,
never an answer.

Eithne Strong

EITHNE STRONG IS A NATIVE of Glensharrold, West Limerick, and has lived in Dublin since 1942. In 1943 she married Rupert Strong, poet and psychoanalyst, who died in 1984. She coordinates and runs creative writing workshops. She has seven daughters and two sons.

Poet in English and Irish, short story writer, novelist, she has had poetry and short stories broadcast and anthologized in Europe and the USA. Some of her work has been translated into French and Italian. She has published eleven books, including four books of poetry in Irish.

One of Eithne's daughters answered the door and led me into a spacious living room filled with dark wood furniture and deep red and blue rugs. Eithne sat in the middle, a woman with friendly eyes and a strong, lined face. She shook my hand firmly and asked, 'Are you of Italian descent?' When I answered yes, she replied, 'That accounts for your face and lovely brown curls. Now, then, Rebecca, what were you wanting to ask me about my writing?' After the interview she took me into the kitchen and fed me lunch. She asked about my family. She was attentive, treating my stories and experiences with respect, often responding with a tale of a similar event within her own life. Despite the vast difference in our ages and experience of life, she treated me throughout as a friend and equal.

I ALWAYS KNEW I WANTED to be a writer, but I did crazy things. I got married young and I was never one who fitted in terribly well, unfortunately – or fortunately, maybe, for the sake of the writing. I think it's good not to fit in if one is a writer, quite honestly. However, I had to do the dreadful thing and fall in love with a Protestant Englishman, which brought its own trauma. My parents were against it and I had to run away from home. I cycled rather than ran. I hadn't any money and he was a student in Trinity College, so we were very poor, but we stuck it out. It took seven years for the family to come round.

Also I began to produce children. I had nine children, and with miscarriages as well I produced about a dozen. My husband only had to look at me and I seemed to become pregnant! The whole business of birth control wasn't really possible in those days. Then, when the children were very small it was quite clear to me that their needs were more important. I really did feel the priority was to keep them and to be there. It seemed self-indulgent to go off to some little cubby-hole and exclude them. Also my youngest child, who was born in 1960, was mentally handicapped and that was always an extra tie. So I gave my energies to them rather than to anything else, although I was writing poetry and one or two pieces did get published. My husband was always very encouraging, but where was I to find the time? A couple of minutes in a mad series of chores, sitting on the edge of the bed or the edge of the sink!

As they grew older and became less dependent however I began to reassert myself. My poetry speaks of that struggle for space, and statements to my offspring that I'm not doing them any harm by searching out these new frontiers of my personality. And despite my youngest child's handicap my first book came out in 1961. It was as if I had determined that if I didn't do it then I never would. It contained poems that had been written over the years. I also wrote a play at that time. Nevertheless, it was thirteen years before the next book came out. I decided I was going back to college and I took up a job because money was needed. There isn't any money in writing in Ireland, unless you are extraordinarily lucky and do something full of sex, violence and horrors, and publish elsewhere.

The next book was very different. It's full of anger against women's condition and expressive of the struggle of a woman to retain her identity or even to define her identity.

In the meantime, in 1968 I wrote and published my first short story and began to write a lot of those. I seem to be one of those people who write in different veins. I couldn't just write short stories. I got my first novel off the ground in 1979 after working on it for a couple of years. I want to write several novels now. I feel I have many things I want to work out in novel form. I hope to be retiring in 1988. I have been teaching fulltime since 1975, which is very draining, so I am looking forward to being able to get up in the morning and get at that typewriter when the energy's fresh and just devote myself to writing.

Is a different process required for writing poetry or short stories? People often ask me that. I don't know. It's an unconscious, spontaneous thing. They're all interrelated in one's very deeps. I have to implement a discipline. I might be writing a poem and feel a flash of an idea for a short story, and put the poem down and start on the short story there and then. I have a book with all these ideas, but I don't say whether this is going to be a short story and this a poem. I just put down these thoughts and later on go back to them.

I see the mind as an extraordinary repository for material, which begins Heaven knows where. I can believe that it starts at the moment of conception, even before. It's an area which is very difficult to define, and I rather feel it defies definition. No matter how scientific people become about these things, I think something always eludes you in scientific analysis. Every single thing that washes over you, or that you undergo, becomes absorbed into you and is stashed somewhere in various levels of the brain. I think the human brain is of inexhaustible interest and when that is again further fused with the mind extraordinary things happen. This is the marvellous thing about the creative process. The material is infinitely rich.

You know when you've got this blank page in front of you, this terrible white page staring at you, there's a great urge to write, but nothing's happening? You do not know where to begin. I think the best thing to do is just close your eyes, relax and become like a jelly. Just be completely receptive and something begins to come. I don't care a damn what it is. Begin to write and it has the effect of loosening up the synapses of the brain and things begin to flow. Free association. I'm very much in favour of free association. Become critical afterwards, but let it come first.

Perhaps a novel gives you the greatest freedom to spread yourself. But I can't say I would separate the processes of creation. For me they merge and I can separate them consciously afterwards. I'm not sure what's going to come up always, but it's very important not to be self-indulgent and wait for inspiration. That's rubbish. Writing's just a job. Call it a chore if you like, but with the chore goes the pleasure of doing it well.

What you must not do is be over-critical. I found that for a period when I went back to university I felt almost desiccated by the process, of the academic superimposition of critical norms and critical expectatons. I felt you had to go find your deepest self again. The one good thing I've learned out of all my study of literature is the line in Sidney, where he said, 'Look into your heart and write.' Shakespeare said it too:

This above all – to thine own self be true,
And it must follow, as the night the day,
Thou canst not then be false to any man.

That is also compatible with having very critical standards, but let it be your own true criticism.

When you're writing, are you writing for yourself? A great deal of the time, yes, if I put aside all temptations to be affected by the market. I'm writing to be true to myself. It's a struggle. But I get weary of cerebral writers. I prefer characters who are built out of flesh and blood and out of one's experience of people, rather than out of intellectual concepts. A person I admire very much is William Trevor. You can't really do a study on Ireland until you also know about the interrelationship between England and Ireland, because it has been part of the history for so long. He is rare in that he can identify sympathetically with both sides. He's also very understated, which I love. I don't like a baroque form or a Gothic style or a page packed with words. I like suggestion and subtlety much more. I also like Jennifer Johnston very much. She has mastered the art of simplicity, one of the most difficult achievements. It's along those lines I envisage myself going.

Is it different writing in Irish? Yes, but that's a part of the joy of it. I have translated a lot of my English into Irish and vice versa. Irish, of course, is in a state of flux. For a long time it was the prerogative of the Irish-speaking areas, but they have been encroached on by our modern technology in order to survive. So new terms have got to come in and it's no longer the language of the heart. The funny thing is that it's being restored, renovated and revitalized by the urban, educated, middle class, who are drawing their sources from what would have been considered the Irish peasantry in the west of Ireland. And from them have come publications of some very good, relevant, modern, newspaper-style stuff, which is essential if ever Irish is going to be back in the streets.

I'm doubtful about that, however. It isn't like the language of the people in any other country you go to. Everyone is very selfconscious about speaking it. There are people who are bringing up their children to speak Irish. There are a few Irish-speaking schools, which are wonderful. It's lovely to hear the little ones getting on the bus in the morning and coming out of school afterwards and speaking it as their first language. But for that to happen universally is going to be difficult. I don't know if it's going to succeed. There are also a few pockets of a working class movement round the Dublin area, but until people like bus conductors and waitresses in cafés and shopkeepers are all speaking it, it won't happen. Even people who teach Irish don't speak it in their normal spontaneous conversations.

I suppose I could be called culpable myself. I didn't bring up my children as bilingual. With their father being English, they seemed to identify more with the English area than the Irish area, only to be sorry later on. I love the language.

When you write does it sometimes just happen in Irish and sometimes in English? Yes. I will get an urge to say something in Irish. I'm working on a fourth book in Irish.

Do you feel then that you have a sense of yourself as an Irish poet? I am very much against frontiers. I don't want to be identified with nationalism. Insofar as I was born here and Irish was the language in my home and I love it, I will, of course, express myself in it. But I could as handily have been born in Italy or Russia. I see myself as much more a European. It is far more important to be a citizen of the world. I am interested in human beings and the business of living with people, and it doesn't matter to me whether they are Irish or Chinese or whatever. I see languages as communication and ultimately humanity as more important than culture. All cultures are changing and you can't keep in the frozen past. There are very separatist things happening all over the world, and I think to our detriment. I am a pacifist. I understand our heritage of hate and violence but I think these narrow nationalist things are divisive and bloody-minded. They make for pain and suffering rather more than any possibility of going forward. Technologically we have advanced amazingly, but emotionally we're still at a very undeveloped level. Culture for me is about standards of values in the human being, as to right and wrong relationships, as to consideration for other people. That's universal. There are a number of young poets writing in Irish who are tremendously important. I love listening to new poets and am really excited about what's being written in Irish at the moment. I very often read their work to my classes, because commercial Irish is so boring and dull. The level of Irish from the students is not good in the main. Nevertheless, if you explain the poem to them, they are always interested.

I really enjoy, however, the new modern poetry. It's lovely to be in flux with it and to see what is emerging. The same is true of English. And people are tuning in their creative production to the exigencies of modern life. You find all kinds of new things coming in what women are writing: the single mother is there, the homosexual, the plural arrangement. Women talk about sexual things much more. This is something very new in Irish poetry. You would have been excommunicated for masturbation at one time. Now it's much broader and more honest, not before time.

How do you think of yourself as a poet? A writer, very definitely, and not as a woman one either. I happen to be a woman, so my experience is going to colour the way I write, but I haven't separatist views about that either. Sometimes I think men are a pain and sometimes I think women are a pain. I don't see how they can separate the human species that way. They happen to be there. I have very strong views about babies, having had so many myself. I think we should give babies a rest for a while, or certainly the family should be very restricted. Now you read there's a scarcity of babies in America and they are bribing people to have bigger families. I think the human race has gone a bit berserk and it would do us no harm to dry up for a bit and review things.

What's your intention in writing? Are you writing to communicate with anyone specific? When you say to me do I write to communicate, yes I do, but I'm more interested now in how to put what I'm trying to communicate in an interesting medium. When you're young it rushes out of you. Lyric poetry has that spontaneity which is itself a manifestation of life and energy. I am much more interested in form now.

Sometimes I think being a writer is most awfully presump-

tuous. Nobody asked you to write. Nobody asked for your
outpourings. It is a highly egotistical occupation. On the other
hand, art is a very egotistical occupation at any level. A singer has
to work a long time to produce a voice somebody wants to listen
to. If you want to dance, you have to have something that's worth
showing. A singer is interpreting life. So is a dancer. And it's the
same about writing. You can't write at all if you haven't lived.
I'm only interested in other people's writing insofar as it's got
something to say about life. Cleverness alone is not enough.

BOTTOMS

All right, so you are crusted hard
in burnt gravy and your bottom
I scrub with a wire scraper, while hers
in the TV corner flashes a shiny bikini
to sell a cocktail, a car or again
– with a number of other rumps –
capers in stretch denim to promote
a line in jeans.

Old saucepan that I clean,
everything is a possible
subject for a poem.

And curiously, scraping yours, I get
a flash of other bottoms in some ways
like yours but different: older,
more battered; younger also –
those of babies afflicted with diarrhoea
that I have treated with
hygiene and affection
through gritted teeth.

And there, facing me, hung on a hook,
the plastic bum of a wash-up basin,
new, and still of untried character.

What about the backsides
of buses,
sixth or ninth in a row
slizzing past
with a contemptuous fart
diminishing the air

leaving me stranded
with whatever load?

And yet again
the posterior of a thought
I do not care to face.

I know a lot about backsides:
every day, many times a day,
I am presented with their lineaments
not needing to see –
I know too well the geography.
And therefore let us celebrate:
Halleluia!

TÓINEANNA

Ceart go leor tá ort cruascreamh
d'anlann dóite agus do thóin scríobaim
le scríobaire sreangach

an fhaid is ata a tóin siúd
ar an teilifís sa chúinne
ag pleidhcíocht i mbicíní sróil
le feabhas manglaim a fhógairt,
d'fhonn oiriúnacht chairr a chur abhaile
nó arís i dteannta scata tóin eile
ag dhamhsa chun gnéasacht úrshaghais
bhriste dhenim a bhrostú chun mhargaidh.

A shean-sháspain a ghlanaim,
is fiú dan ábhar ar bith:

le linn dom do thóin a sciúradh
ritheann liom tóineanna eile
ar m'aitheantas
ar aon dul leat nó dul nach sin
níos sine ná thú, níos batráilte;
níos óige, iadsan le báibíní buinneacha
a ghlanas le sláinteacht is cion –
na fiacla i gcónai teannta.

Tóin bus is bus eile i ndiaidh a chéile
an séú, an naoú', smé fann le hualach málaí
ar chosán tréigthe ag cabhlach bus

a sciúrdann tharam gan dath mo cháis
ag déanamh cúraim dóibh
ach masla broma a phléascadh
sa tsrón orm is an t-aer bocht
a chreachadh tuilleadh

Tóin smaoinimh nach áil liom
i gcónai ar crochadh aghaidh le falla
os mo chomhair amach, réidh le hiompó...

Is eol dom moran faoi thóineanna
gach lá, go minic sa lá
cuirtear os comhair mo shúl a ndéanamh

ní gá dom fiú feiceáil,
rímhaith is fios dom seachas sin
ach, ar aon chuma, abraimis amhrán.

THE CREAKING OF THE BONES

It's a relief, you know, happening this way:
these days I joyfully acclaim my age,
admit the stiffening in the bones. Sometimes
I seize up like an old woman, say, when
I first begin to move having been still
for some time, then I'm locked in my four
joints. (I used to be so limber!)
I do not give too much attention
to the condition, just say hello to it;

give myself a thump, a wallop here and there,
as might a man give a recalcitrant machine
a shake, a jolt without anger, with some affection
even, since it is a machine he has grown somewhat
fond of. Freely now I talk of age who previously
avoided the term: it might put me into focus,
set people, before I was really ready, considering,
speculating. True, though, I always did make
a proud point of being exact, giving the racing years

full count. Only it was not too comfortable doing that;
a certain tightness to it; felt easier if people did not
bring the talk around that way. For, you see, life was
flying too fast. You have felt it too, this fear?
It was all whizzing away while always there had been

far too much hard work and no space to be young-silly
in the silly-young time. Therefore to stretch out
youth seemed very necessary just that
I might have time for more experiment.

I had not had full scope to be nonsensical:
children came too fast; I was myself a child
in much that should have been mature
if mother I were. And so, therefore, fear
of tongues and frightened snatch at flying years;
brittle cheer. How ridiculous would be a skittish sheep!
Somehow now much recedes in importance. To measure
age no longer seems curtailment. A pleased assessment
of the thing is rather what I feel.

Although quiet appraisal sees the seizing bones,
gradual gain of certain ills, and laments indeed
the lessened bounce, the endless surge of energy
even so, I can celebrate; be glad I am no longer
young, that now my hair goes grey I'll wear it so
(no more the instant dye!); accept my flawed self
as is – it has done some battling – acknowledge where
it failed. Refusing to acclaim victories only, I greet
and even sometimes applaud my uncountable blanks.

GÍOSCÁN NA gCNÁMH

Faoiseamh é dar ndóigh na laethe seo
m'aois a fhógairt go haerach,
doicheall na gcnámh a admháil.
Uaireanta, taréis mar shómpla dimhaointis
géag dom, cé amhail seanbhean rite mé,
na ceithre cnamh i bhfostú
– mise a bhí chomh haiclí sráth –
ní bac dom é mar righneas:
beannaím dó,

gabhaim de dhorn orm féin
anseo is ansiúd mar a ghreadfadh fear
meaisín drogallach, gan fearg,
le hiarracht, fiú, de chion
os meaisín é ar a bhfuil a sheanthaithí.
Anois, labhraim go fras faoi aois,
rud a sheachnaínn mar nárbh áil liom

go spreagfaí tomhas mo ré
boidh nár sheanas riamh a chruinneas.

Mar sin féin, b fhearr liom gan tagairt
d'imeacht aimsire arbh mhire a luas:
mo shaol ar cosánairde, tuigir,
ag scinneadh thart sula raibh ceart
baoise agam nuair ba dhual baois
ach mé gafa ag stró dualgas –
bhraithis-se freisin an sceon seo? –
ba mhór liom m'óige a shíneadh
d fhonn cead fiontair ar mo thoil,

cead mo chaoi chun gealtachais,
ach cúram clainne a tharla.
Mise, in ainm a bheith im mháthair,
anabaí do bhí: faiteach roimh lom
na fírinne 'smé ag iarraidh blianta breise:
nárbh fhuar agam é mar óinseach mhná?
Ach anois malairt sceil: ní mór agam
morán ba mhór; ní cúngú liom é
ríomhadh na mblian, ach comóradh.

Anois, cloisim fuarchúiseach gioscán na gcnámh,
'scé braithim laige is fós laige, cé trua liom
trá tuile bhí spleodrach, ainneoin sin uile
molaim an druidim le haois, léithe gan cheilt
lem fholt; glacaim líom féin, lochtach
mar atá; tá mo chiom féin troda déanta agam
'scé gur cliseadh orm uair is uair eile – cuma san:
fógraím cinnte na buanna ach tharsta
beannaím gach teip, fiú ceiliúraim é.

Jackie Kay

Photo: Suzanne Roden

JACKIE KAY WAS BORN in Edinburgh in 1961 and raised in Glasgow. Poet, short story writer and playwright, she lives and works in London.

Her poetry has appeared in *Angels of Fire* (Chatto and Windus), *Beautiful Barbarians, Lesbian Feminist Poetry* (Only-Women Press, London, 1986), *Dancing the Tightrope* (The Women's Press, London, 1987), and *A Dangerous Knowing: Four Black Women Poets* (Sheba Feminist Publishers, London, 1988). Her play, *Chiaroscuro*, was presented by the Theatre of Black Women in 1986 and is published by Methuen. She wrote the filmscript for the BBC Split Screen Series on *Pornography: The Right to Choose*.

I went to Jackie's home in London. It was a warm day and I was running late and so arrived hot and flustered. Jackie met me at the door, rounded by pregnancy, with smiling eyes and a gentle voice. We did the interview in her living-room. Her responses were spontaneous and thoughtful. We laughed a lot. Long after the tape recorder had stopped, we talked. Finally, we hugged goodbye at the door.

I STARTED WRITING WHEN I was about 17 or 18, I wrote because there wasn't anybody else saying the things I wanted to say and because I felt quite isolated being in Scotland and being Black. There weren't many other Black people around, certainly not Black people who were writing, so I think I started out of that sense of wanting to create some images for myself. And also because imagination is one of the most powerful things we're given and I like creating things. I found it therapeutic at first so there were all these depressive, little morbid poems in the beginning! Burnt the lot now!

Ah, you should never do that! No, I don't burn anything any more, but I had to get rid of the lot!

So you were writing to create a space for yourself, is that right? To create an experience of your own? Yeah, I was writing to try to help myself define it. And the more I wrote the more clearly I did define that. So that was good. I remember I read the poetry of Audre Lorde around that time, about 1981, and I was amazed to find another Black lesbian. I didn't even know there were any others in the whole world! So one of the first poems I took seriously was a poem to her. I had this imaginary friend called Audre and I wrote a couple of conversation poems to her. They were the first things I thought worked as pieces of literature. Before that it was just ranting, it was unformed.

Can you talk a little bit about the issue of being Black in Scotland? The poem I'm thinking of is 'So you think I'm a Mule?'. Yes. That poem came about because the question, 'Where do you come from?' is one that probably every Black person in this country is asked too many times for comfort. And the question always implies 'You don't belong here.' That's why people ask it. Either they mean 'Go back to where you came from,' or they just have this obsessive curiosity that is all the time trying to deny the fact that you're Scottish.

This irritates me, a lot, that people can't contain both things, being Black and being Scottish, without thinking there is an inherent contradiction there. So that poem 'So you think I'm a Mule?' is trying to explore that in a humorous way. It was an actual incident. That woman did say, 'You're not pure, are you? You're a mulatto.' All these things in the poem were said exactly like that. So I didn't have to use too much imagination. It amazed me, that whole experience. She didn't meant to be offensive. People don't necessarily mean to be offensive or racist. But it is offensive behaviour nonetheless.

That's the first poem I ever wrote that addresses the whole

issue of being Black and Scottish. Since then I've written quite a bit more because it's part of me. I can't separate one from the other. Other people always try. Like Scottish people will either refuse to recognize my Scottish accent, or my Scottishness, or they'll say, 'Are you American?' And Black people will just hear my accent or think it really funny and say they've never met such a person before. And so being Black and Scottish is always treated as a kind of anomaly, which I suppose it is. But I think that's changing quite rapidly and it will change more.

I was once asked to do a reading at a Celtic-Afro-Caribbean evening, and would I read for the Celts? The Caribbeans were lined up on one side and the Celts on the other, and I just thought this was so funny, because, conceivably, I could have been asked to read for either side! And the man who had asked me to read for the Celts wasn't acknowledging this, so I wrote the poem 'Kail and Callalou' really for him! I don't know if he ever really got it!

That poem was trying to explore different strands of identity. If you're brought up in a place, you get that identity very, very fixedly. And you don't necessarily get a sense of your being Black, because there's nothing else around you affirming that you are. There aren't cultural things to affirm that, like different foods, for example, mangoes and stuff. So in the poem it says, 'I never tasted/mango before I was nineteen/or yam or cocoa root or sugarcane . . .' So, although I was steeped in Scottish culture, of which I'm very appreciative, I never had any sense of Black culture at all, until I went about finding and creating that for myself.

On the one hand you have Scotland, or the Scottish people, not acknowledging your Blackness. How do Black people deal with you, coming from a traditional White Scottish upbringing? Because Black people in this country come from all different places there is more acceptance of each other now. We are scattered to the winds. But some Black people still say, 'It's very unusual to meet you.' I was at a meeting a wee while ago and this Black man came up to me and said, 'Oh, are you really Scottish, because all my life I've wanted to meet a Black Scottish person!' He never knew any existed! So I said, 'Yeah, yeah, I'm the real McCoy!' I think things have changed in that way. Certainly a few years ago, Black people might have regarded other Black people who had been brought up in a White environment as being, well, you know, all these derogatory terms, like coconut, which is being Black on the outside and white on the inside. They'd be

quite shunning of anybody in my situation. But now there have
been so many Black kids brought up in White environments that
it's no longer possible to deny them or their Blackness just
because of that.

*To go back to your own writing process, what happens? Do
you see an image? Do you hear words?* It depends. It's always
difficult to define. It's usually images rather than words. I have a
picture of something I want to say first. The words come afterwards. If it's a play, then I see the characters first. I'm writing a
book of poems at the moment, called *The Adoption Papers*. It's a
sequence of poems about adoption from three different points of
view: the adoptive mother, the birth mother, and the daughter.
All three voices interlink. But it's also a story, so you could read
the whole collection like a novel. Now I might want to write a
poem about, say, the birth mother not wanting the daughter to
get in touch with her, or wanting her to get in touch with her, so
I'll think about an image for that. It might be an image taken
from the land, or it might be an image of this person sitting
behind these really heavy, velvet curtains. Images are more powerful than words, although they are created out of words. So
instead of writing, I was so depressed ... and so on, I would think
of an image for that, so that other people could participate. In the
end, writing is about communication. What you're asking somebody to do is to move into your imagination and see what you
see, and the best way of getting people to do that is to create
things for them visually and then you can bring along your own
thoughts.

*So do you see poetry as coming from your imagination?
How does experience fit in?* You use your experience as a spring-
board from which to leap into your imagination. Lots of writers
say they don't use their own lives at all, but I don't ever believe
that. Everybody uses experience in some way or another. It will
all come into your writing, so whether you're writing out of your
own particular experience, or writing indirectly from something
sparked off in the course of your day, you're still using your own
experience. I use my own experience. I create out of it. But I'm
not trying to be autobiographical in the sense of having other
people recognize it as my experience. I want other people to be
able to read it and think it may be their experience. That's the
difference. I want people to be able to relate to what I'm saying
when I write something.

So you are writing to touch people, or to touch off a reso-

nance in them somehow? I don't think that is the first motive in writing but that's definitely one of them. Otherwise I would just write and never bother getting published. I would just write and put it away in a drawer. The fact that I've decided to be public with it means that I want to give people something. I want to effect some kind of change. I want to make people think about things they haven't necessarily thought about before, or remember things they've forgotten.

What are the other reasons for writing? You've said, 'I see writing as a political activity, one way to contribute to the struggle for change.' Can you talk about that aspect of writing? What I read as a child or as a young adult has made more impact on me than, say, what friend I had at the time or what I was wearing. I can remember with real vividness the way different books affected me. Books became part of my own experience as they were my life. And that shows you that they have a tremendous power to effect change. And therefore I think that power can be used for things you believe in, like I believe in a world that wouldn't be racist or sexist or homophobic and all the rest of it. I don't believe in using polemics, but if I can get my vision of a world through to people, then that's really important. One of the books that really changed me was *The Women's Room* by Marilyn French. I would probably think it really middle-class now! – but at the time I identified with it so much that it became part of my life. And it was reading that book that helped me come out as a lesbian. I probably wouldn't have come out as a lesbian at that particular time had I not read that book. So, that's what I mean. It can help you make decisions and do things you wouldn't otherwise do.

This makes me think of your poem, 'We are not all sisters under the same moon'. You talk about some White women's assumptions about Blackness. When I read the poem I also heard in it a plea for us to meet each other from where we stand, to say, 'This is who I am, who are you?' – instead of saying, 'We are all sisters, we women.' Yes, that's right. That's really important. What we need is to be able to come together on the basis of our differences and not on the basis of our similarities; so that as people we ought to be able to embrace those differences and acknowledge them and not just sweep them under the carpet and pretend they're not there. The only way we're going to have effective change is when that happens. All the divisions in the women's movement, the socialist movements and all the rest of it, are created out of that basic inability of people to acknowledge these differences, embrace them and accept them. You have a competitiveness of oppressions, a hierarchy of oppressions, and I think all this is just ridiculous, playing into the hands of people like Margaret Thatcher. The more divisiveness there is between us, the happier she is.

I wanted to ask you about anger. I was particularly struck by your two poems, 'And Still I Cannot Believe It' and 'Remi'. Can you talk a little about that? That's changed since I wrote 'Remi'. I don't write in such a direct way now. I don't ever say in a poem that I'm angry. I try to use images and humour to create it instead. I don't particularly like 'Remi' because of that. It doesn't succeed in what I would want to do now. But that means a difference in technique, or approach, not a difference in the emotion. So, yes, I've still got a lot of anger about a lot of different things. I just want to find different ways of expressing it, but creative and constructive ways, rather than destructive ones.

There's a play I'm writing now, about two older women who had been lovers. One of them dies, and her granddaughter is clearing through her stuff and discovers she was a lesbian. She's totally shocked – of course! – and very angry. Now, trying to imagine her anger suits me better in that I'm entering into something else, rather than just thinking about different things that I've got to be personally angry about and listing them.

When you project yourself into her anger, does that allow you to understand it? Yeah. But it doesn't allow me to condone it. Whether I condone it or accept it or not is not the point. The point is that she has a journey to go through and it begins with extreme anger and towards the end of the play she changes. She realizes that her grandmother's being a lesbian wasn't any big deal. She was still her granny and she still loved her and got a lot from her. But people have got to understand that anger or else it would have no impact in changing their attitudes.

Anger is only useful when it can be creative. I think it's the same in everyday life. When somebody is literally smashing things up, that's destructive anger. But when someone is ferociously making something, like bread, pounding it down, but making something, well, that's creative anger. It's not that I don't think that anger shouldn't be expressed, because I think it should be. I think many people die from not being able to express it, but the ways in which we express it should be as constructive as possible.

You've talked about the different process for writing poetry rather than plays. Can you talk a little bit more about that? I think it's different in just about every way, especially in terms of technique. As a creative process, however, they're the same. With both you have something you want to say and that you want people to understand. That's why I don't go in for poetry that is too obscure, too oblique. When I'm writing plays I always start off with the character. Afterwards I decide what I want the play to be about.

This most recent play I was commissioned to write for secondary schoolchildren was very broadly about sexuality. So I did some research. I went round schools, asking kids what they felt about lesbians and what their images of lesbians were. And they said that lesbians were big bulky people who worked on building sites, and were dirty and swore! And I said to them, 'What age do you think a lesbian is?' and they said, 'Any age.' And I said, 'Well, do you think she could be about 70?' And they said, 'OLD? NO!' The idea of an older lesbian disgusted them more than anything they could possibly speak of. And one of them said, 'If my nan turned out like that, I'd kill her! I'd kill my nan if she did that to me, embarrass me in front of my mates!' And that's what gave me the idea for this play, that I would have a granny who was also a lesbian. Once I had that I created the characters around it.

In order to create the characters I wrote out long monologues for each of them, so that I could get a sense of them. And once I did that I started writing a play. I had an idea of the structure and everything. Whereas with poems, I don't have an idea of the structure. I have an idea of the form, but I don't have an idea of what what I'm going to say. It just develops as the poem develops.

Now that there are a lot more lesbian women writing about women loving women, do you find that gives you a sense of belonging or a tradition? Or do you find that you're breaking new ground? What's refreshing is that there are lots more lesbians writing about things that aren't just about women loving each other. But I think it's difficult to place yourself anywhere. Other people can place you more easily. I don't know many lesbian writers I would necessarily compare myself to in this country. There are certainly those who have given me a lot of confidence and courage, and the more people who do that, the more strength you get from it. You feel you're not just doing something on your own. That's also what's so good about living down here, rather than in Scotland. I have read a few times in Scotland, but I don't know if I could actually read lesbian poems there. I'm sure I will one day, but I don't know if I could at the moment.

Yeah, you'd shut a few doors if you did, I think. So, how would you define yourself, as a women poet, feminist poet, or what? I usually define myself as a Black Scottish poet because that seems easiest. I think all these long lists after your name, being Scottish, feminist, vegetarian, socialist, it gets a bit much! I don't think the definition in itself is so important. What you write is important, and it's through your writing that people should get a sense of who you are. Because I write directly from my own experience, people do get a sense of the multiplicity of what I am. So I don't feel I need to sing it, all the time. If someone just called me a poet, that would be fine.

SO YOU THINK I'M A MULE?

'Where do you come from?'
'I'm from Glasgow.'
'Glasgow?'
'Uh huh, Glasgow.'
The white face hesitates
the eyebrows raise
the mouth opens
then snaps shut
incredulous
yet too polite to say outright
liar
she tries another manoeuvre
'And your parents?'
'Glasgow and Fife.'
'Oh?'
'Yes. Oh.'
Snookered she wonders where she should go
from here —
'Ah, but you're not pure.'
'Pure? Pure what.
Pure white? Ugh. What a plight
Pure? Sure I'm pure
I'm rare...'

'Well, that's not exactly what I mean,
I mean ... you're a mulatto, just look at...'
'Listen. My original father was Nigerian
to help with your confusion
But hold on right there
If you Dare mutter mulatto
hover around hybrid
hobble on half-caste
and intellectualize on the
"mixed race problem",
I have to tell you:
take your beady eyes offa my skin;
don't concern yourself with
the "dialectics of mixtures";
don't pull that strange blood crap
on me Great White Mother.
Say, I'm no mating of a
she-ass and a stallion
no half of this and half of that
to put it plainly purely
I am Black
My blood flows evenly, powerfully
and when they shout "Nigger"
and you shout "Shame"
ain't nobody debating my blackness.
You see that fine African nose of mine,
my lips, my hair. You see lady
I'm not mixed up about it.
So take your questions, your interest,
your patronage. Run along.
Just leave me.
I'm going to my Black sisters
to women who nourish each other
on belonging
There's a lot of us
Black women struggling to define
just who we are
where we belong
and if we know no home
we know one thing:
we are Black
we're at home with that.'

'Well, that's all very well, but...'
'I know it's very well.
No But. Good bye.'

MY GRANDMOTHER

My grandmother is like a Scottish pine
Tall straight-backed proud and plentiful
A fine head of hair, greying now
Tied up in a loose bun
Her face is ploughed land
Her eyes shine rough as amethysts
She wears a plaid shawl
Of our clan with the seal of an Amazon
She is one of those women
Burnt in her croft rather than moved off the land
She comes from them, her snake's skin
She speaks Gaelic mostly, English only
When she has to, then it's blasphemy

My grandmother sits by the fire and swears
There'll be no Darkie baby in this house

My Grandmother is a Scottish pine
Tall straight-backed proud and plentiful
Her hair tied with pins in a ball of steel wool
Her face is tight as ice
And her eyes are amethysts.

WE ARE NOT ALL SISTERS UNDER THE SAME MOON

and the moon is never the same two nights
running into different shapes choosing
to light up a certain crescent or to be
full and almost round or to slide into
a slither tilted backwards looking up to the stars.

Before this night is over and before
this new dawn rises we have to see
these particular changes speak to
our guarded uncertain before singing
Sisterhood is Powerful. Once we see
that light reflect our various colours;
when we feel complexity clear as an orange sun

moving into the morning maybe we can sit
here in the shade and talk
meeting each other's eyes with a sparkle
that is not afraid to see the lone bright poppy
the dying azalea – the rage in this summer evening;
nor afraid to question the dent
in the dream or the words missing
from the story.

When you see my tone
changes with the sun or ill health
when you realise
I am Not a Definition
perhaps we can move on.

For I am not only a strong woman
with a Scorpio rising I am
not about to dance with daffodils
everyday making putty out of my wishes
to shape my future needs. I have no
definite tomorrow only a longing that
I will write to pick out lights
that cast curious shadows in the dark.

And yes it would be easy to pat
the back of my confidence
smacking out my fears with assurance
saying strong women never hesitate:
looking inward into this particular
Black woman helps me look outward;
only by questioning the light
in my eyes can I refuse to be
dazzled by the lie in yours –
we are not all sisters
under the same moon.

Janet Shepperson

JANET SHEPPERSON WAS RAISED IN SCOTLAND and studied English at Aberdeen University. She taught for seven years in Northern Ireland and after a spell of unemployment now works as a part-time Administrative Assistant. She is married and lives with her husband in Belfast.

Her poetry has appeared in numerous Irish publications, including *The Female Line* (Northern Ireland Women's Rights Movement, Belfast, 1985), *Trio 5* (with Martin Mooney and Denis Greig, Blackstaff Press, Belfast, 1987), *Map-makers' Colours: New Northern Irish Poets* (Nu-Age Press, Montreal, 1988) and *A Ring with a Black Stone* (Lapwing Poetry Pamphlets, 1989).

I was sitting outside Medbh McGuckian's office at Queen's waiting for her writing group to begin. A woman came up the stairs, smiled and said hello. We began to chat. She asked me what I was doing, and I said, 'I've come over to interview women poets in Belfast.' 'Really. Who are you looking for?' 'Ruth Hooley, Janet Shepperson –' 'I'm Janet Shepperson,' she said and smiled again 'Oh! Would you like to do the interview?' 'Sure.' We met several times during the next week at her home, where we discussed current events in Northern Ireland, changes in Janet's personal life and how these things affect her writing.

I WENT TO A GIRLS' SCHOOL where they pushed you to excel. I was good at writing so I had a lot of encouragement there. I wrote poetry and short stories. I also wrote at university. After I came over here and started teaching I hardly wrote anything for two or three years. Then I started writing songs. I always felt that writing was going to be my big thing, but all my energy went into teaching and other things. I got married in 1983. I struggled on for another couple of years with teaching, then made this big decision to leave. It was terrifying. I didn't have an excuse any more. I had to sit down and write.

What inspires you? What happens to you when a poem starts? Anything I get indignant, unhappy or frustrated about, any strong feeling that I have trouble expressing. There's a poem called 'Condolence' about coming to terms with the death of a friend's mother. She gave her children the most awful time and I felt very bad about not being able to feel sorry she had died. But not everything I write reflects a personal struggle. It might be a more general thing. There are certain types of people I keep writing about. The type of man in 'Accusations' I have met over and over again. I've also become more feminist in that I'm increasingly aware of situations where women are taken for granted or take for granted they must do certain things. The whole area of feeling compelled to act in a certain way is something I'm beginning to explore more in stories.

I notice a tension in the poems between things being hard and fast and set in a mould, like the one about the Orangemen and 'Accusations', and the poems which I think come out of you, which are much more complex. That is the whole Northern Ireland situation, people seeing things in totally black and white, very fixed terms, and I suppose I'm always out to undermine that, saying, 'Ah, yes, but.'

Are you conscious of choosing a particular form for a particular subject? Much more so than I used to be. I'm amazed how much Irish poetry is in a very traditional form. It often rhymes. There are sonnets and very carefully constructed patterns. When I was a student, reading Scottish poetry, there seemed to be more that was rhythmically free. Occasionally I find I'm writing something that does turn out as a sonnet. I also find it very easy to fall into iambic pentameter. At the moment I'm questioning whether I want to write in that style. I was reading an interview with the poet Michael Longley, who nearly always writes in a particular form, and he said he has always had this yearning to write in free form but he can't. He can only write things that rhyme or things that have a very close structure. He says that helps him along. I suspect I will always write fairly free poetry.

You seem very conscious of form? The way I create things is that I have to have an idea or emotion and the words come afterwards. There is this enormous struggle to get the idea out. Earlier on I didn't pay as much attention to the sound and the rhythm because of this struggle. But over the last years I have been trying to look at that much more carefully.

Are you conscious of using form for a particular tension or aim? It's hard to generalize. In 'Protestant Street' I had the contrast between the little street looking very innocent and the jaggedness of it after the family has been burnt out. Other than that it's very free. There aren't any rhymes and the rhythm is more as you would say it. In 'The Loyalist Strike' I have the contrast between the longer lines which have a rather 'te-tum-te-tum', reassuring sort of metre, and the short line bit at the end, which is in a totally different mood, stark and full of regret.

It's hard to articulate. A poem has to explain itself. Most of my metaphors begin as real objects, but as soon as I see them they become metaphors. It's an intuitive way of writing, but there's a lot of hard work organizing it so it doesn't come out in a big gush. Occasionally I feel I haven't noticed something I should have noticed, like this image of the woman saying 'I was clenched like a stone at your table' in 'The First Time'. I was just writing about a natural table and her sitting there. But my husband said, 'Well, this is a sacrifice and the table is one of those stone altars.' She's all closed up and inaccessible. I think 'dour' would be the Scottish word. It's not about my own and Nick's experience, but a lot of our experience is in there in the different expectations men and women have. But I like to try to understand why the other person doesn't understand you and you don't understand them, the two different points of view. When I started writing short stories they all had different points of view within the one story, which is incredibly difficult to do in 3,000 words, but I would be reaching after this.

I notice most of your poems are written in the first person. Is that your 'I'? Usually. If I'm going to write from another person's point of view it will probably be in the third person. But when I write short shories the 'I' is never me. It's a created character. That's how my technique has developed. In the poems it's nearly always my point of view.

Are you writing for a particular audience? Very much so with stories. Not really with poetry. I would love my story 'A Word of Advice', my cry from the heart about the awful educational system in Northern Ireland primary schools, to be read by people who have what to me are rather conservative, ill-thought out views, and I would love it to influence their thinking. So, I am trying to be very controlled in the way I project it. I think writing poetry is a wee bit less trying to make points to people. With a short story, I would very consciously sit down and say, What am I saying? How am I going to say it? How am I going to reach people? It's a bit like teaching. The same skill of trying to get a message across.

My poetry isn't didactic, but I am beginning to make points about being a Protestant very much at odds with mainstream Protestant thinking. An enormous amount of Northern Ireland poetry agonizes over ancestry and identity, an Ulster identity or an Irish identity and so on. I don't have that background. My view is more detached because I come from outside. I write about things very much as I see them and it's taken me a long time even to do that. But you get absolutely heartsick of this whole Nationalist-Unionist identity thing. It's been done to death. 'Orangemen' makes my point of view absolutely clear. I'm one of the minority who are not against the Anglo-Irish agreement and we don't feel threatened by the idea of Irish unity. I don't think it's a practical possibility, but I don't feel threatened by it.

I think most Protestants feel very scared because they're a minority within Ireland and they're quite convinced the Protestants in the Republic have a terrible life, but I feel more threatened by the various violent manifestations of loyalism. If you look at fiction, you find a lot written about Catholic schools, the Christian brothers, how repressive and how awful they are. I haven't seen much written about Protestant schools and how repressive they can be. This is something I would like to develop.

To be a Northern Ireland Protestant is a strange thing. They're not really sure what their culture is and they're very, very defensive. If you're an Irish Catholic, you've got the Irish language, Irish myths, Irish dancing, traditional music, a whole welter of stuff. As a group Protestants don't have that kind of culture. What they attempt to have is a very strong feeling about being British and at the moment this is all in the melting pot because it's begun to dawn on them that Britain doesn't actually want them very much. This is where the very narrow evangelical religious thing comes in, the whole growth of the Free Presbyterian Church. It's all to do with Northern Irish Protestants looking for identity and certainty, and in that very conservative type of religion you have very clear rules, like you mustn't drink and you must wear certain clothes when you go to church.

It also ties in with the women's situation and the expectations that go with that. There's the traditional Protestant virtue of being very clean and tidy and neat. And because a lot of Protestant families are anti-drink you have this elaborate thing with food. When visitors come you bring out the tray with the beautiful tray cloth and the nice china and you offer them a cup of tea with a whole lot of wee scones and wee sandwiches and barmbrack. Everything has to be done just so. I suppose there is a certain type of wee woman the world over who goes in for these things, but it's almost pathological with Northern Irish women. It can be very stultifying.

I admire people who have come from the Protestant culture and stepped outside it, who have realized that life does not just consist of defending your own interest. It fascinates me, the different reactions to situations, such as a relative being killed by the IRA or whatever. Some will really clench in and get involved with paramilitary groups. Others will be able to make the imaginative leap to see that by becoming more and more violent you are actually perpetuating your problems. It's very difficult to write about. It needs fiction. It takes space. It's quite difficult to get it into poetry because there you're painting pictures, making moods, not creating characters and analysing their attitudes.

How would you define yourself writing about these religious and political issues? I'm not consciously writing from any particular position. I don't start with a hidden agenda. A lot of my poetry could be written, not necessarily by anyone anywhere, but it isn't specifically about all the local things I have been talking about. I wouldn't like to categorize my own poetry. I would like to do more political poetry, and I would like to write some religious poetry. My faith is enormously important to me, but so far I haven't been able to get it into recognizably 20th century poetic language. Also, religious life in Northern Ireland is fairly depressing. You're struggling against the way language has been misused in talking about God. I've written songs for the peace programmes done by the Corrymeela Singers, so maybe a lot of my effort is going into that. It's probably a good thing I have that other outlet.

Would you consider yourself a female poet, a feminist poet, or what? A female poet. Definitely. I became very exasperated reading all the poems in a recent issue of *The Honest Ulsterman*. They were all written from a male point of view and some were very sexist. The women are seen as objects, as flowers or bits of landscape, towns or whatever. You get fed up with this. Starting off as a woman, I don't have to see a woman *as* anything particular. I am already putting a woman's point of view. I'm putting more direct emotion into my poetry than you often get with contemporary Northern Irish male poets. They tend to write obliquely, in a dry, unemotional way. Not to be afraid of emotion, to be able to bring that out, is quite a female thing.

I was thinking about your willingness to write about the woman having a nervous breakdown. I don't think it's an enormously good poem, but when I read it at readings the response was quite strong. I don't know whether there are more people in Northern Ireland having nervous breakdowns than there are elsewhere, but there are certainly an awful lot, and you would think this would be something gone into by writers, but it isn't. All the female experiences of sex and marriage and childbirth you would think would have been written to death, but because there haven't been that many woman poets who have been widely read, there has been so little said about that.

But I've got to be a bit careful. There is a feeling among men, some men and some women, that women will write about personal relationships, marriage and babies and houses, and men will write about the corporate things, work and groups and politics. But for anyone writing pretty seriously there should be both. I think there is a female point of view in both. When I started writing, I wouldn't have said I wrote as a woman particularly. I just wrote as a person. You live your life as a person and you write as a person. I am now coming round more to the idea that being female is enormously important in everything you write. The female point of view is not there in a lot of contemporary literature. I wouldn't say that fewer publications are accepting my poems because I'm a woman, but it does make you notice how many of the ones that are accepted are by men.

Some of the reviews of *The Female Line* complained that all the women in the book were writing about families, mothers, sisters, babies and so on. But if you take that point of view too far you end up saying, 'Well, these are not the real things of life. The real things are work and politics and so on.' In fact, some of the most vital things in life are who produces breakfast and who cooks the meal at night. So many women are shouldering all that responsibility because they feel they must or because they feel that men can't quite manage it. And that's affecting every other area of their lives. So what happens inside people's houses is one of the most important things you can write about. The symbolism of homes and what people choose to put in them can tell you so much about them. There shouldn't be a feeling that if you are writing about fast life in the streets, it's much more interesting and important.

I would never have said I was a feminist until fairly recently and I would still probably not say that. I'm all for equality of opportunity and equal sharing of domestic tasks, but then I've always been encouraged to express myself and prove myself; that was a burden, too, but I've never had the burden of feeling I had to be a very womanly woman and make a nice marriage and have nice kiddies and so on. Academically I was very much pushed and it took me a while to realize how much some women are kept down, not just always by men, but often because they feel they can't shoulder public responsibility and must keep the home going instead, encouraging their men to talk about their feelings and so on. It's still very often the women who will introduce emotional topics. The man won't be able to. There's an enormous amount men have to learn in talking about their feelings, and women have to learn not to do themselves down, not to feel that they and they alone must look after this little man – who is really quite capable. There's an enormous amount of that in Northern Ireland.

After I got married I was talking to a fellow woman teacher in Newtownards and I made some comment about my husband making the tea. And she said, 'Good heavens, you mean he can actually cook!' And then she said, 'But how does he know what to cook?' And the next thing was, 'How does he know what to buy if he goes into a butcher's? Do you give him a list?' She couldn't understand he had been looking after himself for years and was perfectly capable. She felt she couldn't sit there and watch a man cleaning up or cooking. He would make such a mess of it and she would have to do it to make sure it was done properly.

Would you consider yourself an Irish writer? I feel very Northern Irish. I never did see myself as Scottish at all. My parents are English. I also have an emotional connection with

England, although I have never lived there for any length of time.
I am very much at home in Northern Ireland. I find it hard to
express what I find so congenial. I can be myself here. It's a small
country and people are very friendly and will chat away to you
like in the west of Scotland, in spite of all you hear about
everybody being dour and taciturn and so on. And there's the
sense of humour. Ruth Hooley was saying that when she went to
a feminist book fair in Norway with Frances Molloy everybody
assumed that because they were Irish they must be very repub-
lican and anti-British. I'm very anti- a lot of things the British
army do, but I don't see myself as Irish in the sense of being
anti-British. I'm fascinated by Irish culture and I'm very keen on
traditional Irish music. And when I leave Northern Ireland and
hear Northern Irish people speaking, I feel this great nostalgia.
I've got to come back. I don't think I would have as vivid a life
anywhere else.

LOYALIST STRIKE: IN THE SUBURBS
(March 3rd, 1986)

All February, no rain fell. Not a whisper
to lick the dusty glass, just frost
having a long lie, stretching over the garden,
ignoring the dry cracked soil round its edges.
That morning, the little houses sat sullenly
tensing themselves for the power cuts, drawing
back into their shells like frightened snails,
waiting. But nothing shook their quiet. The message
had gone home; the shops were shuttered, metal
faces blank in all the streets, closed stiff as ice.
At night, some cracks, some splintering; but sirens
repeated again and again that the fires were distant
and the shots, and the shouting. We thanked God
we'd kept just on the right side of trouble
again.

    And then it started.
    Black, heart-bleeding rain,
    bitterly cleansing the glass,
    seeping through our compromise,
    mourning in its own slow way
    the closing of doors.

SWIMMERS

The Ladies' Class rotate and clutch each other,
their rubber-capped heads bobbing helplessly
in colours surely too youthful: pink,
turquoise, lemon, mauve, with petals
that wobble as their lumpy arms
engage with the unhelpful water,
flailing, twittering, fanning out
like sparrows round a bird bath.

A serious swimmer, I shake them
off like drips from my sinuous back
and strike out confidently,
younger, faster, thinner.

Lunchtime lets in the men,
grim, with their quota of furrows
to plough dead straight. Sleek water rat heads
and held-in stomachs, elbows sharp
and purposeful, eyes blanked by goggles;
unflinching, business-like.
Do they really do this for fun?
Or is somebody paying them?

Across wet tiles, slow, careful,
I retreat to the chirrupping shower,
content to sag in comfort
with the other plump middle-aged birds.

Ellie McDonald

ELLIE MCDONALD HAS LIVED all her life in Dundee. She left
school at 15. In the early 1970s she began attending creative
writing classes at Dundee University and was encouraged by the
then Writer in Residence, Anne Stevenson, to start writing in
Scots. She works part-time in a department store and is a cultural
nationalist and champion of the Scots language.

Her poems have appeared widely in Scottish Literary magazines, including *Akros, Chapman, Seagate, Seagate II, Lines
Review* and *Twa Chiels and a Lass*, a taped reading distributed
by Scotsoun in conjunction with Alastair Mackie and William
Tait. In addition, many of her poems have been broadcast on
radio.

I was introduced to Ellie at a poetry reading in Dundee. She
gave me a big grin as she shook my hand. I had read some poetry
in Scots, from the Aberdeen area, and thought I had a pretty good
grasp of the language. I got hold of Ellie's poems the day before
the interview. To my chagrin, I realized that her language was
quite different and that I understood about one word in ten!
Nevertheless I went ahead with the interview. She gave me lunch
in her tiny kitchen. She had two friends over who came into the
living room with us for the interview, turning it often into a

four-way conversation. Ellie read me two poems, took one look at my face, and burst out laughing. 'I guess you don't understand very much of it, do you?' I laughed, 'No, but I enjoyed it.'

MY FATHER WROTE POETRY and my maternal grandfather wrote poetry, and although we were really very poor, there was always an interest in poetry in the house. We had books and were taken to the public library and museums and art galleries in the city. So I'd always had this bit of background and I'd often written funny things easily. When anyone wanted a verse or something I just made them up.

I wasn't very sure what a creative writing class was all about, but I thought, This is great. I'll go and listen. So I went along and discovered that writing poetry came naturally to me. Then in 1973 they brought in Anne Stevenson as creative writer, and the chap who'd been taking the class, Jim Mackintosh, said to me that I should take what I'd written along to her. So I took my poems along and she hummed and hawed about them and seemed quite interested and said she was going to try something on a Wednesday afternoon and would I like to come along to it? So I went along and it was very free. There was nothing structured. Sometimes we just talked about other things. I'd only written a couple of things in Scots. I'd attempted writing in English, but I wasna really that happy. I think my command of the language wasn't that good. It didn't work. OK, I could do some things, but when I did them it was with my brain, but it wasn't with my heart. And it was Anne who said, 'You should really write in Scots.'

I didn't really know anybody who wrote in Scots, but Anne said, 'OK, just do what you've always done when you don't know anything about it. Read everything you can.' That was a revelation. So I started doing all this reading and I thought, I could do that. That's nothing! I speak the language. I could do that. It wasn't as easy as I thought, but Anne encouraged me. She has a way of driving you on without a stick! I seemed to be awful lucky, in that the right people got my name and when I sent them my poems they took them. I didn't have to struggle to have them published. But there's not that many people writing in Scots and people know it should be encouraged.

So what inspires you to write? I get a line, a line of poetry, two words, something like that. I don't know what the poem's going to be about. The last one I finished, I got this line 'Kirk bells and carnivals' and I had to work on from there. I've always wanted to write a poem about being different from other people, because if you're creative you are different. One of the greatest things for me was when I met Anne and moved in among people who were creative. For the first time in my life I felt I belonged. So this poem is about the difference between the creative and the non-creative, and how the non-creative don't understand the creative and yet feel slightly uncomfortable about it. They try to push you into their way of being. They don't want to know about this other thing. They don't understand creativity. People who aren't creative simply don't understand creativity.

Then what happens? Does it happen very quickly or does it take a while? I've written only one poem in my life straight off, and that was a poem I wrote in my head in the middle of the night when I was half-asleep. I wrote the whole thing out in the morning word for word. But mostly I'll write down the first line that comes to me, and then other things come too, and I'll write them all down on a sheet of paper. Then I'll throw that sheet aside and start working on this next bit. I always keep the first sheet and when I get what I think's going to be my first line I write it out, and then add to it, and go on like that. At the end of the poem, when it's finished, it's as if I've done a jigsaw, because all the words that are on the first sheet of paper are always in the poem at the end. It's quite odd. It's as if I'm just manipulating a puzzle. It's all there and I'm the person who puts it together. That's what I'm for.

Who are you writing for? Do you have an audience in mind? Not at all, no. I write because I can't help writing. I don't think you have any choice once you've got into doing it. It's the most annoying thing sometimes, because it doesn't come to you when you've got plenty of time to write. It usually happens when you're in a frazzle, and all sorts of things are happening in your life, and all of a sudden this thing comes along and you've got to write.

I'm not happy now with what is happening with public readings. There's an awful danger you're thinking about how this will come over to an audience. Most of the time your best poems are not readable because the first impact is what an audience is looking for. They just want to hear something that's light, that can be comprehended immediately. I don't think they're going to get the real message unless they see it on the page What is important about poetry? Is it the sound it makes? Or is it on the page? I would far rather people read poetry.

Do you have an intention when you're writing? Yes. I'm writing in a language which is threatened, and the more I can write, the more I can communicate this language to other people. I'm not just doing it for poetry, but doing something for my own language. *Can you talk more about that?* I'll try. I write in Scots because it's my first language and it's the language I care in. I can feel things in Scots that there's no way I could express in English. I can use the right words in Scots. It also has a strength. You can use words in Scots that the English just do not have. It's also important because there's so much threat to Scots. You feel as if you're fighting a battle all the time just to have it recognized as a language. MacDiarmid broke the biggest barrier ever for Scots, probably since Fergusson and Burns. From Burns to MacDiarmid there's this enormous gap. You could count the good poets on the fingers of one hand. And because I speak in the normal everyday language I can manipulate it and show it really properly. And I'm talking about simple grammar which is going because people are not using it. And that is important. There are an awful lot of people who can string words together in a kind of half-Scots, but the grammar they use is English. That's no good. I know the language well enough to be able to get it right. And I have to make sure that I keep getting it right because that's a political statement about my country. If you don't have your own language you don't have your own country. That's the only distinguishing mark you have. That's why the English tried to root it out...

So would you consider yourself then a Scottish Poet? Yes, I would. *Would you consider yourself a female poet, a feminist poet, or what?* I've never had any problem with this feminist issue. Partly because I'm Scottish and we originally were a matrilinear society, and Scots women are very strong, very strong indeed. In the area I belong to in Dundee, women have always been very strong. Most of the time they've carried the men and been equal to them and been respected. It's a great place for that. Sometimes in Scotland, way back, women kept their own names after marriage. You can still keep your own name. It was often done because power was handed down through the women. It didn't matter who the man was. There's still a sense of that in this country, and for that reason I've never felt any need to be feminist, or even to be a female poet. I don't believe in female poets and male poets. Creativity's a thing in itself. I feel as close to a male poet as I would to a female poet.

What forms do you write in? Free verse mostly. I've written one or two in a rhyme scheme, like villanelles and sonnets, but it's mostly the music of the line that I go by. I can feel when it's ending. Sometimes a poem comes out because of the music of it. It works with six lines in the verse. But I don't start off doing that. I think it's something to do with the inside music. *So it's not a conscious decision?* Never.

Where do you see the Scots language going? Is it altering? Well, it's still alive, so it's always changing. But it's been dying off faster in the last 30 years than it did in the last 200. That's the influence of the media. Even the accents on Scottish radio have changed. There are all these people trying to speak some kind of English which even the English don't speak. I think some linguist should study it. I've never heard anything like it. They can't even pronounce Scots words properly. It's got nothing to do with language. Nobody would try to learn French and not attempt to use the vowel sounds and the consonants as they do. But with Scots they're saying, 'This is a second rate country and a second rate language and it's English we should all be talking.' The sad thing is they won't give enough voice to the people who really know what they're taking about. The schools are very bad. The teachers themselves have been educated at university in an English department, not a Scots department. And the ones who know the language themselves are all trying to speak what is known in Scotland as 'properly'. They all want to imitate the English. They've lost their history and they've lost their culture. I don't know what the future is. They said 200 years ago that Scots was dying. It is. More words are lost every year, with every dying generation. Nobody wants to encourage their children to speak the language. They want them to 'get on', and the only way to get on is not to speak Scots. You go for a interview, and people say, 'It's a pity about that terrible dialect.' How would you like someone to say that about your language?

Do you do any other kinds of writing? I've done a bit of translation and a couple of short stories. Both in Scots. I'm not any good at anything else other than poetry. I love drama and do drama as well. But I don't work hard enough. I'm a very slow writer. I don't produce that much. This is the sum total of what I've written. Maybe 30 poems I've kept in fifteen years. That's not a lot. I know people who can run that off in a month!

What other things do you do in addition to your writing? I work part-time in a big store. That's what keeps me in touch with my language. The people I live with around here, they speak the same as me, and the people I work with, and the people who come into the shop. You can't keep writing in Scots if you're not speaking the language. A lot of people try. They maybe have the language from their childhood, but it's not their living language. It's not what they speak. They intellectualize it. They're not living where it's spoken. They don't even get on a bus! We don't see enough of other people nowadays. We don't make enough human contacts outside our own circle. It's getting tighter and tighter and more and more closed in, and that's not any good for anybody's creativity.

Maybe in the next few years a lot of good writing will come out of Scotland because we're in a semi-war situation. There's only five million of us and around fifty million English. That's a hell of a lot of English against us. Not that they would articulate that. It's just that we don't exist, we're not important, we don't count. And in the last few years this government's emasculated this country. We've gone to the wall first every time. And it may be that when you get a situation like this you have an upsurge of good writing. In every country when you've got trouble you get this big blast of creativity. It's happened in Ireland. A lot of the poetry that's coming out of England has no content, no feel. The language has been beaten to death. They can't do what Keats, Wordsworth and Shelley did. They've exhausted the language. The best writing in English is coming out of countries other than England.

If I can get along, if somebody somewhere gets something out of my poetry, if I've done something that's hit this wonderful thing in somebody else, that's great. That's what I want. I want poetry to live in people's hearts and mean something, maybe even just a line that does something for them. That's all we should hope for, not praise and prizes and Arts Council awards and shelves full of books in your own name. That's not important to me.

THE GANGAN FUIT

Whit ist that greets outby the nicht,
that fakes tae find the sneck?
It's juist the wind, my bonnie lass
gaen speiran i the daurk.

Whit ist that greets outby the nicht,
that keens abuin the ruif?
It's juist the glaid, my bonnie lass
gaen seekin i the lift.

The glaid gangs free, my bonnie lad,
kens nocht o daith nor birth.
The wind but cairts aa human pain
tae ilka howe o earth.

Whit seeks tae come inby the nicht,
nae bield has ever haen
but haiks its gangrel body whaur
eternities cry doun.

FAIRINS

Abune the raivellit claes
my heid gaes birlan.
Drunk? Naa, glorious.
Lippan owre wi life's
illyased intoxication.
Sae bonnie hochmagandie
wha cried ye gorkie names?

For aa begoud
wi sicca celebration.
An Athole-brosian,
halliracket reemle-rammle
cuist up frae the glaur
tae ligg there, crimson-mou'd
upon a bolster.

Out owre yer jizzen bed
rowed aa the warld's wunners.
Sinsheen an siller licht
ain wi the sang I sing
i the mornan's glory
Sae bonnie hochmagandie
thrum on ayont the snorl.

Glossary
greets – weeps; fakes – searches; sneck – latch; speiran – prying; daurk – dark;
abune – above; ruif – roof; glaid – kite hawk; lift – sky; cairts – carries; ilka –
every; howe – hollow; bield – shelter; haiks – drags; gangrel – vagrant; fairins –

gifts from the fair; raivellit – disordered; claes – clothes; birlan – spinning; lippan owre – brimming over; illyased – illused; hochmagandie – physical love; gorkie – smutty; begoud – began; sicca – such a; Athole brose – a mixture of honey, oatmeal and whisky; halliracket – giddy; reemle-rammle – racket; cuist – cast; glaur – mud; ligg – lie; jizzen bed – child-bed; warld's wunner – world's wonders; sinsheen – sunshine; siller – silver; snorl – confusion.

Nuala Ni Dhomhnaill

NUALA NI DHOMHNAILL WAS BORN in Lancashire in 1952 and grew up in the Dingle Gaeltacht in Kerry. She spent seven years on the *seachran* in Turkey and Holland and now lives in Dublin with her Turkish husband and four children.

She writes in Irish and her publications include *Selected Poems* (1986), *Fear Suaithinseach*, *An Dealg Droighin*/Selected Poems (1988), and *Selected Poems*, translated by Michael Hartnett with additional translation by the author, all published by Raven Arts Press, Dublin.

Nuala and I had had several in-depth talks on the phone long before I went to Dublin. Once there I called her and set up an appointment. I took a taxi to her house, went up to the front door and knocked. No answer. I waited half an hour but no one came. I left a note saying that I was sorry I had missed her and that I would call to reschedule. When I got back to my front door the phone was ringing. It was Nuala. I had gone to the wrong house. 'I can give you forty minutes on Wednesday', she said. 'Will that do?' Grateful for a second chance, I accepted. The woman who answered the door in no way matched the image in my mind: I had expected a tall, Amazonian woman, and before me stood this small woman with a mane of auburn hair. 'Is it okay if I talk

about the male muse, as that's what I'm currently working with?'
'Fine.' I turned on the tape recorder and Nuala did all the work; I
think I asked three questions in forty minutes.

I HAVE AN UNCLE WHO TELLS ME that I have been telling stories
since I was a small child, that I would have dreams and would see
all these strange things in my dreams and would spend all day
making up stories about them. Then I started a diary at the age of
twelve in boarding school, in code, in Irish, because I was so
unhappy there. I think I started writing poetry about the age of
fourteen, again at boarding school, and again because I would be
upset by something and couldn't sleep because of it. These words
would go running through my mind and I found the only way I
could get to sleep was to write them down. I get these bouts of
insomnia when my mind races, races, and I can't get to sleep
because of the words.

I was writing poetry in English and my journal in Irish.
There was something wrong, although I didn't know what it was.
I was nearly there, but something was missing. It suddenly
dawned on me I was writing Irish poetry in English. I was
working with Irish prosody, but through the medium of English.
The rhymes and the half-rhymes, the whole underpinning of the
poem was actually Irish. I thought, 'Why don't I write it in what it
should originally have been written in – Irish? Get on with it.'
And I did. I made a big jump then.

The second thing was that I had terrible trouble with my
family because I wanted to marry a Turk. All hell broke loose! I
got a huge shock. Then I made another jump – into poetry. What
I had been writing at first was nearly poetry, or verse, efficient
enough verse. I think there's a lot of misunderstanding about
what poetry is. People think words come to poets as they come to
politicians. They don't. It's a completely different kettle of fish.
It's another layer of language altogether. A lot of what passes for
poetry nowadays in our generation – and this has been true of all
generations – is just very efficient, nicely turned, graceful verse.
For poetry to occur it has to come from a deeper level of the
psyche. I call it the *lios* or 'faery fort'. There's supposedly sixteen
hundred of them in the Irish countryside. We know now, archae-
ologically, that these are settlements, anywhere from the Iron
Age to the Middle Ages, but at home, and as a child, you think,
'That's where the fairies live.'

My attitude is that the *lios* is not there at all. It's within, the subconscious, which generally you can't get into, and poetry is bringing stuff from that other world into this world. Anything that comes from there will be imbued with an extraordinary charge, a luminous quality that will make it jump off the page.

People ask: Do I have a discipline? I do, a very rigid discipline. I sit down at the desk about five hours a day, but I won't be writing all that time, just sitting, brooding. It's even more difficult to sit and do nothing until the tension builds up. I have to be away from everyone. I have to get terribly lonely, or to get a terrible emotional shock before it comes out as poetry, and then it just comes out. It doesn't have to be mediated by intelligence, or the rational side of the brain at all.

That's the medium side. On the craft side, though, you also have to work very hard at language. I work with dictionaries and will tease out the meanings of words for hours. I will be working with the language for up to five or seven hours a day. I try to reach thirty hours a week, but with the kids and all, I really only do about twenty-four, but that's OK.

There's another level of poetry that I don't think people understand, and it's got to do with the muse. I am a muse poet. I can only write when there's a muse about, somewhere in the vicinity, maybe in another country, so long as he's there. Now I say 'he', because at the moment I'm writing a lot of male-muse poems.

The muse doesn't necessarily have to be a man. We've all heard about the muse from male poets and they have always said that the muse is female, everything from Botticelli's Venus to I-don't-know-who, whether in pictures or in writing. They are talking about their inner woman and projecting it on to us. Actually, I've done a bit of research on this, and women have had a male muse. Emily Dickinson is full of him, so are Emily Brontë, Virginia Woolf and Sylvia Plath, and Anne Sexton has a bit of him. Each one of those women came to a sticky end, because the male muse is ferociously dangerous. Number one, being a man, he's inclined to all or nothing action: killing yourself, walking out of a relationship, black or white, right or wrong. Number two, he's allied with society against you, against your deeper levels of femininity, because he's male. There's a poem I'm working on about this that comes from Irish folklore.

The story is about a woman breast-feeding a child. She goes out to do some washing and the baby is taken by the fairies. She goes to her godmother and asks, 'What should I do?' And the godmother says, 'You have to go into the *lios*. The fairies have taken him into the *lios*. You had better take a black-hafted knife and a bundle or a wisp of wool from a black sheep, and armed with those you can go into the *lios*. The first person you will meet is a black man, a tall, black, dangerous man.' And that's where I am. The folk memory is telling you about journeys, previous journeys done over the centuries into the *lios*. You are going into the *lios* for your own child, and the child is the potential, the image for the new or future dispensation, and you are going into the *lios* to get it back. And the first person you meet is this shadow black man who is dancing.

Right now I have an eleven-year old daughter and when she was nine, she had a dream of dancing with this black man, and it brought it all back to me: being fourteen and dreaming I was dancing with this black prince, and then waking up in the morning in boarding-school and all the nuns saying, 'Praise be to Jesus', and realizing it was a dream and sitting down and crying about it. I didn't realize at the time that there was nothing to cry about. He's a dangerous fucking bugger, that fellow, I tell you!

How do you work with him then? It's a wrestling. It's a wrestling with the Angel, and, like Jacob, I will not stop until he releases me, until I get that creative energy into my consciousness. But that might mean that I don't write poetry any more. I might write something else. But the only way to find out is to work through it.

Now in the story, when you get to the black man, you tie him with the woollen wisp from the black sheep and immobilize him, and then you come to a blackberry briar with is two heads in the earth. You take the black-hafted knife and cut that and go through. You find yourself in the *lios*, where the fairies are passing your child from hand to hand. And just as they are doing that, you swipe it and run like hell. And that's the end of the story.

Can you say more about your creative process? How does it work for you? You have to give poetry its head. My poetic function is about two or three years ahead of the rest of me. It's only looking back on what comes out in a poem that you realize where you're going. Each of my poems has been a milestone on that journey and what might have worked for me ten or fifteen years ago won't work for me any more. I don't think this is emphasized enough in poetry workshops. You have to break through into deeper levels. Nobody seems to be approaching that, or even articulating the need for that. It's a terrible loss.

What women find when they go in there is very different from what men have written about. That's the really exciting thing. Lots of women's poetry has so much to reclaim: there's so much psychic land, a whole continent, a whole Atlantis under the water to reclaim. It's like this island, again in Irish folklore, which surfaces from under the water every seven years, and if somebody can go out to it and light a fire, or do something, it will stay up forever. I had a whole series of dreams about this last summer. But nowadays you can go out in jumbo jets and have trouble with passports and customs and duty-free! That's what you would call 'threshhold difficulties', the stuff that's just near the surface, but not quite coming through.

I find that when I go through one of these 'threshhold' periods I'm very tired and weak. Recently I spent two years sitting there in a stupor of lethargy. All I could do was look out of the window. So I sat there, because I knew this was the real biggie, if I could hold on to it! It's only coming in now. I've had some breakthrough periods and I've gone a bit high and not been able to concentrate. It's a huge energy you need to bring it into this world, to harness and bridle it – I use these words because it often appears as a horse.

There's a thing in Irish folklore to do with the water-horse. The water-horse lives in the deeps of the lakes, and sometimes in the sea, and can change into a man – his spirit takes the form of a man. The trouble is, when he takes the form of a man, he still has horse's ears. So be prepared for the next time he puts his head on your knee, check his ears! 'Come all ye young maidens and listen to me' – when he puts his head in your lap, have a feel of his ears. *Before you let him into your bed!* Exactly! Because the water-horse is very dangerous. When he appears as a horse he persuades you to get up on to his back and then he races into the lake and you're drowned. He actually hauls you, he does. He brings you down into that lake, and that's what's known in clinical terms as depression. At one stage I had about fourteen years of it. I'm only coming out of it in the last two years. I wrote some poems then but I don't know how I did it. It was my disembodied energy, something else outside me. Time and time again I felt that.

You say you've worked with a female muse. How was she different from your male muse? She's much softer. But I got a shock when what I saw at nineteen was the *cailleach*, the hag.

The story goes that there's a corner at every road, and invariably there's a spirit there, and invariably that spirit is female and ugly. I know you can say it's the male fear of the female, but it's not just that. It's neither fashionable nor popular to say that, but I have felt her as well. Being a poet means that you are mediating between the other world, the *lios*, and this world. Robert Bly is very good on this, and people say, 'Oh, he's a man', but, no, I tell you, time and time again my best poems have been written out of a response to the unspeakable, because you're not supposed to talk about this. Women aren't supposed to have this quality in them, these negative, destroying teeth. What's in the middle of the labyrinth isn't necessarily the maiden in the tower. It's something that destroys you, creates psychic dismemberment literally, sends teeth and hands and legs flying all over the place. But I have also written out of the other side of her, the ecstatic side. Sometimes I write love poems through the female muse and that feels right. The veritable experience of that female energy, which is not particularly goal-directed, is to do with the joy of being.

Because males have told us about the muse all the time, we have accepted that she has to be a woman, and a woman in their way, like the distant Beatrice. But I don't think that's so at all.

Ultimately, in me, the deepest image would be one of the Mothers. But you see, as Robert Bly says, when you set out on the journey towards your Mother's, you think you're going to meet the Great Mother, the Good Mother, the Ecstatic Mother, but what do you do when you meet the Teeth Mother?

But the muse doesn't have to be either male or female. It can be animal, vegetable or mineral, person, place or thing. The greatest muse in Ireland is the country – Eire, again seen as a woman, and the whole sovereignty of Ireland. That's what lies deepest in our hearts here in Ireland. There has been an ongoing love affair between people and the land and the land and the people here for millennia. And we have lavished our imaginations on it until we have projected on to it the depths of our own psyches.

So what I am saying is that the land can be the muse. I noticed this when I was in the States. You realize that the land there still really belongs to the Indians. Somehow the white men have not made their peace with the land or with the Indians as co-inhabiters. This need to do so is very strong in me, because I have a similar attitude to Ireland and to West Kerry, my tribal stomping-ground. I'm obsessed by it. I have to know every story and every stone, and I spend my whole life walking around, meeting people, listening to stories and telling them, or just wandering round the countryside, just being in it.

There's a book called *Arctic Landscapes* which is about the land being the muse and being an echo of an inner landscape. And it's this inner Atlantis that I'm trying to bring up again, this whole continent lost in a dark sea that Western man has lost his way of getting to. I'd be very pleased to return to that state. It would be outrageous. I know we can't go back exactly to our original existence, but we can gain an awful lot from, for example, how the Aboriginals live. They spend two thirds of their lives asleep or working out their sacred dramas which they get from their dreams.

I think there's an enormous capacity for that still alive in Irish people. I think I'm very lucky in being Irish because the Irish language wasn't industrialized or patriarchalized. And many things, including this idea of a deeper quality, this negative femininity, this Hag Energy, which is so painful to mankind, hasn't been wiped from our consciousness, as it has in most cultures. Irish in the Irish context is the language of the Mothers, because everything that has been done to women has been done to Irish. It has been marginalized, its status has been taken from it, it has been reduced to the language of small farmers and fishermen, and yet it has survived and survived in extraordinary richness, but not necessarily in a literary form, rather a paraliterary form. The real richness of Irish is not found in the literature of the last two hundred years, but in places like West Kerry, among the speech only of the ordinary people. They were reduced to their tongues as their medium because they didn't have even enough money to buy musical instruments, and so all their creativity went into their speech.

I'm working on a poem at the moment which is based on a beautiful flower which is very rare in the British Isles but is very common in West Kerry. It's the same word in Irish for the liver fluke. I've been fascinated by how the name of a beautiful flower could come to have the same name as a devouring parasite that can eat your liver from the inside. There's another theme for the muse!

I've also written a poem called 'The Mermaid'. First of all I thought it was about being cut off from a man, and then I thought it was about the state of autism which I'd investigated at the time.

Only recently has it dawned on me that, as well as all those things, it's about language. If you call Irish the sea and English the land, the rationality of the land which comes with English which we've had to crawl up onto has been terribly painful. I know the sheer psychic distress of it in my own family, and it's happened in most Irish families in the not so distant past. It doesn't go back more than two or three generations, but it's still there. It's just been buried. Probably because I've always had English as well as Irish, I've maybe been more aware of it.

AUBADE

Is cuma leis an mhaidin cad air a ngealann sí; –
ar na cáganna ag bruíon is ag achrann ins na crainn
dhuilleogacha; ar an mbardal glas ag snámh go tóstalach
i measc na ngiolcach ins na curraithe; ar thóinín bán
an chircín uisce ag gobadh aníos as an bpoll portaigh;
ar roilleoga ag siúl go cúramach ar thránna móra.

Is cuma leis an ghrian cad air a éiríonn sí:–
ar na tithe bríce, ar fhuinneoga de ghloine snoite
is gearrtha i gcearnóga Seoirseacha: ar na saithi beach
ag ullmhú chun creach a dhéanamh ar ghairdíní bruachbhailte;
ar lánúine óga fós ag méanfach i gcoimhthiúin is fonn
a gcúplála ag éirí aníos iontu; ar dhrúcht ag glioscarnach
ina dheora móra ar lilí is ar róiseanna; ar do ghuaille.

Ach ní cuma linn go bhfuil an oiche aréir
thart, is go gcaithfear glacadh le pé rud a sheolfaidh
an lá inniu an tslí; go gcaithfear imeacht is cromadh síos
arís is píosaí beaga brealsúnta ár saoil a dhlúthú
le chéile ar chuma éigin, chun gur féidir
lenár leanaí uisce a ól as babhlai briste
in ionad as a mbosa, ní cuma linne é.

AUBADE

It's all the same to morning what it dawns on –
On the bickering of jackdaws in leafy trees;
On that dandy from the wetlands, the green mallard's
Stylish glissando among reeds; on the moorhen
Whose white petticoat flickers around the boghole;
On the oystercatcher on tiptoe at low tide.

It's all the same to the sun what it rises on –
On the windows in houses in Georgian squares;
On bees swarming to blitz suburban gardens;
On young couples yawning in unison before
They do it again; on dew like sweat or tears
On lilies and roses; on your bare shoulders.

But it isn't all the same to us that night-time
Runs out; that we must make do with today's
Happenings, and stoop and somehow glue together
The silly little shards of our lives, so that
Our children can drink water from broken bowls,
Not from cupped hands. It isn't the same at all.

(rendered into English by Michael Longley)

KUNDALINI

Na bain an leac ded chroi,
thios faoi ta nathair nimhe
ina lui i luba.

Einne a thaighdeann an poll,
geobhaidh se ina codladh ann
an ollphiast ghranna.

Eirionn si taobh thiar ded dhrom,
is uafar agus is gear a glam
ar fuaid na duiche.

Caortha agus tinte teo,
coinneal a sul ag at, is ag reo
na fola i do dhearna.

Is ni cabhair duit, a Naomh Cuan,
dramhlach na mine a chur ar a ceann,
ta si romhor dhuit.

Is ni feidir leat dallamullog
a chur uirthi seo mar a dheinis fado
le cleasaiocht focal.

Atann is tagann clipi ar a drom,
d iosfadh si trian agus leath don domhan
gan cead o einne.

Cinte, ceainte ta si ann,
go breith an bhratha, go brach na breithe.
Amen, a thiarna.

KUNDALINI

Don't unblock your heart —
in there a serpent
lies in loops.

Who explores this cave
will find asleep
a grim Medusa.

She rises up behind you
sharp and terrible her voice
throughout the land.

Hot coals and glowing fires
her swollen candle eyes
freezing your pulse's blood.

No good, St. Cuan
putting the meal-tub on her head.
She is too tall.

And you cannot blind her eyes
as once before you did,
with punning sentences.

She swells, spines on her back:
she'd eat five-sixths of the world
without permission.

She's there indeed —
sempiternally.
Ay! Senor — c'est la vie.

Sara Berkeley

SARA BERKELEY WAS BORN IN DUBLIN in 1967. She studied English Literature at Trinity College, Dublin.

In 1984 a selection of her poems appeared in *Raven Introductions* (Raven Arts Press, Dublin). Since then her work has appeared in numerous journals and magazines. Her first collection, *Penn*, was published in 1986 by Raven Arts Press and her second, *Home-Movie Nights* in 1989.

Sara and I arranged over the phone to meet outside Trinity College. I came clutching *Penn*, hoping to be able to recognize her from the photo on the back. She spied me first. The stylish young woman who introduced herself in no way matched the photo of a girl that I held. We did the interview over coffee in the student café, which was crowded, noisy and warm. Sara's friends kept passing us as we talked. They greeted Sara and stared curiously at me. It was an awkward conversation. Perhaps we were too close in age. I felt as if we were dancing round each other, each checking the other out.

WHEN DID YOU START WRITING? I've written poetry since I was about nine and bits and pieces since I was very small. I keep diaries and things. The earliest poems in *Penn* I wrote when I was fifteen or sixteen.

Do you write fairly consistently? It seems to go by how hard I'm working. Under pressure I write a large volume, but if I'm slacking, like during the summer, I don't usually write as much.

What about the idea of inspiration? Do you feel you're inspired? Yes, I do.

What happens when you start writing? What motivates you? I keep notes all the time and write bits here and there, any time of day or night, and then at some stage I begin to work them into a poem. It's not one particular event that sparks it off, more impressions from different events that make me write down certain images. Then I can transfer the emotion in one sentence to something else. It's like clay to mould.

Do you just give yourself over to it? What happens when it comes in class? Yes. I don't care where it happens. I always put the writing first. It may sound selfish. I've often written in lectures. It's one of the best atmospheres. Everyone's concentrating and you know you should be doing something else!

Do your poems come out quite quickly? A few have. I wrote 'Curious George' in half an hour when I was fifteen. I couldn't do it again, or anything like it. I wouldn't try. I don't know where it came from. The average poem takes me a few weeks or a few days.

Do you work over your poems a lot? Much more than I used to. But once they're finished I never go back and change them, or very rarely, just a word here or there. I hate changing stuff when it's done. I feel it's ruining it.

So you have a sense when a poem is finished? Yes, definitely. I don't know what it is. I just know. I feel satisfied.

Is emotion a strong factor in your writing? I think so. It must be what sparks it off. Writing with no emotion in it is dead. And yet you need a lot of control as well. If it's too emotional it's just embarrassing.

There's a lot of screaming, crying and ripping in your work. Are you conscious of that? Yes. I try to keep that to a minimum. It's very much an adolescent phase. Too much angst! It's embarrassing to read over poems that are too full of that. It's too violent. It might be a sincere expression of people's thoughts but a bit of control is in order. Maybe I'm hung up on control but I'm always conscious of not letting it get out of hand, conveying the feelings without getting too explosive with the language.

My experience of reading your poems is that they make you very vulnerable. They probably do but that's all part of being truthful. If you don't have a certain amount of yourself in them, people are going to recognize them as being phoney.

Do you have an audience in mind? Never. That's really inhibiting. I prefer to imagine that it's just going to be for me. *So you're writing primarily for yourself?* Yes, although with the book you have to have an idea in the back of your mind that people are going to see it. It's hard to say. I can't just be writing for myself, I suppose.

Some people say they're writing to communicate, to touch other people. Do you feel that way? It's not the most important thing. You want to get it out of yourself, for your own therapy or enjoyment or necessity, and if it touches other people then that's great.

Has being published changed your work? Yes. Slowly. It puts pressure on you and expectations, which I try to ignore as much as I can, but it's hard. You can feel under some kind of onus to be producing. *Producing a certain kind of writing?* Yes. Or if you've written a slightly off poem, it's much easier to sink into the mire of, 'Oh, no, I'm never going to write again!' Or if I haven't written for a few weeks, it's very hard to convince myself it's OK, that it's happened before.

Sometimes you write in free verse and sometimes in rhyme. How do you choose what form to write in? I only started using rhyme about a year ago. I was very turned off rhyme and poetry in metre before. I found it difficult to enjoy, stuck with this necessity to rhyme. Then I discovered you can use it without being tied to certain strictures and it's much more interesting that way. You can use internal rhymes. But I'm still experimenting. I'm afraid of going too far into rhyme.

You seem very conscious of form. I'm much more conscious of it now. Partly from people asking me questions about it! You start to analyse, which I would never have done otherwise.

Do you think it's a good thing or a bad thing? Too much of it is a bad thing. I suppose it's good up to a point.

Do you work more from the content of the poem? I work more from the words. The ideas come afterwards. Sometimes I'll be halfway through a poem before the idea comes out. I'm not even sure what I'm saying. It's just the words that are there.

Is writing poetry different from writing prose? It is, but it's like different members of the same family. Writing an essay is a creative experience as well. There's the same sense of relief, of achievement, when it's finished. It's maybe not so concentrated as a poem. It's not as personal. It's an exercise set for me. It's for someone else. But it's within the same kind of experience. It's just not as good.

A lot of your poems seem to come from dreams. Yes. 'Brainburst' came from a dream. Some of the others have bits of dreams in them, but that one came from a full dream. I'm a prolific dreamer. I write them down. It's really interesting, because normally they just disappear as soon as you wake up. It's different from writing prose. The happenings are so unusual. *A cross between this reality and unconscious reality?* Yes. Dreams are amazing.

Do you think of yourself as a poet? Not if I can help it. It's too intrusive. I can't live an ordinary life here at the college if I set myself up as a poet. People immediately expect things of you. I hate when people come up to me and say, 'I hear you're a poet', or when someone introduces you to someone else as 'This is our poet. She's our great poetess', immediately there's a barrier between you and other people. Naturally, if you've had stuff published, you have to be a bit responsible about it. I've made my statement and have to take the consequences. But I prefer just to say, 'Well, I write poetry.' I might stop tomorrow. *How would you feel if that happened?* Devastated. It's a constant fear. *Writing is very much part of you.* Yes, it is. It's very important.

Do you have a sense of yourself as a female poet or a feminist poet at all? I don't want any labels. That's partly why I called the book *Penn*. I don't want to make any statement whatsoever if I can help it. I don't want to say, 'I'm a woman writing in the nineties' or whatever. And I'm definitely not a feminist. I appreciate that there probably has to be a difference between a twenty-year old guy writing poetry and me, but apart from the natural difference, I don't think there needs to be a big distinction. Feminism has made its point. They've gone overboard and I'm just tired of it.

Do you have any sense of yourself as an Irish poet? Not very much. I think Irish poetry is great and it would be a shame to lose the language, but I don't write in the language. I haven't been brought up in a strong Irish tradition. It's much more cosmopolitan here. My mother is English as well, so there was never any Irish in the house. And I've lived all my life in the city so I'm really not that much in touch with the country.

Is it possible to be an Irish poet living in the city and writing in English? Oh, yes, because our main language is English. But I think of an Irish poet as being someone very in touch with the whole tradition of Irish, probably writing about things like the ecology. Probably there are Irish influences on my stuff, but I've never heard anyone say that. If you just picked up *Penn*, would you know I came from Ireland? *No, I don't think so.* I don't think so either.

In the poem 'Crossing I' I was interested in the tension between wildness and the city. It was just the idea of the horse being mad. He's crossing a boundary between being a slave horse and being free. In the madness there can be no restrictions on him.

Would you say there is a fine line between reality and madness in your poetry? Yes, I think so. *How do you keep sane?* Other people. If I spend too much time on my own I go crazy. I really need other people and small talk, silly things, getting drunk now and then, just doing ordinary things.

Is it different writing a poem in a persona than speaking as yourself? It's not difficult because normally it is an imaginary person and I have total play anyway because it is my person. I don't think I would attempt to write from somebody else's point of view, a real person. I could never try to consciously write someone I knew into a poem because I would feel I was taking too much of a liberty.

You said 'My Person'. Are you comfortable with that? Yes. It's not necessarily me, but it's my own creation. There's the whole realm of imagination where it's OK. That's when I feel happy.

Is it any different working out of your imagination versus working from experience? I don't work much from seeing things. It'll be more small things rather than an event I witnessed the whole of. It might just be the look on somebody's face that will stay in my head and I'll write it down. Then later on things will add up. But I never really see something, a big event, and then write a poem about it.

Are your poems about death imaginary? Yes. Most of them.

Some people would argue that writing from your imagination rather than your experience is less honest. I see the point. But writing from your imagination there has to be some influence from things you've seen and done. So it's not really a lack of integrity. It's rather a truth that has been much more processed and filtered down. *Where does imagination come from?* I don't think anyone who had lived his whole life in a dark hole would be able to imagine things. You have to have some kind of experience to get imagination from.

Are you a strong Catholic? Yes, I am. *Does that play any part in your creative process?* Yes, well, I feel that God would have a part in it, but I wouldn't like to make it too overt. It would turn people off. I would hate for it ever to get classed as religious poetry. If I could weave it in with other influences, then it's OK. I'm sure it does quite a bit without my realizing it.

Do you read much poetry? Yes. I read much more, obviously, since I've been published. Before I came to college I didn't read much at all, just the stuff in the school courses and a little bit on the side. It needs a lot of discipline, reading poetry. It's something you have to decide to sit down and do, unlike a novel, which you can read on the bus. I've read a lot, but it was all fiction. Now I also read things like biography, some non-fiction, which I wouldn't have read a few years ago. But poetry is very difficult. You can't read too much, especially of the same person. *I've also found that reading too much has stopped my own writing.* Yes, I'd be afraid of that, too. Also I don't want too much influence coming in.

What do you plan to do when you graduate? I don't know what to do with an Arts degree these days. I'll probably travel for as long as I can. I want to travel and, if I can, keep writing. Maybe journalism but I'm not sure. I'm not sure I would choose a career that would use the creative writing, because it might sap my energies for my own writing. I hear teachers say that when they're teaching English they have no ideas left over and I don't want that to happen.

CROSSING I

I saw a horse's madness in this street today:
The whole afternoon becomes his tangled reins
Hot midday stillness splintered by his madness
Like a lord he writhes and rears
In every frantic leap a hundred struggling colts are thrown from
    the womb,
Strange harmony of lunacy and reason
As the walls of stares break before him like matchwood
Tread and tumble; he will not spare our fragile restrictions
A circle of frenzied vaulting
And he has marked this street forever

But something breaks even above the mad horse froth and rolling
    eyes
Sweet melody of sounds and sighs
As he breaks against the spitting cobbles
And the dying afternoon loosens its white anger grip.
This world deals so capably with death
This street does not tremble in taking one of its own.

IN ST. ETHELDREDA'S

You do that small thing.
Know nothing, think nothing,
Where the unlit stone
Supports dead prayer of seven centuries
Massed in drifts against muted glass.

The slow beat of awakening consciousness
Is the one you move to
And climbing, memory on memory,
Remain unsure of the presence, three-personed, whole,
Which moves to your side after so long,
And doubt, and climb back down.

In St. Etheldreda's
The echoes are prolonged
And purple is worn
Brushing up against the candle flame
And you have been close as you will ever be
To an admission that the flame,
That same flame, burning,
Is causing you pain.

Although you know nothing
And may soon stop wanting
The reassurance of feeling again,
For now, you do that small thing –
Understanding nothing, believe all,
And the certainty is awful, reverential, calm.

Ruth Hooley

RUTH HOOLEY WAS BORN in Belfast and studied English Literature at Queen's University, Belfast. She has recently completed a
Masters degree in Philosophy at the University of Ulster based on
the work of local author Janet McNeill. She lives in Belfast with
her daughter.

Her poetry has appeared in numerous journals, including
Poetry Ireland Review (No. 11,1984), *Fortnight, The Belfast
Review,* and *The Female Line,* an anthology of Northern Irish
women writers, published by the Northern Ireland Women's
Rights Movement, Belfast, 1985. She was sole editor of *The
Female Line,* the first collection of Northern Irish women writers
to be published. It includes prose, poetry and playwriting.

I first made contact with Ruth in her capacity as the editor of
The Female Line, which had impressed me by its breadth of
writing styles and vitality of female experience.

We sat in her kitchen, both initially rather shy with each
other, and talked about our families and our writing. When we
talked about *The Female Line,* it became clear that the book had
allowed her to explore in depth her own work in relation to the
politics and *literati* of Northern Ireland.

I STARTED WRITING WHEN I WAS SIXTEEN AND I REMEMBER getting a real buzz out of thinking, 'This is a poem, my goodness!' I felt an immense sense of power and satisfaction . . .

Had you had any formal training in creative writing? Not really. Studying English literature was obviously a formal education in the arts, and that would have influenced me. I also went to a couple of writing groups. But then the tables turned and I became a tutor for things like literacy.

Creative writing is useful in basic education. I also feel strongly about the gaps between esoteric writing and writing as self-expression or therapy. Both are important. That's a barrier to poetry, both for the reader and for the woman writer here in Northern Ireland. It is the last bastion of male authority. Literary poetry wants to cut its links with the primal creative instinct. Many people write poems but they wouldn't call themselves poets. That self-expression you have in childhood, which is often therapeutic, but is creative and regenerative as well, is very important. I don't want to lose that link. But now I also want recognition that this is good, 'poetry' with a capital 'P', that the two are part and parcel of something which should be recognized as valuable, and not pigeonholed into poetry that's printed and poetry that's for people who want to go to a writing class to get something off their chests.

You said that this dichotomy between esoteric writing and writing as self-expression exists particularly for women. Can you say more? I remember going to poetry readings and very rarely was there a woman reading, and if she did read she was fairly apologetic, and then it was a real inverted ego trip of a performance. That is generalizing, of course, but self-projection always seemed so difficult. Poetry is a form in which you have to have confidence in yourself to come out and speak it. I'm not talking about over-confidence. There are several successful women novelists in the North and there always have been. In short stories, less so, but there are some, and in playwriting there are some up-and-coming women. But in poetry there's only one, Medbh McGuckian. She's in a category of her own. She's not writing with the sharp, clever wit that the Ulster poets are known for, so she's not competing with the same style. I admire some of the male Ulster poets, certainly, and I don't think they have purposely excluded women. It's just that all the jokes, all the camaraderie, the poems too – it's all-male, and so harder to break into. It's like everything. Once a tradition is established, it's very

hard to break it down, and that's why the imbalance has perpetuated itself.

Concerning your own work, what inspires you to write? An
idea or an image. I find I need to write. Quite often what I begin to
write doesn't end up in the poem. It's a basic need to express my
impressions of the world and my experience of it, so that even if
something comes out as fairly polemical, it's usually come from
some image I want to communicate.

*What happens when you begin to work with an idea or an
image?* It usually explodes in lots of different directions and I find
it very difficult to know what direction I want to go in. Quite
often it goes in a direction I didn't intend, but that's part of the
process. The most important thing is to be selective. There are so
many ideas. You have to cut down all the things that are drawing
away from the central focus.

I just enjoy writing. It's the most absorbing thing to do. It
worried me that I didn't write very much when I was doing *The
Female Line*. In a year and a half I'd hardly moved at all, I was so
much more involved with other people's writing. But in the last
six to eight months I've started writing a lot more, and it's falling
into poems that want to be poems in themselves and more
broadly political writing.

In doing readings I have become aware that there are poems
that work when read aloud but don't work so well on the printed
page and vice versa. It's ·enjoyable to engage people with
something immediate. I like injecting humour into it. That's how
I've got more interested in performance and communication. But
the few poems I am really happy with are the quieter ones, more
formal, that you can go back to and get more out of — hopefully!
It's again the dichotomy between élite poetry and the plebeian,
between the things you want to be there for everybody and the
things you want to be there for yourself, and perhaps for some
sort of recognition. You haven't just got one voice. The dramatic
quality of poetry is very important, especially if you want to
communicate conflicting views. What I'm interested in, in the
whole male-female and the north-south issues, are the complexities, not the extremes.

*You said there is a difference between poems for the printed
page and those to be read aloud. Does this parallel your own
work, in that there are poems that come from an 'I' that seem to
me very clearly from you, and those that are personas of other
people?* Yes, if you are writing in a persona, that is a way of

dramatizing and projecting a stance. I don't think you can only write from experience. That would be terribly narrow and unimaginative. That's why I feel writing for therapy is limited, and to say that it's really good for women is a handicap – if that is all you are saying. It's very important if you have experiences you want to express, but there are lots of other things you might want to do, that are just as accessible to women. To say that women don't write the same way as men, or aren't capable of projecting their imagination, or being intellectually articulate is terribly crippling. That's partly why I'm disappointed *The Female Line* doesn't have more that is politically or intellectually challenging in it. Poetry is challenging in its many functions. A persona, for instance, is an interesting way of conveying a viewpoint and a lovely way of liberating energy in yourself.

Is there a difference for you, as a process, when you write from your own experience as opposed to writing in a persona? It's becoming increasingly difficult to write from my own experience. I'm not sure exactly why. I think perhaps the warning signs have come up for me. I don't want to write only about my own experience. I don't like exploiting my experience. It's a bit like fields you should leave fallow sometimes. There are also many issues that I am not immediately involved in, but I feel strongly about and want to write about. In the last six months my mother died. That's probably the worst thing that will ever happen to me, and I suppose that's why I'm not involved in writing from my own experience. It would just be black, either manic or self-indulgent.

Are you writing with an intention? Sometimes, but it doesn't always work. The poems I am pleased to have written are the ones that use a metaphor to carry their message. They've got something of their own for other people. They don't just depend on my own subjectivity.

Do you have an audience in mind? I find that very off-putting and debilitating, so I try not to think of one. Obviously some poems are more geared to women, but usually it's just the world outside I am addressing, whoever that is.

What for you is the relationship between form and content? I don't often use conventional forms, like sonnets, but I still want a certain rhythm. That matters a lot. If I'm using stanzas I like them to be the same length of line. It's what feels right. The form is geared to the meaning, but it's usually not the initial concern. Recently I tried to write a rondo, a medieval form, to express something about the way women are treated in the north and the south. But the more I tried to do it, the less the initial incentive was being expressed, and the more I was getting bogged down in the technicalities of getting it all to work, so I have left it for the time being. That often happens when you're trying to fit an idea into a straitjacket, although if it does work it can be an advantage. I also like to use as plain a language as possible.

I was conscious you were using rhyme in an unusual way. I'm not sure if it works for everybody, but I like doing that. I like echoes and internal rhymes. It's like changing the tempo. Poetry is more like sculpture than, say, illustration, and I find that very satisfying.

How would you define your own work? Would you say you are an Irish poet? It's very hard to figure it out. I think I would say I was a Northern Irish poet because I live here and am familiar with its politics and its people. But I don't identify with either of the two traditions. I was brought up in neither religion. I can't speak Gaelic Irish. Nor do I have any of the Orange Order tradition. I suppose I was brought up with a liberal Protestant background. I'm also partly British, but I'm not English. I live in Ireland and ideally I would like to see it united, but I can't imagine that happening.

How would you see yourself as a poet in relation to feminism or being a woman? When it comes to writing you're a writer. This is very important for women, to identify themselves as writers, rather than women writers. The category is very dangerous, but I feel it's very much a transitional thing. As long as there is an imbalance you have to have some way of redressing it. I am a woman who writes poems, and the fact that I am a woman essentially informs what I write. So I am really a woman poet, but I prefer just to be called a writer. I'm concerned with women's issues. I would say I'm a feminist, but that doesn't mean I'm a feminist poet. I'm not consciously being a feminist whenever I'm writing a poem. A lot of people seem to be scared of the term feminist. They say, 'I'm not a feminist, but...!' They feel threatened by it.

You said that being a woman informs your poetry. Can you say more about that? I'm writing primarily from a woman's perspective. With a lot of my poems the gender of the poet wouldn't matter, but knowing the gender of the poet does make it different. It comes across in the imagery. A lot of the poems in

The Female Line couldn't have been written by men. They couldn't have said the same things.

Have you ever, or would you ever, think of writing in the voice of a man? Yes, I've written a couple of poems like that. One was about a relationship between a man and a deaf and dumb woman who had died. He was communicating his memory of her, and because she couldn't speak, things like her smile meant very much more. Sometimes the emotional side of men is locked away. Very few of the men I know talk about their relationships, whereas the women I know do. There is this immense problem of the silent, strong person who must not show weakness. What happens instead is violence or alcohol or just complete indifference. It's an obvious generalization but it still stands.

These are marvellous poems. Do you like them? That's very good. It's only in the last few months that I've started thinking seriously about trying to get things together. I haven't sent off any poems for publication in the last two years and it frightens me that the hesitancy about doing so has returned. You can retreat into a real lack of confidence. And if you have a few blows, you just curl up into your little shell. You're afraid of going out in case something else happens to you.

Sometimes you really have to retreat and heal. It takes time and effort to appreciate what it means to be there for yourself. My mum was never there for herself. She was always there for other people, and always giving a tremendous amount.

I feel a strong dilemma about this. Women should have a right to abortion and to be on their own. In order to be creative they have to cut off a link or blood line. I am arguing for all these things, but at the same time I would claim that the most important thing is bringing up your own child. It's the most special thing, the greatest privilege you can have, and an immense responsibility. But why should you only be defined through that role? To define yourself in that role is to make it a substitute for your own. It's meaningless if you're trapped in it and patted on the head. And yet, if you do all these other things it doesn't mean you're going to be happier. In fact, it might be a lot more painful. But what I want is for women to grow up and outgrow these restrictions. It's easier to retreat into roles already made for you. At least you know where you are. Women aren't required to be adults, and yet they endure extremely maturing experiences, like childbirth. It's only when women hit thirty that they start thinking about what they want in life. They have a lot more to look

forward to as life goes on. A lot of poets use female imagery to
convey beauty or fertility or feeling, and yet women have really
strong qualities as well. I don't want women to be more like men.
I just want them to have a fair share of recognition. But I don't
know how you can gain that, except through a more plural
society with less fear of the unknown, of the things that aren't
you.

MY MOTHER'S HOUSE

You, coming downstairs
with a mewing black cat in your wake,
coming to the door with wet hands
or into the room with a tray of porcelain cups.

The day you went away
curtains hung unopened, rooms
held their breath, stagnant without
you to open doors and windows to the light.

It grew too tall for you in the end;
cobwebs hanging from corners of neglect
reflected nothing of your bright
attentive ways to make us all important.

I lived there a while
each wall untouched,
in your room where fingers of firstlight
poked through holes in the blinds to lace my bed.

It wasn't the same. Your house
shuttered within the one fading over the fireplace.
Each time I wanted it
to be you in the mirror, without white hair.

Finding a way to house the past
I see you better, back to the light
And when you visit me
It will be always summer in a shady room —

I will not need to ask.

CUT THE CAKE

Our Lady, dispossessed
on some alpen ice-cap
would not look out of place
in ski-pants, zipping
down virgin slopes
to the sound of music.

But wait for her second
coming round the mountain –
the icon-shattering thaw.
Our immaculate image, white-iced
and frosted for two thousand years,
might melt to nothing more divine
than a seething woman, cheated
out of sex and a son in his prime.

Rosalind Brackenbury

ROSALIND BRACKENBURY WAS BORN in London and studied at
Cambridge University. She has two children and lives in Edinburgh where she teaches creative writing.

Between 1971 and 1985 she published eight novels. Her first
book of poems, *Telling Each Other it is Possible*, was published
by Taxus Press, Stamford, Lincolnshire in 1987.

We held the interview in Ros's living room on a summer
afternoon. It felt like a writer's room, full of light, books and
paintings, papers and pens scattered about her typewriter on the
desk. She was very relaxed. The interview flowed from talking
about her life and her writing to her teaching. We seemed to talk
for hours.

I MOVED TO SCOTLAND FROM LEICESTER nearly five years ago.
The man I was married to at the time got a job, which he no
longer has, and I'm no longer married to him! But I'm here and it
suits me fine.

When did you start writing? I've always been at it. When I
was very young it seemed the most exciting thing you could
possibly do.

You went to University? I did. I went to Cambridge. I started out reading Architecture, failed that, then went on and got a History degree. I didn't write at all when I was a student. There didn't seem to be any time. Also, what people were writing at the time seemed quite intimidating stuff and I didn't understand what they were doing. I never thought of myself as a poet or a writer at that point. *How did you get back to writing after that?* Desperation, really. I started again properly just after my daughter was born in 1968. I remember thinking, Well, it's now or never. I really have to do this. I was quite depressed. It was a matter of personal survival.

So how did the first novel come about? It was quite an angry novel. I was furious about a lot of things at the time. I still had this idea of myself as a novelist and I thought, If I'm a mother and I'm going to spend all my time doing nappies and looking after babies, I'm just going to go under. I had to become a novelist in a way I could believe in, and if I allowed myself to drift off into domesticity I'd never get back.

And how did you manage to juggle your writing with being a mum? I've always found it difficult, as lots of people have. With one child I used to write when she was asleep, and luckily she fell asleep quite often. I kept going with my first two novels in that way. I gradually worked out a solution to two children. They both have disabilities, which has made life more complicated, and when my son was born I paid someone else to come in the mornings. I was more organized then than I am now. I had to be to keep doing it. So it's been a bit of a juggling act. It still is. Teenagers need your attention just as much as babies in some ways. And they stay up later at night too!

What inspires you? What motivates you to write? It's difficult to say. It's probably changed over the years. When I was young it was definitely making up another version of my life from the one that was going on at the time. At boarding school I had this thing about girls who'd run away with gypsies or gone to sea and done exciting things. I used fiction to escape from my life, which seemed pretty boring and awful. Then, when my first novel was accepted, I was writing as a kind of lifeline. I don't know that I thought I had anything to say. I just had to keep doing it. It's changed again now. I have more of an idea of what I want to say about things. It's more deliberate. I think of novels as informing and moulding the way people think and there's an awful lot I want to challenge at the moment, a lot of assumptions, old stale ideas about the way society has to be.

Talking about the way your novels challenge the way people see things, is that the same when you're writing poetry? There must be a thread of the same thing in it, because it's all me. But writing poetry surprises me more. Sometimes I don't know where it comes from. It feels more mysterious.

What happens when you write a poem? There's usually a quick first draft. Sometimes I don't change things but I tend to meditate over them and keep coming back, changing and pruning, trying out various things. It's like fishing, throwing a line and hauling things in. It's as if even the words are somewhat submerged and I think I know when I've got the right ones. There are some you have to chuck back. It's like letting down buckets into wells and waiting to see what comes out.

Are you writing more to be read aloud? I write both to be read aloud and on the page. I think it's a very good test for something if it reads aloud well. It's something to do with how it fits in with the way you breathe and everything.

Do you think of yourself as an English writer or a Scottish writer? I'm an English writer, but living in Scotland has made me much more conscious of what being English means to other people and to me. It brings it into sharp focus. From the historical point of view, England has colonized Scotland and given the Scots a bad time on the whole, but I don't feel people here are hostile. It's like being an American in Europe. You have to be conscious of what you've done and what your country's policy is towards these people at the moment. Then there's the language. You have turns of phrase that people don't understand. The way I talk and write has changed since I've been here. I've begun to take on Scottish expressions, partly because it appeals to me and partly to be understood. I dropped a few particularly English expressions I would have used five or ten years ago, and when I go back to England and do readings, they say, 'Your writing's full of Scottish words.' And I think, Well, there's a richness of language here, and phrases I really like. I'm not a Scottish writer, but I'm in contact with and close to lots of Scottish writers, so I don't feel out on a limb, but I realize that I'm outside a lot of their experience and they're outside a lot of mine.

So do you feel that your writing reflects an English literary tradition? Yes, because I've read a lot. Lots of English writers have influenced me. It's a great literary tradition and a tremendous one to belong to. Sometimes I'm not conscious who I'm quoting, but I think every writer goes through a stage of falling in love with other writers. I wanted to be Virginia Woolf. Every-thing I wrote was trying to be her. I've done this with various different people. You absorb what you can from them and then try to do it your own way.

How do you define yourself? As a poet, female poet, feminist poet? All of those in a way. I didn't think of myself as a poet for a long time. I'm a feminist. I'm a woman. And I suppose I write from those points of view. But it's difficult to define. You write from who you are and I'm now more of a feminist than I was twenty years ago. Then feminism was under cover, and I was brought up to think that poets were men. I would once have thought of it as a bit dangerous to be known as a woman poet, but now I would be proud to say that.

Did you feel that as a woman poet you would be dismissed? Yes. It was to do with that mystification I got at university. The poets I knew were men. They all wore black shirts and white ties and stayed up all night and were very decadent! And they wrote completely incomprehensible things. That stayed with me a long while. They were very extreme and dramatic about everything and that didn't seem to fit in with my own experience at all. I used to try to copy that in my attempts to make it as an existentialist poet. I didn't know any women who wrote poetry. And yet there's an odd thing there. My tutor at Cambridge was Kathleen Raine and I didn't know who she was. She operated under her married name, Mrs Madge. She was just the person who was keeping an eye on my architectural studies. It tells me how much women's poetry wasn't talked about then.

I felt when I read your book of poems that you were writing from your own experience, not as a persona. Nearly always. I mean, 'The Seal Woman', you could say it's me, but it's also a story. The 'I' is the woman in the story, but I'm quite close to her.

What drew you to that? A story in an anthology compiled by Iain Crichton Smith. I read it in a bookshop in the Highlands and began to feel quite peculiar. It's the kind of story that makes the hairs rise on the back of your neck. For me it was about women. It's about this young man, a fisherman, who comes across these beautiful women swimming and playing on the beach, but they're actually seals. There are lots of stories in the Highlands about silkies, who are human but seals as well. They leave their sealskins while they become human. The fisherman falls in love with one of them and takes her skin and hides it and asks her to go home with him and marry him. She says, 'All right', and

they're moderately happy, although she has the sense that she's
lost out somewhere. They have a child – I made her a girl in my
poem, I'm not sure if she was or not originally – and she finds this
beautiful sealskin wrapped up and hidden high up in one of the
barns. The mother whips it on and is back in the sea in a minute
and disappears. In some of the stories she comes back regularly,
which is nice and generous and housewifely, with presents of
fresh fish for the children. It's the whole thing about women
marrying and having children. You've often a feeling of giving up
on your own freedom and creativity. These silkie stories have this
ambiguity about being both animal and human, of being not
quite the same species as the man in the story. I felt intrigued by
that. It was new to me.

*Do you think about women as associated with nature and
animals?* Yes, very much so. *I also noticed a tension between
order and disorder.* Yes, the chaos breaking in from outside and
being bigger than the thing inside. Again it's to do with being
indoors and being domesticated. Like the seal story, you fit into
it, but you give up on something as well.

*In contrast, your poem 'Card Trick' is a powerful and vital
female image – 'I am the queen of magic'.* Yes. It pleased me a lot
when I'd written that. It's about that fantastic self-confidence
sometimes pre-adolescent girls have. They don't care if anyone's
watching or not. I used to have it myself when I was young, doing
cartwheels. I've seen young girls do things brilliantly and
beautifully in a sort of off-pat way and then something happens
when you're adolescent. You lose your nerve and begin to feel
clumsy. Or if somebody puts you down, you think, Oh, I
shouldn't do that. You shrink away.

*Then there's this amazing contradiction in your relationship
with your children, offering the poem, 'For a Writer's Children',
almost as an apology for having been writing all the time, being
an absent mother.* Yes! I often read that to other writers and a
little ripple goes round the room and they go, Ah! Yes. They feel
guilty. *Do you read it to your children?* My children are awfully
incurious. I don't think they're uninterested but they don't read
what I write very much. I think if my mother had been a writer I
would have been curious about what she said. But maybe it's
self-protective as well.

You teach creative writing. How did you get into that? I
started doing it with the WEA when I lived in Leicestershire. The
university wasn't keen. The English department didn't like

people coming in and assuming that anyone could write. It undercut their élitism! When I came to Edinburgh I wrote to the university's extra-mural studies department saying that this was what I wanted to do. They were very kind and said they were actually looking for somebody to do that. So I've been doing it since I've been here. It's been really interesting, because you begin to realize there's a tremendous amount of talent around and that people often just lack confidence to work on it as much as they'd like. It's a nice way of talking about writing and being in contact with people if you spend a lot of time solitarily working on something. So I enjoy it. There are people of all ages, and since unemployment has become more widespread there are now young men in the groups where there never once would have been. It's no longer just retired people and young mothers who couldn't depend on someone to look after their children.

Is it different working with women than with men? It depends on the balance. I've had to tell men to pipe down sometimes because they've much more of a habit of speaking out than women. But if there's a group which is mostly women, then men feel intimidated. Then there have been a lot of men, people of retirement age, who wanted to write about their war experiences, which they've kept bottled up for forty years. Some very moving stories come out of that. They just needed the encouragement to get down and do it. And you realize that was a time when men were shot out into something completely unusual, which challenged them, scared them, shook their lives up. Women on the whole have not had experiences like that, so their writing tends to be different. I think there's a great curiosity about what each other has to say. It teaches women a lot about how men really feel. Similarly with young women writing about childbirth or how they feel about being married. Some of these middle aged older men have never heard this. They're amazed! Their wives never told them what it was like. Sometimes they're quite shocked and upset by it. It's very important they hear it, I think.

Do you see writing as an act of power? Yes, I do. You lay hands on your own experience, and you make it thoroughly yours by writing about it. At the same time it's taking a step out of your own experience. It's saying, 'My experience is valid and what I want to say about it is valid.' You may have behaved like a victim in a particular situation, but writing about it transforms it.

What about a muse? I've been intrigued by this idea. Men have lots of variations of muses, but she's basically female. Quite often women poets use a man for a muse – the masculine bit of ourselves, if not an actual man. I don't think my muse is female, but I realize that I have to move on. I have to free myself from masculine imagery and ways of doing things. I often address things to a male figure, then say, 'Get out. I'll do it on my own.' This fiery energy I've referred to in one of my poems, I want to say, 'It's mine. It's ours. Not just me. It belongs to other women too.' They can't take it away from you. There's a wonderful bit Adrienne Rich wrote about walking through an airport to meet someone and knowing that the energy of going to meet this person could actually be used for lots of other things. You suddenly realize that this energy doesn't depend on the other person. It's all here anyway. You are generating it.

In one of my novels, *Sense and Sensuality*, the muse is a surreal encounter on a train to Edinburgh. He's not meant to be realistic. He's not a real person. But he's there all the time somewhere, sometimes helpful, sometimes mischievous, stirring things up, and the woman, who is a poet, keeps meeting him in various guises. Lots of people have criticized that. But that en-counter on the train – it's like a dream sequence – was for me the centre of the book. It was peculiar. It kept coming back to me like an obsession. I keep on exploring it.

One of the other poets I interviewed said she saw muses much more as antagonistic. I would agree with that, but you can't not do it. I've talked to feminists about this. Sometimes people have taken that episode in the train as being a portrayal of a rape, but it isn't at all. It's all to do with finding the other side of yourself. People have been investigating goddesses and female muses and finding out what they get from them, but I think you have to work with what you were given. I've been reading about George Sand, and I was very interested in this mythical figure in her life, not real, but very much in her imagination, in her grandmother's garden, that she had to keep hunting for. She wrote about him endlessly.

THE SEAL WOMEN
(from a traditional Scottish story)

The cold sea it is that knows me,
The water my lover as no man can be.

Fifteen years I waited in your houses
Dry-eyed in your beds

Awaiting transformation;

I am almost changed, almost:
But winter evenings pace by the cold strand
Picking from wet sand what the sea has left.
The horizon closes its low gleam
As I go home.

On other beaches I see them,
The women whom the sea has reached;
In their kitchens, through their shutters,
Whispered to them at their winter firesides
Lured them singing from beds and embraces.

While we are in your arms, yes and
Holding children, setting the table,
It is there, there is no forgetting it;
How can I say this to you who have so loved me?

The day of my marriage I forswore the sea
Turned inland, drew blinds, lit lamps
Awaited instructions.
I thought it could be done, the salt rank passion
Purged and tidal pull annulled,
Water and its urgency be stilled at last,
Water that carried my breasts weightless
And spread my fingers, gave my body speed,
That entered me all ways, washed out my womb
And slapped my buttocks flat
Carried me as the wind splays bird flocks
Pulsing in the slip stream
Made me one of many, moved as one.

I am one of them, the seal women,
There are others,
Wives, mothers, daughters,
Pacing the shore of this island
For the incoming tide
Waiting till the gap of sea and rock is closed
Waiting till there are no more margins.

I hear them sometimes, the others,
They were wedded to the sea in their infancy
Girl children left too long on the uncovered sand,
The sea has stroked between their shoulder blades

And washed their dark heads smooth
Already; they are won
They are the free swimmers
Nights they struggle with the sea in their souls
It washes and floods their dreams
Woken by the moon they turn and tremble
The men they sleep with fling out hands
Across the bed, and dread to find them gone.

They have daughters
And their daughters plunge easily in
Into the small waves, their wet heads round
And eyes staring with pleasure;
One day their daughters
Or their daughters' daughters
Will not return.
And here are the emptied houses
The kitchens, bedrooms, food cupboards
Chairs upturned; here is a house ransacked
For the one thing needed.
Daughter, little daughter,
Tell me where it is
My skin, that was taken from me
In love; tell me where it is, my freedom.

FOR A WRITER'S CHILDREN

I see you go, in other directions
Down through the wet grass on Sundays
At a time – afternoon – when families
When couples, when children –
Through the garden gate and out, I see you go.

The house, as suddenly emptied, settles around me
And once again time opens fresh as a box of pencils
At once there is possibly
(You whom I love in your absences)
A way forward (as your outward footprints track my page);
Eased of you as after a long labour
Myself again, flat-bellied, taut, knit
To my own purposes, I sit behind glass
At a table with yellow chrysanthemums.

Silence comes that is not ringed and rippled

With your voices, but pooled for deep fishing.
You are not here to reproach me,
I breathe out as once, tiptoeing from your rooms
Nightly with fingers crossed I breathed,
Gambled for time and lost with a bad grace.

Older, you expect less but look angrier
As others, mothers, pack thermos flasks
Sandwich in outings, Sundays, when couples
When parents, when families –

Yet how will you know that I love you now
Unless seeking the word that will truly draw
Your mackintoshed backs departing
I can let you go?

Sheena Blackhall

SHEENA BLACKHALL IS A POET and surrealist painter. She writes in North-East Doric Scots as well as English. She is a single mother and lives in Aberdeen with her two sons and two daughters.

Her poetry has appeared in numerous Scottish magazines including *Orbis, Chapman* and *Lines Review*. She has published five collections: *The Cyard's Kist* (1984), *The Spik o the Lan'* (1986), *Hame-Drauchtit* and *Nor'East Neuk* (1989) all published by Rainbow Press, Aberdeen and *Fite Doo/Black Crow* published by Keith Murray Publications. A collection of short stories entitled *A Nippick O' Nor'East Tales* (1989).

The first time I interviewed Sheena the tape recorder died. A year later we tried again. We sat for a long time swapping stories. When we started the interview, both chain-smoking, we were interrupted by one of her children returning home from school. I have never seen anyone put out a cigarette so fast! When two more kids arrived, Sheena said, 'I have something to keep them busy.' She ran cold water in the bath and poured into it green oil paint diluted with thinner. The oil floated on the surface making swirling green patterns. Every child, including myself, was given a scrap of wallpaper, which dipped across the water. The results were an array of abstract images. 'It's called marbling. We play a game of how many things we can see in each one.'

I DIDN'T START WRITING, I started painting, primarily to express things visually. I wanted to become an artist when I was about five! Everything from then on was geared to that end. Later I tried to work out what the appeal of painting was. I think, basically, it was the idea that if I saw something beautiful I wanted to capture it and, in a sense, perpetuate it for myself. Rather as people like cave painters started out. There is an element of magic attached to the image. Image equates the thought. I think in images as opposed to words. There's very little dialogue in my mind. So, when I couldn't further my career in art, after an initial period of readjustment I rechannelled it into trying to do the same thing in words.

You told me a story, the last time I interviewed you, about your dad advising you to write to the laird. That's right! When I started writing I became very involved in local history and in poetry. I've written poems since I was fourteen or fifteen, and I had a collection of poems ready. But it's very difficult to get into print and difficult to know where to start if you haven't gone through the normal academic channels of university or what-have-you. So I asked my father what he suggested and he thought I should contact one of our Deeside lairds. My father was sure that he would be able to further anything artistic or literary as there's a long tradition of that.

The laird's wife, actually, was very helpful. She sent me the name of an agent in Glasgow and took a copy of the collection for the agent to read. So they helped a little, and they did invite me up to meet them but I couldn't do that. Our family have been tenant farmers on the same farm since 1622, almost as long as the laird's family have been on Deeside, and when you're in that feudal set-up, there's a tremendous block against overstepping yourself and meeting on a one-to-one basis.

Crossing boundaries? Yes. My grandfather used to compose bothy ballads. He was a fine singer and would be invited up to the gentry's houses if they were having an evening. They used to invite some of the particularly talented tenants and he would go up and sing. So we're very adept at touching the forelock!

So what inspires you to write? Different methods of writing. The main method I use, in the simpler poems, is a straight run of surrealist or straightforward imagery. I was greatly influenced by

René Magritte and what he'd written on image as thought and the power and mystery inherent in the image. So a lot of my poems fall into that category. The second method, which I don't use so much, is based on the sound of words, onomatopoeia. I've written some pieces purely to exploit the rhythm and sound of words. The rhythm comes through my being born in an extended family where my maternal grandmother and I shared a room when I was little. She had a store of ballads which she had been taught as a child and she passed these on to me. Also my father delighted in singing. So the strong natural rhythms sometimes come through.

Later I was lucky to meet one of the travelling folk, John Watt Stewart. I taped him and he taught me the tinkers' ballads that he knew. I'd had professional singing lessons as a child, but in professional singing lessons you're supposed to sing from the score. And John said, 'Tear up all that. Ignore all that.' You let the music take priority. The song is supposed to come through you, you don't mould the song. You're just the vehicle for it. And to do that, you have to let it take you over, which is a different method altogether. They prefer it unaccompanied as well. If you feel that the particular song requires to be projected or heightened, then you do as the song dictates.

The ballad rhythms also came through at school. At secondary school we had a teacher who was very interested in the old Scots ballads, like 'The Twa Corbies' and 'The Ballad of Otterbourne', and we had to learn these. I enjoyed that, again because of the rhythm.

The most difficult method of writing poetry that I've found, but possibly the most rewarding, is using the Buddhist technique of meditation. That's bringing the mind to one-pointedness. It's an extension of concentration. You're required to be completely alone, very quiet. You still the mind as much as possible. It's as if you were panning for gold. If you can think of your past as a river and yourself as panning for the little gold bits lying at the bottom, you can take a moment that was important to you, or an object, or an animal. I've done it with deer. The first time I saw a deer I was probably about five. The one way you can recapture the freshness of that is to try to imagine the meeting as it was when you were that child, not as an adult with preconceived ideas of what the thing was. It's much more vivid if you do that. You sit as still as possible, until the particular image of the meeting begins to cluster around it linked images or emotions.

And only then would you sit down and try to write about it.

Does it happen very quickly when you write? I went through a very productive phrase for about three years when I wrote about three poems a day. Moods were alternating very quickly. I would write something in Scots which was quite light, then there would be something in English which was very serious, and maybe on the same day I would do a surrealist painting. That output continued for about three years. I amassed about five hundred poems in that time. Latterly it hasn't been so easy, possibly because I'm on medication to slow the mind, which is fine in a way, but it's putting a brake on the creativity. I haven't considered the option of risking coming off it to capture the push because the imagination is a very powerful and dangerous thing.

I did learn that much from the Buddhists, that in the West you're taught what to think, but you're not taught how to think. So practices of meditation have been helpful because they teach me how to think, how to control thought and, in a sense, how to control imagination. I found that I was so involved with the image I was working on that when I finished a particular charcoal sketch one day, the image moved, which is, of course, a hallucination. It wasn't frightening and it didn't last long but I knew I'd reached a dangerous boundary and possibly it was time to draw back. It's a little alarming because you aren't able to tell the difference between conscious use of the imagination and something involuntary. It's a question of finding the balance between the two.

I write in Scots sometimes and sometimes I write in English. If I'm writing about something intuitive it'll come in Scots because it's my first language. If it's conceptual or cerebral then I use English, because I was trained to think logically in English at school.

Why are you writing or painting? Is it for other people? Is it for yourself? Do you see or hear an audience? No, I don't hear or see an audience. We were a very insular family. People say, How can you be born in Aberdeen and have this cultural background of the North-East so richly from the farming side of it? It's because we were so insular, so contained within the family unit. My greatest difficulty came when I started school, when I had to leave the family unit and was confronted with what was to me an alien English culture. I couldn't handle that. I divided, consciously. I kept my home life as separate as possible from school life. I adapted very quickly, as children will do if there's any sort of ridicule, to using English, but I left it at the door when I went back home, and comfortably adapted back to Scots. What it does, eventually, is to make you tremendously insecure, and for self-preservation in any sort of company, you tend to be better in a one-to-one situation. Put into a crowd, I disintegrate.

I had to give a reading once in Edinburgh with about six other poets. One spoke in Gaelic and when I spoke with him I went into a West Coast lilt. Another was a Glaswegian and I went into Glaswegian. Another talked in English so I went into English. There was also a Caribbean and I found myself going into Caribbean. It's like mimicry but it's unintentional. It's not even flattery. I wouldn't like to say what it is. It's mirroring. I didn't know what I was doing by the end of the night. I got plastered. I didn't know what else to do! When I was so drunk, I couldn't speak at all, and I found that very helpful!

Possibly this is why I prefer painting. I'm happier painting. It's a universal language. You're expressing exactly what you want to express.

I'll tell you what I occasionally do in short stories, which is an extension of the day-dreaming I did as a kid. People used to say, 'What are you smiling at?' or 'What are you laughing at?' and of course I was right in the middle of something very interesting, and they hadn't a clue why I was wandering down Union Street with this laugh on my face. Possibly I was working out something particularly nasty that had happened at school and turning it the other way around, so I came up on top. But I found I did better in writing short stories if I went into the past tense and changed persona and wrote it as a male. I could work out various little things through my stories, if anything particularly bothered me, and I couldn't work it through otherwise.

From the way I write people expect me to be much older than I am. Perhaps it stems back to the fact that I wasn't brought up in a young household. My grandmother was eighty-odd when she died, and my parents were fortyish when I was born. Their perspectives were different. They didn't particularly value materialistic things. They set a higher value on achievement, which is a bit of a sharp sword. The Celts are a highly competitive race. But in the academic world the concentration's on team effort. I found that extremely difficult. I couldn't cohere as part of a team at all. I would excel in things where you tested yourself to the utmost, but when it came to holding myself back and fitting in like a jigsaw, I couldn't do that, and I didn't like it. I hadn't been brought up to be a team effort person, I had a very strong competitive drive.

Well, of course, later on you question what is the worth of winning competitions and of being aggressively ambitious. In some ways, it's spoiled quite a lot because it means that, as the tinkers tried to teach me, if you are geared toward winning you're not doing justice to the music. The music isn't the end in itself, it's what you can get from it, a certificate for this or a cup for that. And in doing that, you've destroyed the enjoyment, the nowness, of the music or the art. So I'm trying, a little late, to unlearn some of the competitiveness, and just settle down to take creativity when it comes, and not force it.

I spoke to a woman in Southern Ireland who talked about muses, and she talked about male and female muses, and that different poets work with different muses. I was struck by what you said, that you would write short stories in the voice of a male, and then you talked about the imagination being very powerful. Do you experience it as a muse in any way? I was given a book to read called The Horned God, which deals with the animus-anima. It basically said that there's male and female in all of us and that we should come to terms with that. Possibly the ideal would be a well-balanced hermaphrodite personality. I think a lot of people are coming round to this.

I have found, in talking to women writers, that there are male ways of thinking. And there are people who seem to have a very original cast of mind, to whom you would almost say, 'That's a masculine way of thinking', which I suppose is an awful sellout for your own sex! But when I was younger I used to say, 'Why did I get the short straw?', because you're not very old before you realize that boys and men are esteemed and women really aren't. And people would say, 'Why do you want to do this art-thing, you'll just get married and have kids'. I used to be furious because I couldn't see why that should be, or why I should be forced into that role. I didn't like pink dresses and frilly knickers and I didn't like dolls.

I was absolutely terrified the first time a doll arrived at the house. I'd never been interested in them. I just wanted to paint and draw, and I think my mother felt I was too much into that. So this doll arrived. I think I was about five. It was called Deirdre. It was one of these china creations and it was absolutely dead. It was like looking at a little corpse. It was very cold and hard to touch. My mother went into raptures and all I wanted to do was smash it. I thought, 'Why has she bought me this thing?' I thought, this was my replacement. This was what I was supposed to be. They like this, but they don't like me. They can't accept me. I never played with it. I shoved it in a drawer and my mother was furious because it had cost her about five pounds, which was a lot of money in those days!

I was never interested in girls' things. At school we were channelled according to how well we did in our IQ tests. If you passed reasonably well you went into the Classics section which meant you got academic subjects and didn't touch cookery. That agreed with me very well because there again the female was being put down, and I thought, 'Oh good, they really think I'm beyond this. I couldn't accept that there were women who enjoyed cooking. I couldn't accept the very feminine women I met. I still can't. I squirm when people gurgle and goo into prams.

You think when your own children are born, that this great surge of motherhood is going to come upon you, and you're going to become a mother with a capital 'M'. I remember when my son was born. They brought this child and I thought, 'That's a stranger.' What I saw was a new individual and I thought, 'I don't know you and you don't know me. We are going to have to do a lot of learning with each other.' I think the child intuits that. He knew I wasn't comfortable changing him or anything, because I didn't know how he operated. I didn't know if I would break his arms if I tried to take his vest off. Everything was difficult. It didn't come naturally, as all the books and all the hype say it should, and I'm still working on it!

I went to one of the Polygon book launches in Edinburgh where a woman read a story about a teddy bear. When her child was born the mother could get no sleep. It screamed itself hoarse night and day. The health visitor arrived at the door and said, 'You must get your sleep', and she had just managed to drop off to sleep when this woman arrived at the door again and said, 'Oh, it's good you're getting your sleep'. She crawled back to bed, completely shattered, and tried to get back to sleep, when the child woke and started to scream again. She clutched this teddy bear – she was reverting to infantile ways; she couldn't stand it anymore – and shook it so hard its head flew off! Once she'd read this story, there was a woman in the audience who had wandered in with bags of shopping and she was quite aghast. She thought it was a horrible story. How could you write a story like that about a child? I felt like saying, 'Very easily'. It's such a thin line because the child doesn't understand that not everybody is an instant mother. It's not like coffee. It doesn't turn brown automatically. Some people never get to it! In some ways you envy men, who aren't similarly encumbered. They are free to do this and that.

I wouldn't be without the children. They are a hold on the realities. One of my functions as a single parent is to see the children up and settled to the best of my ability. That is a very good reason for me to continue when there may be darker passages. If you're having a creativity block, or you're extremely down, then you hold yourself together for the children. I don't know if a man would do that. They can walk away. So there's sufficient of the woman in me not to walk away. It's difficult to say how much it affects writing. I've got a lot of stories out of it – not exploiting it, but working it through, trying to understand how families interact on each other. You have to learn compassion. If you're going to try to understand other people, you've got to try to be that other person. It's good therapy. Role-play and story telling help me a lot.

Do you see yourself as a Scottish poet? I find my hackles go straight up when people write 'poetess'. I don't want to be judged as a woman. I hate that. It's like what Samuel Johnson said about the woman preacher, 'When it is done, it is not done well, one is only surprised that it's done at all.' And when people say, 'Oh, woman writer,' it's as if they're making allowances for you. I would rather be judged on the merit of my work, not by the fact that I'm female.

The Scottishness makes for individuality. I couldn't conceive of myself as English or anything else. Sometimes I swither, because it decreases the size of your reading public. This is not any reflection on the language, it's just a statement of fact. You may write what you think is an excellent story in Scots, but only a certain percentage are going to understand it without a glossary. And that means that your work is being read in translation. So I think anybody writing in Scots should be able to write in English as well. I write in Scots because it's easiest for me.

THE TEA PAIRTY

English bedd in the wireless.
We let it oot, whyles,
Turnin a knob, fur a bit diversion.

Min', we hidna a doonricht aversion tilt,
It jist didna belang;
Keepit fur Sunday best,
Like an auld psalm.
Cam the day o' the pairty.
'Ye'll enjoy't,' quo mither,
Hale an hairty.
'Say please an thanks.
Dinna be quanter,
Ye canna gae wrang.'

The genii wis oot o' the wireless ...
Somebody'd clapped a bin-lid
Ower the Scots.
There wis a rowth o' fancy pieces, I mind that,
An a wummin, dragon-dreidfu, in a green frock,
Speenin broon saps, intil a dish.
'Fit'll ye hae?' she speired,
(The genii did some sma translation,
Takkin peety on a stranded fish)
'I'm easy. I'll tak onything.'
An did the dragon nae blaw rikk?
Reid's a labster, ower ill-natured tae spikk?
'A conscious decision,' quo she, 'is little tae ask
Efter aa my scutter.'
'I'll takk the mochie mousse,'
I managed tae hubber.
'Wis't a nice pairty?'
Speired ma mither.
'Fit wye are ye kickin the wireless?'

bedd – stayed; whyles – sometimes; min – remember; tilt – to it; quanter –
awkward; rowth – abundance; fit – what; speired – asked; rikk – smoke; reid –
red; spikk – speak; scutter – messy work; mochie – mouldy; hubber – stammer;
fit wye – why

THE LINTIE

The lintie lichtit on the bough
Abune twa lovers true
An' sweet an' lang she sang her lilt
Fin love wis fresh, an' new.

Fin love grew auld, the bird cam back
Bit didna hinner lang –
For 'Fegs,' quo she – 'there's nocht bit strife
A spittin' futterat's man an' wife
I widna waaste ma sang.'

lichtit – alighted; abune – above; lilt – tune; fin – when; bit – but; hinner – hinder; futterat – weasel

THE SERPENT

Gin I wis ivy, I wid twine
Yon lang, lean limbs, unyieldin's steen
Sear laggard thocht, a kinnelt vine
Wi leaves o' langin, fill his een

He'd learn tae loe me, quick eneuch
Gin he waur bane, an' I waur bluid
A flytin tide, I'd draw awa
Leavin' him pale, as I am reid

I am the serpent i' the stoor
Tho lower than the dust I lie
I haud the knowledge o' delicht
Oh wha daur pass me by?
A thoosan-fauld, they crush my heid
I hissin rise, an multiply.

laggard – tardy; kinnelt – kindled

Tessa Ransford

TESSA RANSFORD WAS BORN in India and raised in Scotland. In 1981 she founded The School of Poets in Edinburgh, which offers advice, criticism and support to practising poets. She was also instrumental in founding the Scottish Poetry Library of which she is currently the Director. She has three daughters and one son and lives in Edinburgh.

She has published two books as Tessa Stiven, *Poetry of Persons* (1976), and *While it is Yet Day* (1977), both published by Quarto Press. She has published three books with Ramsay Head Press, Edinburgh: *Light of the Mind* (1980) which was awarded a Scottish Arts Council Book Award, *Fools and Angels* (1984) and *Shadows from the Greater Hill* (1987). *A Dancing Innocence* was published by Macdonald Publishers in 1989. She is also editor of *Lines Review*.

I had corresponded with Tessa in her capacity as Director of the Scottish Poetry Library as well as a poet. Going to the library I had no idea what to expect. Tessa materialized as a gentle, warm woman. We got to know each other over the following weeks as I worked and read at the library. We did the interview in her living room which looks out over Arthur's Seat. We started quite formally, sitting in chairs facing each other. Ten minutes into the interview, Tessa said 'I'm writing a series of poems about the view outside my window. Would you like to hear some of them?' Soon we were on our hands and knees, with Tessa's poems spread all over the floor.

I STARTED WRITING WHEN I was about six. My father was in India and my brother was at boarding-school, so I was living on my own with my mother. She has a letter from my father saying 'Please thank Tessa for her poem'. So that's how I know. Later it's been when I've been thrown back on myself that I've written, when I was pretty unhappy at school in my teens and then when I was a student. I did get a poem in the student magazine, which was quite a thrill, but I didn't think of myself as going to be a poet. I was just working out what I needed to do.

So you trained yourself basically? Yes. I didn't have any contact with other poets at that time. I graduated when I was 20, was married at 21 and then went to Pakistan. I did occasionally write things, but it wasn't until I returned to Edinburgh in 1968 that I started writing more seriously.

What inspires you to write? Is there a difference between your earlier writing and what you wrote after coming back to Edinburgh? It's always been some sort of passion, although it might be some idea rather than just an emotion. I get excited by ideas and have crazes for new thinkers I discover. I've had a Teilhard de Chardin phase, and a Rilke phase, and a David Jones phase, and an anti-nuclear phase, which still goes on. I also had a long struggle with religion, but I'm finished with that now.

When an idea comes into your mind, how do you work with it? It has to be more than one idea. An idea has to link up with something else to make a poem. It's got to have an 'objective correlative', something else to be projected on to or reflected in. Sometimes the thing will give me the idea and sometimes the idea the thing. Rilke's good on this. He says that poets are always transforming. They take from outside and transform it inwardly. They also take from within and transform it outwardly.

People have said I'm not a visual poet. I'm not good at remembering details of things I've seen. It's more the analogy I'm looking for. But I have attempted to change. Since I came to live here two years ago I had the idea of writing poems in the form of a diary. I have experimented in writing poems based on what I see from this window. I haven't done it every day, but I did about 50 over the course of a year. Each poem isn't entire in itself. I want the whole sequence to be the poem. I'm editing them down now to make them into a book, perhaps with photographs. That was a deliberate attempt to set myself an outward focus. Rather like painting an icon. Arthur's Seat is my icon, and each poem is slightly different: different colours, different moods, different effects. Any time you write about landscape you're really writing about your inscape as well. I tend to write about myself. I'm not very good at projecting myself into other people.

There's a funny story about a dramatic monologue I once wrote about a Pakistani woman lamenting the birth of another daughter! It was published and a year or two later I sent some more poems to the same editor, about Dido and Aeneas this time, and I got them back with a note saying, 'These are not an authentic woman's voice. I liked the one much better about the birth of your daughter!'

I was interested in your fascination with Dido and Aeneas. Yes, that seems to me a marvellous parable for what happens to women. *How do you mean?* Well, you pour out your riches and then some duty always comes first with men. With women love comes first. I think duty is a very evil thing in many ways. If it's going to cut across personal relationships, then what sort of a duty is it? There is a conflict, there's no doubt about it. Men are very scared of women. And many women, I think, have not written because of this, or have written under pen-names, or have written and not published. Until recently, with the encouragement of supportive families, women have just kept quiet about their writing, and especially poetry. Novels can be projected into another age, another place and time, but poetry has to come from the power of our experience and our own mental fight. It's a fight all the time to believe in ourselves and to keep our thoughts clear when people keep telling us we're wrong or stupid.

You use a lot of rhyme and metre. How do you make the decision about what form goes with what content? It's very instinctive. Usually I'll start writing down my ideas fairly freely, and if they seem to be taking an intrinsic rhythm and shape, then fine, but if not, then I think, maybe this needs a stricter form. With a number of poems I've tried them several ways until I've found what seemed right for them, because I'm looking for the best form for what I'm trying to say.

As a student I studied German. I steeped myself in the German poets, and English poets, like Hopkins and Donne and D. H. Lawrence, and I would imitate them. I also learned a lot from translating the German poet, Hölderlin. Discovering the Greek metres he used was a revelation. There are things to learn in poetry and I get a bit impatient with people who think you're born a poet or you're not and there's nothing to learn. I like using rhyme and metre, but I wouldn't do it in a mechanical way. They have to come from within you. You take them in and absorb them.

You talked about women trying to find new forms. How do you see that happening? I'm interested in the theory that women shouldn't have to conform to forms which have been devised by men over the years and that they should explore new forms that suit them, but what these are I don't quite know. Possibly we should just use the old forms with freedom, make use of them and manipulate them for our own purposes. Somebody said to me recently that women are more interested in process and men in project, that men want to achieve something and women are interested in what they're doing and not necessarily in any finished result. I find this a very useful way of analysing attitudes. It's something to work on.

When I wrote a long Irish epic based on the story of the 'Peace People' I tried to experiment with form and to vary the forms according to who was speaking or what was happening. I remember telling someone from the university English department here that I was writing an epic and he said, 'Oh, is it in blank verse?' And I said, 'No, as a matter of fact, it's in *gestic* verse.' And he was wonderfully perplexed because he didn't like to admit he'd never heard of gestic verse. He obviously didn't know because I'd just made it up! I meant verse suitable to a heroic deed, like the *Chansons de gestes*, but also the gesture, as if you were gesturing while you were speaking. So, if you're a soldier your gestures will be short and sharp, and if you're an Irish Catholic woman from the Falls Road you might have a certain urgency. I tried to vary the rhythm to indicate what was happening: the urgency and chaos of the situation, the sense of desperation the women had when they started these marches. That's the kind of thing I mean about women exploring new forms. How do we speak? How do we feel? Are the forms reflecting that?

How did your ideas for the Poetry Library and the School of Poets come about? The School of Poets has meant a great deal to me. I started it because I needed to. I went to America and stayed with the poet, Julia Budentz, in Cambridge, Massachusetts. There I met her friends, all very active, intelligent, confident women who seemed to expect me to be the same. If I said I was a poet, which I hadn't really dared to say in Scotland up till then, they were interested and wanted to know about my work in a way that nobody had been in Scotland, not even other women. And when I came back to Scotland I felt I couldn't breathe. But I couldn't leave either. My children were here. My life was here. So I decided I had to change the environment.

I don't know how I did it. I was fanatical. I had to be at that time. I had no one to discuss my work with and then I met one or two other people who were the same. I discovered that there were many talented people and I was terribly lucky to have been published because I wasn't any better than them. It was a very humbling experience.

The Library grew out of the School although many people who support the Library wouldn't support the School. There is still the idea in Scotland that you shouldn't share your poetry with other people, that you should simply shut yourself up in your room and write. Most of the well known published Scottish poets despise the idea of getting help from other poets, and yet I know many of my poems have been greatly improved by other poets' suggestions. It's a learning situation, but the idea of learning in that way is very alien in Scotland. With most of the workshops here it's a visiting poet who comes and talks about himself and that's meant to be terribly enlightening to other people. That's not what we do in the School of Poets.

Another thing we've done is we've tried to link up with art and music. We've had conferences on poetry and art and poetry and music to try to get composers, artists and poets to meet each other. There's far too much segregation of the arts and they really do inspire each other. I'm inspired by music and painting a lot, and I'm sure that painters and musicians might be inspired by poetry if we could all have a bit more sharing. The same is true of the *Women Live* programmes which started in 1982. Women came from all the different arts together to do them. But that needs to happen right across the board – much more interaction and less fear of stepping out of your own specialization.

Do you consider yourself a poet, a woman poet, a feminist poet, a Scottish poet – any of these? First of all, it's important to be able to say that one is a poet. We should also be able to say we're student or apprentice poets, as you can say you're an art student or a dance student. This business of being either a poet or not a poet, and only a poet if you're published and someone's read you, or only a poet after you're dead and someone says you're some good, like a saint – you mustn't call yourself a poet, you must wait for someone else to call you one! What's so great about being a poet? It just happens to be what you do – no better or worse than being a cake-maker or a gardener.

I'm unhappy at being categorized as a woman poet, but on the other hand I'm not scared of admitting I'm a woman. Feminism has been a great help to me, although I was quite old when it came along. I had always believed in myself, but for a long time I allowed myself to be put down. Then in the late seventies I went to a Quaker women's group and that was also a help because you could talk about your own ways of dealing with life and admit to what was difficult, instead of pretending that everything was fine as we tended to do in the old days. To admit that things were difficult then was to admit to failing. Feminism confirmed my belief in myself. But I don't want to be put into any slots. There was an extraordinary review in *Akros* of my collection, *Light of the Mind* – really quite a pure and religious book, most people think, but this review said it was full of 'blood, tears and mammary glands!' When you think of the average man's poetry, full of explicit erotic detail, it's quite extraordinary! Women poets can be totally different and I daresay I'm more intellectual than some women would like, but I don't want to be told what's an authentic woman's voice by anyone, man or woman.

What about being a Scottish poet? Inasmuch as I regard Scotland as my home I would say I am Scottish. But I don't write in Scots. I didn't learn it at my mother's knee. It isn't my native tongue. I do understand it quite well and appreciate its richness, but I couldn't write in it authentically. And I haven't got round to learning much Gaelic. So I write in English.

Scotland is my home. I don't know England. I've only lived there for three years of my life. I belong to Scotland. I love the country. I don't altogether love the people, but I feel I understand them, the complicated mixture that they are. It's got tremendous strengths, Scotland, tremendous richness and variety, but one of the things I find most difficult is the lack of spontaneity, the taciturnity and the reticence about feelings. I tried to express it in a poem called *Ode to Edinburgh*. A lot of one's own spontaneity gets limited by a lack of it around one. Part of me is very spontaneous and when I was in India and Pakistan I felt very much at home. I loved the way people would express their feelings, the way they would cry and laugh and when anyone was ill they would cry and moan and wail. They would hug you and weep over you and give you flowers. I can identify with that. But in Scotland people only get to that state after several glasses of whisky!

The problem is that the only emotion that's acceptable in Scotland is anger. Obviously one should be able to express one's anger, but here people, especially men, express *all* their emotions through anger. Fathers seldom cuddle their sons. It's a real sensual deprivation. And anger is so debilitating. It crushes people. It's using anger as the vehicle for all the other emotions. You can't cry, you can't be tender, you can't weep, you can't embrace, but you can be angry.

ODE TO EDINBURGH
(from *Light of My Mind*)

City of my north
of dispassionate views,
calculated contours –
to your volcanic remnants
we lift not eyes
but only intellect...

when rain and mist caliginous
obscure the skyline
we adhere to stone structure
and regain lucidity...

How sharply you defined me and indelibly!
Early I was persuaded
that nothing is but north...
even east and west beyond our compass...

Much I admire uprighteousness
and your grey endurance
but it has cost me warmth

Among the startling gorse
I am asunder
torn with endless loss;
identity is northern,
my south, my soul remedial
but unremedied
for ever.

FEBRUARY 14TH
(from *Shadows from the Greater Hill*)

The scene is set for me daily.
Again and again I paint it
as if an icon:
shall I make the cloak of the Virgin red?
How much to incline her head?
What proportion of sky
and cherubim, if any?
Where the square trap
door that leads to Hell?

Today's beauty lacks mercy:
calm, pale, unperturbed
in sleet, hail, keen wind.
Show it by nothing:
the hard edge of Hell's cliff,
by the very vacancy:
a walker straining forward
like dog on leash
but his dog unleashed in the wind.

Or shall I paint the mountain
as an elephant-god
fat, sleek, pregnant,
feet turned up
navel protruding
and wide, flat ears?
He is detached from predicaments
of weather or winter;
laughingly knows of desire's flame
never quenched to nirvana,
but lit anew in rock and sinew
year by year.
He is complete, content to be
gross, yet noble,
inevitable yet enabling.

Anne Hartigan

Photo: Christine Bond

ANNE LE MARQUAND HARTIGAN, poet, painter and playwright, was born in England and studied Fine Art at the University of Reading. She has lived in Ireland since 1962. She belongs to the Women's Studies Forum at University College, Dublin. She has six children and lives in Dublin.

In addition to receiving numerous bursaries for poetry, play-writing and batik, her award-winning epic poem *Now is a Moveable Feast* was performed on Radio Telefís Éireann in 1980. Her publications include *Long Tongue* (1982) and *Return Single* (1986) both published by Beaver Row Press, Dublin. Her paintings have appeared widely in Ireland and England. Two of her plays, *Beds* and *La Corbière* were performed as part of the Dublin Theatre Festival.

I met Anne at a poetry launch in Dublin. I explained my research project and asked if I might interview her. She questioned me thoroughly as to what exactly I was doing and to what end. Satisfied with my answers, she consented. We met at her house late one morning. As she made the coffee, I had a chance to glance at some of her paintings. They were strong, colourful portraits and abstractions, done in bold brushwork. We sat

outside in her back yard. It was like sitting in one of her paintings; it was April and there was a heatwave in Ireland and all the
flowers in Anne's garden were in bloom. The air was heavy with
the scent of cherry blossom.

I STARTED WRITING IN the sixties when I was still a farmer's wife.
I probably started for two reasons. I had six children and I was
isolated from my painting sources. I didn't give myself the space
to paint. I would have had to claim it. Writing can be done almost
anywhere and very privately. I met a woman who didn't even
have a shelf to put her work on. She used to carry her notebook
around. I wasn't as bad as that! Also there's much more confirmation in writing than there is in painting. I put that down to the
historical factor. This was an occupied country. Things can be
destroyed, houses and possessions. You have to have a certain
amount of wealth to possess paints and paintbrushes. People say
the Irish are not visual. I don't think that's true. But they could
write, and if they couldn't write they could sing. So the word has
a great strong use behind it in this country. It has in England, too,
but England was richer and able to have a painting tradition.
Here it wasn't so. It was mostly the élite who could do the
painting. So I felt more affirmation for writing.

Is it a different process, writing and painting? I don't really
know. I don't think it is. It's just a different medium. We all use
words so in a way we all have a training as talkers, word users.
The poetic impulse is the thing that moves you, that makes you
want to write or paint. I think they have a different effect on you.
I find it more stressful to write. Then again, you can do that and
nobody need see. If you're painting a picture you're making a
statement which is very hard to hide. Just recently I've been
painting very small, but I used to want to paint really large! A lot
of women of my generation wanted to, and had to. They had to
say, 'Look, bloody hell, we're here!' When I trained as an art
student, if anybody said, 'That's feminine', I would have been
appalled. I felt that meant wishy-washy anemones in a bowl,
something incompetent, weak, feeble. It sounds terrible treason
now, but then there was only one woman painter put up to us as a
model, Gwen John. Reverse that – if I was a male and only saw
one male painter. That puts it in proportion.

What inspires or drives you to write? I used to say I just had
to. It was a matter of survival. I always knew I was going to do
something in these fields. I had this passion, this energy. Without

energy you can do nothing. It's a great word: 'energy'. It's gritty.
It's gutsy. It's like breeding. It's a belief in life, a confirmation of
life. Laura Huxley said in a rather dotty but lovely book, *You Are
Not The Target*, that war is energy used destructively, whereas a
work of art is energy used creatively. War is followed by appallingly ruthless, relentless passion and in a way you have to have
something similar. It doesn't need to be ruthless. The only time
you should be a perfectionist is with your own work.

Have you always trusted that passion and energy? Yes, I
think so. Why do you ask that? *I was thinking about an article
which described the conflicts a woman feels when she's writing.
You have no role models, no history, no tradition.* We do have
role models, but we've been denied them. Particularly in this
country. The modern movement this century was brought into
this country by women painters. All these women were either
unmarried or married for a very brief period of time. Many had a
very big output and yet they still aren't given their place. It's part
of the whole pattern of the history of this country which I've had
to learn. I'm an Irish-Jersey woman who has returned. This
doesn't often happen. My father was a Jerseyman living in
England. He was very pro-Britain and anti-Ireland. My mother
was Irish and brought me back to her village every year. I was
very torn between the two. And here I am now, the weeping
mother on the shore with six children and four of them out of the
country. The wheel goes on.

*How do you juggle painting and writing and having six
children?* The basic thing behind that, too, is energy! If you
haven't a heap of it, you haven't a hope. I went through enormously desperate periods. I used to feel a lot of anger and despair.
Women of my age are a pioneering second movement. I've a good
friend of the same age who also had six children and who's now
having an exhibition in Lausanne. It was contact with people like
that which got me through those tough times. Moving from
England where my painting roots were, where I'd trained, where
I had made friends, to come here did leave me appallingly isolated. We only lived four miles from the town and thirty or so
from Dublin, but when you have six children you can't browse in
bookshops or go to poetry readings or have a free life like I do
now.

I don't regret the children, but if I were in my twenties now
I'd plan more, and of course that would be more acceptable than
it was then. People used to say to me, 'Well, it's nice for you to

have a hobby.' The little view. You have to take yourself seriously. That started from my father. I wrote a play called *Strings*,
which is about the inter-relation of women with men. I have a
woman and a man on the stage to play all the parts. She is
daughter, mother, wife and lover. He is father, husband, lover,
son. That's how it is. This awful mixture of pressures. It's only in
the last two years I've been without family around. There was a
stage in the seventies when we moved up here and I said, 'Well,
now I'm working. I'm doing my stuff.' My youngest child was
then about six and I deliberately left everything in the kitchen
after breakfast in the morning and walked over it straight up to
my studio. I painted and wrote poetry like that for about two and
a half years.

Do you have an audience in mind? I don't know. I do and I
don't. I find it very hard to think that way, and yet you're a fool if
you don't. Women haven't been very commercial about their
ideas. One of the things that made me write poems was feeling
something that nobody talked about and wanting to say it. I want
to feel I'm communicating, that other people enjoy or suffer the
same things. You release something for yourself by saying this is
a human experience. The artist is the person who takes the
licence to cross barriers and break taboos. I think an Arts Council
is a very strange thing because the artist should be on the side of
anarchy, the court jester who says what cannot be said and can
play the fool. If you're going to be honest, you're bound to be
stepping on other people's toes.

Can we go back to rhythm in poetry? I think the tunes words
make very important. I love the interior sounds in poems. Music
in each poem will have different notes, different movements. I
find a lot of poetry written now excessively dull because it's
over-influenced by Eliot's 'ordinary voice'. It comes from the
spoken voice, rather than from someone like Yeats who has
powerful music all through his poems. Some form of experience
is expressed, but I don't think that makes a poem. I get bored
with flat voices. A poem is very distilled and chiselled. The
musical beat is very important. When a reading is good it actually
gives you music. And there should be as much variety as possible.
There's so much you can do in a poem. Adrienne Rich in her
essay 'When We Dead Awaken' says 'But poems are like dreams:
in them you put what you don't know'. I also remember writing a
particular poem without my glasses and so not being able to see it
very well, but I could feel the balance between my reason, my

rational, tough side, and the unconscious, dreamlike side. I quite often let my eyes go out of focus. It crystallizes things. Sometimes, too, you may start writing and suddenly the poem begins to start somewhere else. That also happens with painting. The world was supposed to be made out of chaos and I'm quite keen on chaos. It's the other side of simplicity. Writing a poem, doing a painting, politics also, is trying to create a new order out of chaos. There's an awful idea that the arts are peripheral. They're not. They're central. It's to do with absolute, basic, inner essentials, like a lifeline.

How do you see yourself as a poet – as a female poet, woman poet, feminist poet? Labels have their uses. They help me find things. But I don't want any labels on myself. I could say 'yes' to everything you've said, but that has dangers. You limit your vision if you belong too much to something. Yes, I'm a feminist, a woman, a mother. I have been a wife, a lover, a cook, a gardener. Why should I wear any of those labels? On the practical day-to-day level one prefers to be incognito, like a fly on the wall. If people really want to know, they had better read my work – what's available of it. Robert Graves said you had to give total allegiance to the muse. That's just a mythical word. I could say the same if I was talking about the conscious and the unconscious.

I don't practise any religion now, but I was brought up strictly Catholic. I haven't had the extremely restrictive Irish Catholic influence, but when I found the church didn't give me a viable programme – it was very anti-woman – it was like being let down by a parent. So with much pain I threw it out and was horrifically surprised how little I missed it! But I'm also deeply grateful, because I did get an incredible richness from it – from the masses and all these prayers and collects. There's great ritual, great drama, great use of words, great music.

But I do see myself as a woman writer. I'm much more interested in what women are saying and writing, and have consciously been reading only women's work for at least two years. That's part of looking back to find my heritage. The whole area of what words we use is very exciting. It's very interesting that we appear to use words men don't use. I've done a lot of work with the Women's Study Forum for the last three years and that's definitely feminist. We've had very extensive programmes and I organize poetry readings for women. I feel that's where my politics lie, with the women's movement. I don't think any order will come out of our political situation in the whole world except through women. There doesn't seem anywhere else to go. There's the grip of capitalism, or the grip of communism, and socialism doesn't seem able to survive. So, although I'm not a separatist, I really do see women as the new political force.

Do you consider yourself an Irish poet? Yes I do. Initially I was fearful of being criticized because of my English connections, but now I feel they're valid. So many Irish people have gone to England, why not celebrate someone who has come back? It's all linked up with identity. I feel Irish in my guts. You know the part of Ireland we're in now, this narrow strip from Wicklow up to the border, is called the Pale? It was once surrounded by palings to keep the Irish out. That's where the expression 'beyond the Pale' comes from. So English, or British, influence, was particularly strong in this part of Ireland. In 1975 I went to a writers' week in Kerry, in the far south west, and had a marvellously mad time. It was probably the first thing I'd done on my own since I was married. That confirmed me in my sense of Irish identity. I knew this was right.

LONG TONGUE

'Long ago in Ireland the poet was thought to have fearful powers. It was a misfortune to have a poet in the family: doubly so if the poet were a woman, as her powers were twice as strong as a man's. A poet was recognized by the possession of an extra-long tongue.'

> If, as the old ones say,
>   None is as poison as I,
> That my long tongue can
>   Pierce more death,
>
> Brew more potent words
>   Make rats remember or forget,
> Swirl the bucket, pudding spoon
>   The sailor, stir him to his doom;
>
> And yet, if wished, good do;
>   What spawned this twice
> Deceiving gift, did I feed
>   On white serpent flesh, or

Press small teeth to the
   Sweet salmon's neck,
Suck the tit, wild milk
   From sun struck fairy cow?

Can my cypher pushed beneath
   The door keep dancers' feet
Pattering, pattering, more more,
   The death beat shreds life

With a Beheading Howl. Curdles
   The spirit in a drunken speech;
Press the vein; the Word,
   Cries cease.

Do I carry dark blame
   And sorrow double deep,
Because I sing a woman's song,
   So therefore, must I weep?

IF

If you were a jug,
Round, fat,
Comfortable;
I would fill
You to the brim;

Then dive in.

HEIRLOOM

My father said
It's always good weather
in bed.

Dilys Rose

Photo: Hilary M. Morrison

DILYS ROSE WAS BORN and raised in Glasgow. She has travelled extensively in Europe, North America, Central America and South-East Asia. She lives in Edinburgh with the Scottish writer Brian McCabe and their two daughters.

She was awarded a Scottish Arts Council Bursary in 1985 and was literary editor of *Radical Scotland* in 1984. Her first collection of short stories *Our Lady of the Pickpockets* (Secker and Warburg) and of poetry *Madame Doubtfire's Dilemma* (Chapman) were published in 1989.

The first time I heard Dilys read her dramatic monologues I was impressed. Her work was difficult to get hold of as it had been published in a variety of magazines and anthologies. The first time I called at her flat she had a stack of poems and stories waiting for me. She asked me to interview her in the afternoon when her daughter, Sophie, would be down for a nap. We tip-toed into the living room and closed the door. Her desk was neat: blank paper on one side and a pile of stories and poems in progress on the other. I got out my recorder and we sat on the floor by the fire and talked.

I STARTED WRITING WHEN I WAS 16. I wrote for a year or two at school. Then I came to university, studied English and lost all interest in writing. All we were doing was critical work. There was no creative work at all. Things like creative writing courses didn't exist at the time. So I suppose I didn't start writing seriously until about 1980.

Do you find writing poetry different from writing short stories? Yes. I have a different feeling about it. There's more of an emotional drive about a poem, but there's more of an interest in the outside world in a short story. That's why I want to write more fiction. At the moment I'm so interested in fiction that poetry seems a little removed from me. You have to have a different way of life from what I have at the moment to find space for a poem to work. It seems contradictory, because a short story takes much longer to write, but I don't have as much time to think about what poetry is about as I used to have.

What inspires or motivates you? The impossible question. I don't think I have a clear idea when I sit down to write. Something is given, a line, a character, a situation, a word even. I think it's the exploration that inspires me, the sense that I might establish something I don't know, either about myself or other people. Usually my ideas come from things I have experienced or know something about, which isn't to say they're autobiographical. I don't want to write fantasy. Sometimes I want to say something, as in 'Snakes and Ladders', which is about a woman who needed to move house. I had been working in a housing scheme on the outskirts of Edinburgh with a lot of problems and I wanted to convey something of that life to people outside that area, and to people there too.

If it was just a question of information, getting a point across, then I would be better to write a newspaper article. Although I have political beliefs I don't feel the best way of getting them over in fiction is to preach about them. I find I'm turned off something which preaches its point too much, whether it's feminism, socialism or nationalism. I found that when I was literary editor of *Radical Scotland*. So much of the poetry that came in was only concerned with the message and not how the message was given to the reader. Those people already knew exactly how they felt and all they wanted to do was state the case and that to me isn't very creative. It's maybe honest, it's definitely justifiable. There is a need for it, but I don't think fiction or poetry is the best way to go about dealing with these things.

My experience of reading your short stories was that they were about particular situations and they are written in such a way that you experience them by reading them. Well, I would hope that. One of the main tasks of the writer is to make the reader experience the action of the story or the character, not to persuade them.

Are you writing for an audience? Not a specific audience. I'm certainly not writing for women only or feminists only or socialists only. I don't think that's particularly useful. The problem for me is that it seems to work for people who have already sorted out their lives. There are so many other people, especially women, with normal working or middle class lives, who feel the same things but aren't able to deal with them in the same way as more liberated, educated women can. I wouldn't want to be seen as writing for an educated audience particularly, but an audience can be chosen by the magazines or radio stations who take your stuff. That in itself has probably more of an effect than what I write in the first place.

Do you have an intention when you're writing? To be true to the characters I'm dealing with, or to the voice I'm dealing with. That puts drastic limitations on the point of view, which I like personally, but some people criticize my work because it doesn't uphold certain ideas, certain more positive aspects, let's say, of women today.

How does the relationship between form and content work for you? Every character has his or her own way of telling their story. Every story or poem has its own particular way to be written. That's why I use voice. The way people speak says so much about them. I don't think I could separate form and content. I couldn't say that I decided to write this in this way in order to do such and such, but that it started in a certain way and therefore had to go on.

I don't want to write about myself. Having a chance to imagine how another person might think, how another person might act in a situation, what's important to another person is much more interesting. It doesn't always work. People say a man can never write anything from a woman's point of view and vice versa. I think you should try to do things that stretch you a little. You have to imagine quite thoroughly in order to bring characters to life. I try to build things up as I go along. You have to have certain details that are crucial to the character, that couldn't be anyone else at the time. Using voice helps in that you can check back to see that the character isn't saying anything out of keeping. I've often seen pieces of writing where there's a confusion because the writer's own way of thinking intrudes on the characters and forces them to think unnaturally. We all have our own way of imagining certain things. Fiction is a construct. It's not so much mirroring reality as taking things from it and creating something new. That way speech isn't just speech as it is. It has to be selective realism, if you like.

Do you hear those voices in your head? Yes. I have to or I couldn't do it. Then there's always the divide between what is actually said out loud and what is thought. Stories which have too much straight dialogue become very artificial. They're not getting at the undercurrents of what's going on. Also, although we use speech so much all the time, our ability to use it to say what we mean is very limited.

Does that tie in with the people in many of your short stories being in powerless situations? Maybe. I find that a common situation and a sad one, and maybe I'm trying to give a voice to characters who don't necessarily have one. *Giving voice to areas of silence.* Yes. *But what about relationships?* Some of my themes are a bit unsavoury, about prostitute characters basically, but usually these things tend to be glamourised, tend to be very much good and evil situations. I felt that there are too many other things going on, too many other pressures not talked about between people, economic pressures, etc. I suppose I feel that most people who aren't in the top five per cent who go to university and things like that have a rough time, and generally aren't given credit for the fact that life is a lot harder for them. I had quite an easy life relatively. I was cared for well. My parents had great expectations of me. I don't think I've fulfilled them, but you can't make very much of yourself if you spend all your time scrubbing around trying to make ends meet. That takes up your life. You don't have anything left to be creative or independent, or even good, necessarily.

Tell me about the doll poems. They started off as a poem about the wooden Russian dolls which open up and up and in the end you get left with this little solid one. I'd always found them fascinating and I began to think of them in terms of an idea of women, and the rest of them came from that. I'm not obsessed by dolls. I've never been interested in them as playthings except I once wanted a foreign doll with a fancy dress on! But I found it was quite an interesting field. I would like to do more, not necessarily on dolls, but on images of women as portrayed on the screen.

In some cases I used the voice speaking. In some I didn't. In some I used someone else's voice. I read a book about doll-making at one point, just out of curiosity. Then I went to the Museum of Childhood here in Edinburgh, which I enjoyed. All the dolls seem to be constructed with separate aims in mind. For instance, The china doll was porcelain so a child couldn't actually play with it. So I imagined this mother constantly telling the child to be careful with it in the same way as she was being careful with the daughter because she was very precious.

The fertility doll was made originally to encourage the crops to grow, but the actual figures of the dolls looks so uncomfortable. They're very badly balanced, with tiny little feet and huge hips. The way I saw it they were a man's idea of a pregnant woman. They looked nice in the sense that they were going to produce something, but they weren't anything in themselves.

Then there was the rag doll. It speaks for itself, made up of cast-offs. When I was little I got cast-off clothes from people. All children get them and most children at a certain age don't want them any more. They want their own things. They want to be independent. So I was just thinking about the doll who wanted to be independent. 'Give me a new life'!

How do you define yourself, as a poet, as a writer, as a female writer, woman writer, feminist writer? Only as a writer, I think. I hope I can say that now. I'm a woman writer because I'm a woman. I believe in feminism, but I'm not setting out to promote that in what I write. I write stories about men as well. I live with a man. I can't deny that part of my life. It's a big part of it. I don't think labels are useful. They restrict interest rather than create it.

There seems to be this incredible categorization here, that if you're a feminist writer you write about particular things. And not only that, you have to write about them in a particular way to be accepted. I remember having a huge argument with somebody about my poem 'Sister Sirens' because she objected to the way I portrayed women in it, but I feel that a lot of women are still like that and need to break free from it. The same thing used to happen with some of the feminist presses. They would ask people to change the endings of their novels if the endings weren't positive enough. It was as if they wanted to say, OK, we've done with the heavy stuff, everybody knows about this, now we want a joyful progression into the future. But the world goes on and people still murder, rape and bomb each other and people are still trapped in their own little domestic settings.

Do you think of yourself as a Scottish writer? Only in the sense that I live here at the moment. I've been too interested in other countries to feel that Scotland is my only frame of reference. I may get around to writing more about the homeland later, I don't know. I don't know what this Scottish writer business is all about. It seems to be an argument that's been going on since the Union of the Crowns, trying to work out the differences between a Scottish writer, an English writer and a British writer. I would like Scotland to be a little more international. We're a small country and we have the advantages and the disadvantages of that. I think nationalism is something we should shake off a bit. Not because there aren't a lot of things that are particular to Scotland to write about, but that being Scottish is not a virtue or a vice in itself.

How do you juggle having a daughter and teaching and writing? With difficulty. I hold her in one hand and my pen in the other! But it works. The problems were overwhelming at first, tiredness and the upheaval of moving house twice. In the first few months my concentration was dreadful. I found it hard not to be constantly thinking about her and what she needed, even if she wasn't there. I do get frustrated, but I've learned a little patience. I would like to be able to sit down, close the doors and say, 'Go away. I want to do this.' But I can't. I have to work within very strictly defined hours and I'm not necessarily settled down at that point. But over the months it gets easier. I hope it will, once she's able to do more herself. Hopefully she'll be typing away on the little toy typewriter sitting in the corner!

She's been quite a good discipline for me. Before I had so much time and I don't think I ever used it particularly well. If you have all the time in the day there's no real need to do something. Now, if I have only four hours in the day I do attempt to do something in that time. I have to! I'm very glad to have had her, although it's been hard going. It's closed off nightlife and things like that, which I'd had enough of for a while anyway, and taken me into the world of hospital surgeries and playparks and all kinds of places where I meet people completely different from me. That's why I like it, not to see the people whom I work with or people involved in writing. Meeting almost anybody is possible in a playpark, or almost any kind of parent anyway, and children have a way of introducing you to people by themselves. It's amazing the number that come up and speak to you, or to the baby actually. They don't speak to me that much. But at a certain point I'd like to go travelling again. I do get itchy feet. In a couple of years maybe, once she's old enough to have a little rucksack on her back!

SISTER SIRENS

Another boat veers for the perch
Where we're tethered.
We preen our feathers,
croon seductive duets –
the sailor is deaf to all else.
He ignores omens,
Throws sense to the wind
Sets course for the harbour
of our twin smiles.
The moon conspires with us,
improves our allure.
How gorgeously we glimmer.
Our glamour takes his breath away.
If only we'd squawked a warning –
    Beauty is only a trick of the light
    Beneath our flightless wings
    We've talons to tear out your heart –
If only we'd screeched,
    Block up your ears, hide your eyes
    If need be, bind yourself to the mast.

More monster than myth, we'll pick you clean.
Later we'll toss on this rocky bed,
Unable to sleep. We'll bitch, squabble
Over whose good looks charmed him ashore.

But to ourselves curse the gods
Who blessed us with the songbird's voice,
The hawk's claw.

MATRYUSHKA

the wooden doll widens her lidless eyes
unbinds her swaddled middle

(*I rouge my skin, tint*
alabaster lips a life-blood shade)

the doll inside unsnaps her clasp
unfolds her braided limbs

(*I curl my hair and straighten seams*
wind up my hour-glass waist)

the smaller inner wooden doll
spins and rattles her pillarbox grin

(*I slip on rings and knife bright shoes*
I sheath myself in silk)

the even smaller wooden doll
undoes herself discards her shell

(*I insulate my flesh in fur*
perfect a veiled smile at the mirror)

inside the even smaller doll
sits the tiniest of them all

she's shapeless
faceless
plainly solid

(*we're both indestructible now*)

Val Warner

Photo: Edwin Madge

VAL WARNER IS FROM MIDDLESEX, England. She has been
Writer in Residence at University College, Swansea, and the
University of Dundee. She lived in Newburgh, Fife for a time, and
now lives in Harrow.

She has published two volumes of poetry, *Under the Pent-
house* (1973) and *Before Lunch* (1986), both by Carcanet Press,
Manchester. She translated the work of Tristian Corbière in *The
Centenary Corbière* (Carcanet, 1975), and edited *The Collected
Poems and Prose of Charlotte Mew* (Carcanet and Virago
Presses, 1982). She has received a Gregory Award for poetry and
her short stories have appeared in *Pen New Fiction II, Edinburgh
Review, Encounter* and other magazines.

I talked with Val several times on the phone and finally made
it through to Dundee to hear her read. She stood on the podium, a
tall, stooping woman with long black hair and anxious eyes,
reading in a deep voice. We agreed to meet later that week at her
home. I knocked on the door. She opened it halfway and said
'Hello, come in, and watch your step.' I found myself in a narrow
hallway, climbing over sacks of cooking oats and boxes of books.
We made it into the living room, which was awash with papers
and books. I stood, paralyzed, carrying my bag of recording

equipment, not sure what to do. Val cleared a small section of the floor for us to sit on and we began the interview. As we talked, it became apparent how completely committed she was. It was the first time I had seen the sacrifices some writers are willing to make in order to give themselves over to their writing.

As a child I wrote in the way children do. I knew I wanted to write. I wrote a full-length novel when I was a schoolgirl, but I burnt it a couple of years later. I wrote more seriously when I was a student. I suppose the crunch came then. I was studying History and had the choice between working for a good degree and going on to some kind of career, which would probably have been research or just getting a second class degree and spending as much time as I could writing and reading things that would help me to write. I decided that writing was going to be the thing and I would look for part-time jobs when I finished my degree in order to have more time to write.

What inspires you to write? People, I suppose, are my main interest. I've nearly finished a novel which is based on a series of character studies. It's about a woman writing a biography of an imaginary dead poet of the thirties, in whom other people are also interested. It's the story of how the biography came to be written and the different personal motivations of the people who want to write it. It shows the censorship that goes on in a supposedly free society like Britain. I always wanted to write prose, but it took me so long to write poetry that I never really had time. I feel I'm much more of a prose writer, and even if I fail I shall always believe I should have been a prose writer and not a poet. I'm very interested in the use of language. There are things you can do in poetry that you can't do in prose, but also an awful lot in prose that it's very difficult to do in poetry – it would take so long you'd never even finish a single book.

Are you writing for a particular audience? Yes, I would always have some kind of audience in mind. I don't believe in just writing for oneself, although ultimately you are writing to please yourself. I wouldn't have a particular audience in mind, other than somebody who loves reading and borrows books from the library. Also I'm not terribly interested in writing work to be read aloud. I tend to have in mind the person reading the poem on the page. Some of the poems do work when they're read aloud, but some of them are difficult to get across in a single reading. There's so much word play, ambivalence, allusion, irony, and so on, so that you do have to give the text at least a second glance. Also dialogue in a poem is very difficult to read aloud, unless you're an actor. So I would write for the solitary reader, and I would pick a man rather than a woman. I would like to appeal to women as well, but I would be very disappointed if I were told most of my readers were women. I would like 50 per cent of each. My idea of a good poem is one that you can get something out of on the first reading, but you also pick up a sense that there's more there to go back to and re-read again and again. I don't like poems where the surface is so complicated you realize after line 1 that 'this is a very difficult poem' and the poet wants you to work at it. Poets sometimes defend that kind of poetry by saying they do want the audience to work at it, but I don't see poems as intellectual puzzles. I would be very sorry if anyone puzzled over a poem of mine. I'd rather they moved on to another one, and if they found them all too difficult I'd rather they moved on to another poet.

What forms do you write in? The new book I'm working on is in two long sequences, the first in iambic pentameter, the second in free verse, or very corrupted pentameter, although all the lines work out to much the same length. It's not the kind of free verse where you have a line and then a huge space and then one word, and so on. All the poems are the same length, more or less of 17 lines. The first part is set in 1939 and the second in 1984. I wanted to make a technical difference between the two parts which might reflect the time gap. But I don't think you can divide form and subject. With me the subject would suggest the form. I can't imagine the form suggesting the subject.

What happens to you when you have an idea? I wouldn't use the word 'inspiration'. If it was a long sequence I would plan it in a broad general sense, but leave it sufficiently flexible to include changes as I go along. I would have a pretty detailed outline in my mind before starting and then modify it if I needed to. In my novel, for instance, I haven't written the chapters in the right order and I'm quite happy to write the last chapter at an early stage because the main outline is there. Then I rewrite a lot.

What word would you use instead of 'inspiration'? Craftsmanship. Writing to me is a craft. The word 'inspiration' to me has mystical, religious overtones, or vaguely sentimental ones. I would prefer the word 'feeling'. The poems do come out of what one might be feeling at the time, but it's not a matter of day-to-day feeling, and also I do go back and revise poems written many

years before when any feeling that sparked them off is probabl
long dead. That doesn't worry me at all.

*Would you say you've trained yourself to write just by
reading other people all the time?* Yes. A lot of people when they
begin to write simply don't read enough. You're not likely to
write anything good unless you know what other people are
doing, and hopefully you'll do something original, but if you
don't know what other people are doing, you can spend a lifetime
doing things that other people have done already. Reading other
people is the only way to learn, and practising, writing stuff that
isn't very good and then revising it. You might have an early
poem where you'd hit on a good subject, but the technique
mightn't be very good. That's why I'm so interested in going back
and revising.

*You've been in Scotland for a long time. Would you consider
yourself to be a Scottish poet?* Well, I'm British, I suppose. Even if
I stayed in Scotland for the rest of my life I would never become
an adopted Scot, as some English people have done. In England I
never thought of myself as an English poet. I consider myself as
somebody writing in English. Most of the writers I most admire
are American, particularly in poetry. So it doesn't seem very
meaningful to talk about nationality. The historical influence is
more important in Scotland. In England one doesn't think about
history, certainly not earlier than the 18th century, because the
English came out on top. In Scotland it's the reverse because the
English were the imperial power and absorbed Scotland, as it
were. The victors forget whereas the defeated remember. English
people don't realize how real history is in Scotland and Ireland.
When I lived in France for a year it seemed much less of a foreign
country than Scotland or Wales because nobody is very
interested in nationality, but living in Scotland or Wales you're
conscious of it the whole time. You never forget you're English.

*Do you consider yourself a poet, a female poet, a feminist
poet, or what?* I consider myself a writer. I wouldn't want to tie
any label on. I don't want to say I consider myself a British writer
or a woman writer. One writes the best one can. One does the
best one can and one's ideal audience would come from every
section of English-speaking readers.

How would you define your poetry? Well, other people,
particularly about *Before Lunch*, which was published this year,
seemed to think I tend to concentrate on unhappy people,
especially those towards the bottom of the pile, generally fairly

hard up. Politically I consider myself a Socialist, but people who call themselves Marxist wouldn't consider me one. A strict Marxist would say I was writing too much about the individual rather than the class.

It's a cold observation about your work and what people see. Yes, 'observation' is a word that has been used about my work. But all the writers I like have powers of observation. I try to write about people whom I empathise with and wouldn't want only to observe from outside, people whom I feel I have some insight into, which again is perhaps more a novelist's attitude than a poet's. Some poets achieve very good poems from external observation, but that wouldn't be my way.

Do you see yourself as sometimes stepping into another persona? I wouldn't be as confident as that. No, I would say there's an element of guesswork. Take the characters in my novel. There's a bit of myself in all of them. There has to be because I'm the perception that's bringing them to life. There's more of myself in some of them than in others and there's bits of other people as well. Somebody once said writing a novel's a confidence trick. It sounds very cynical, but I agree with him in a way. I would never use the phrase 'putting yourself in someone else's shoes', because you're always blinded by your own perception. You use observation, you use people you've known, you use your reading, you use insight and empathy and you try to project yourself. In the end the one thing that makes the leap, I suppose, is imagination, which in some ways is the least trustworthy of the lot.

Do you support yourself completely by your writing and your teaching? Yes, well, I have an extremely low standard of living. I don't think many people would be able or willing to live as I do. Two or three years ago I worked out I could spend only £100 a year on food. I think I spent a little bit more, but it really was at that level of basic subsistence – a sackful of oats, cheap vegetables, textured vegetable protein and buying things in bulk. For about three years I didn't buy any books at all, which is an amazing thing for a writer. When I was a student I'd always bought books. I got a few review copies and one or two people gave me books, but that was all. I was simply determined to get a lot of time to write. My part-time jobs never left enough time, nor did other literary work, like translation. I had a lot of poems I wanted to finish or revise and organize into a book. That took two years of doing nothing else. I also wanted to write new

poems and novels and short stories. By 1981 I was in my middle
thirties and I really didn't care what price had to be paid. I had to
get into a situation where I could get up every morning and do the
work I wanted to. And it has paid off. In the last four years I have
completed far more work than in many years before that.

AT THE DENTIST

I recall that session, run of the mill,
gagged by the usual ironmongery
stuffing my mouth. Half-choked, I understood...

the dentist's gentlest touch was an affront,
near rape. Boring my mind like hail, the drill
rock-drilled, irrelevant before the storm's
eye: pure thought's clarity. He'd interrupt
with his cliché remarks, or that forked tongue
of lightning pain – the nerve jagged, my eyes welled
crocodile tears. Silently, my tongue wagged
narrating you the story of my life,
begged understanding. Craved mirage? Who wants
a doubtful gift of tongues, the forked ... nude mind
fig-leafed by questionable ironies,
half truths – *ah si j'étais un peu compris* –
doubtful asides, more doubtful images?
I understood, I craved your tongue's response.

BOTTLED MOON

A packet, slipping down the oceanic deliquescence...

Once in a blue moon, I'd broach that envelope,
plundering that kangaroo pouch of the past, flip

through papers, aged by dead suns beyond
their age, after some legal document, only meaningful *in absentia*. God knows how it came
there, your Ernst card growing blue

gentians and olives between gilded typescript
sheets. There, a baby-face and drink-ruddy moon glares on
a post-Armstrong moonscape, the landscape
of our common form, slitheringly over-

lapping ... under the belljar of the night, pickled
strange fruit. Shades of Lady
Day. The message in the bottle on the moon-

tied tide sings 'Why don't we meet sometime
if you like?', signed only by your hand
on a Tate postcard, franked in Dover.

AUTUMN PETS

Gently, gently, with the flat of her hand,
she's seeing off a small spider abseiling
down from the lintel, framing her against my summer

garden threshold: 'Spiders are pets, practically
twining around the heart strings, through the year's

twilight. They live with me a while and then
they go. I dread to think just where they go,
sprung from a glassy sea of white-wash

to a Giant's Causeway of crumbs or worse
along the wainscot, or the unspeakably sheer face

of a newspaper tented on the floor. Meantime, they know
their place and stay there, moving a foot

a day, before they disappear
as if vaporised.' Alone, she's a prisoner in the cells,
hormonally. Yet, her pores suck this gilding sun. In all

conscience, what of the prisoner in the cells,
whose world's ... the motion of a flea?

List of Poets with Selected Poems

Sara Berkeley: 'Crossing I' and 'In St. Etheldreda's', from *Penn* (The Raven Arts Press, Dublin, 1986).

Sheena Blackhall: 'The Tea Pairty' from *The Spik O' the Lan'* (Rainbow Enterprises, Aberdeen, 1986); 'The Lintie', from *The Cyard's Kist* (Rainbow Enterprises, Aberdeen, 1984); 'The Serpent', *Lines Review* 97 (Edinburgh, June 1986).

Eavan Boland: 'Mise Eire', from *The Journey* (Arlen House, Dublin, 1986; reprinted by kind permission of Carcanet Press, Manchester, 1987); 'Anorexic' from *In Her Own Image* (Arlen House, Dublin, 1980).

Eva Bourke: 'Fish' and 'Two Times Two Domestic Interior' from *Gonella* (Salmon Publishing, Galway, 1985).

Rosalind Brackenbury: 'The Seal Women' and 'For a Writer's Children', from *Telling Each Other It Is Possible* (Taxus Press, Stamford, Lincolnshire, 1987).

Valerie Gillies: 'Young Harper', from *New Writing Scotland* 2 (Association for Scottish Literary Studies, 1984); 'The Negative', from *Each Bright Eye* (Canongate, Edinburgh, 1977); 'Infertility Patient', from *New Writing Scotland* 3 (Association for Scottish Literary Studies, 1985).

Anne Hartigan: 'Long Tongue', 'If' and 'Heirloom' from *Long Tongue* (Beaver Row Press, Dublin, 1982).

Joy Hendry: 'Death-Eve', published here for the first time.

Rita Ann Higgins; 'Middle-Aged Irish Mothers' and 'Poetry Doesn't Pay', from *Goddess on the Mervue Bus* (Salmon Publishing, Galway, 1986).

Ruth Hooley: 'My Mother's House' from *The Female Line: Northern Irish Women Writers* (Northern Ireland Women's Rights Movement, Belfast, 1985); 'Cut the Cake', from *Map-Makers' Colours* (Nu-Age Editions, Montreal, 1988).

Kathleen Jamie; 'Poem for a departing mountaineer' and 'The way We Live', from *The Way We Live* (Reprinted by kind permission of Bloodaxe Books, Newcastle upon Tyne, 1987).

Jackie Kay: My Grandmother', from *The Adoption Papers*; 'So you think I'm a Mule?' and 'We are Not All Sisters Under the Same Moon', from *A Dangerous Knowing: Four Black Women Poets* (Sheba Feminist Publishers, London, 1988).

Liz Lochhead: 'The Bride', from *Poetry Broadsheet* (Edinburgh, 1985) and 'Dreaming Frankenstein', from *Dreaming Frankenstein and Collected Poems* (Polygon, Edinburgh, 1984).

Mary McCann: 'On not going to Greenham Common', from *The Edinburgh Women's Liberation Newsletter* (1986); 'Dragon Nonsense', published here for the first time.

Ellie McDonald: 'The Gangan Fuit' and 'Fairins', from *Seagate II; An*

Anthology of Dundee Writing (Taxus Press, Durham, 1984). 'Fairins' also appeared in *Chapman: Woven by Women* (27–28; Edinburgh, 1980).

Medbh McGuckian: 'The Flitting' and 'The Flower Master', from *The Flower Master* (Reprinted by kind permission of Oxford University Press, 1982).

Catriona Nic Gumaraid: 'Eilidh' and 'Rodhag 2000 AD', from *Cencrastus* (Edinburgh, Winter, 1987–88).

Nuala Ni Dhomhnaill: 'Kundalini' from *Selected Poems*, with translations by Michael Hartnett (Raven Arts Press, Dublin, 1986).

Mary O'Donnell: 'Antarctica', published here for the first time; 'Rehearsals', from *Poetry Ireland Review* 11 (Dublin, Autumn, 1984).

Tessa Ransford: 'Ode to Edinburgh', from *Light of the Mind* (1980); 'February 14th' from *Shadows from the Greater Hill* (1987); both collections published by the Ramsay Head Press, Edinburgh.

Dilys Rose: 'Sister Sirens' from *New Writing Scotland* 4 (Association for Scottish Literary Studies, 1986); 'Matryushka', from *The Glasgow Magazine* (1984).

Janet Shepperson: 'Loyalist Strike in the Suburbs', 'Swimmers', from *Trio 5* (Blackstaff Press, Belfast, 1987).

Eithne Strong: 'Bottoms' and 'The Creaking of the Bones', from *My Darling Neighbour* (Beaver Row Press, Dublin, 1985).

Maud Sulter: 'Delete and Enter', published here for the first time; and 'Thirteen Stanzas', from *As a Blackwoman* (Akira Press, London, 1985).

Val Warner: 'At the Dentist' from *Lines Review*, June 1988; 'Bottled Moon' from *The Poetry Book Society Anthology, 1987–88* (Hutchinson, 1988); 'Autumn Pets' from *Encounter*, December 1988.

Notes on the Editors

Rebecca Eureka Wilson was born in San Francisco, California, in 1962. During the course of her college education, she worked as a waitress, nurse, housecleaner, stable hand and artists' model. In 1986 she graduated *Phi Beta Kappa* (National Academic Honors) from Scripps College, California, with a Bachelor's Degree in Cultural Anthropology/Anthropology of Women. She was awarded a Thomas J. Watson Fellowship in 1987, funding for a year of independent study abroad, the basis of which became this book. She is currently living in Muir Beach, California, and working as a columnist and reporter for a weekly newspaper. She is still waitressing and has begun her first novel.

Born in Glasgow and educated in Edinburgh, *Gillean Somerville-Arjat* has had a varied professional career, taking her from English teaching through university administration into freelance writing and editing. She has had several short stories, articles and reviews published in Scottish literary magazines and contributed to an oral history project based on the Tollcross district of Edinburgh, published as *Waters under the Bridge* (Aberdeen University Press, June, 1990). She is currently working on various fictions based in Edinburgh and Morocco and a reminiscence project based on the former George Watson's Ladies' College, Edinburgh.